Reflective Activities

NCTE Editorial Board: Pat Cordeiro, Bobbi Fisher, Xin Liu Gale, Sarah Hudelson, Bill McBride, Alleen Pace Nilsen, Helen Poole, Jerrie Cobb Scott, Karen Smith, Chair, ex officio, Peter Feely, ex officio

Reflective Activities

Helping Students Connect with Texts

Classroom Practices in Teaching English
Volume 30

Edited by

Louann Reid
Colorado State University

Jeffrey N. Golub
University of South Florida

National Council of Teachers of English
1111 W. Kenyon Road, Urbana, Illinois 61801-1096

Staff Editor: Tom Tiller
Cover Design: Evelyn C. Shapiro
Interior Design: Doug Burnett

NCTE Stock Number 17554-3050

©1999 by the National Council of Teachers of English. All rights reserved. Printed in the United States of America.

It is the policy of NCTE in its journals and other publications to provide a forum for the open discussion of ideas concerning the content and the teaching of English and the language arts. Publicity accorded to any particular point of view does not imply endorsement by the Executive Committee, the Board of Directors, or the membership at large, except in announcements of policy, where such endorsement is clearly specified.

Library of Congress Catalog Card Number 85-644740

ISBN 0-8141-1755-4
ISSN 0550-5755

Contents

Introduction ix

I. Establishing a Climate for Reflection 1

1. A Well of Mirrored Mirrors 3
   Dan Chabas

2. Lightbulbs and Pandemonium: Thinking about Thinking 11
   Jeff Schwartz

3. Responding, Reflecting, and Evaluating 15
   Kathleen and James Strickland

II. Reflecting and Connecting through Reading, Writing, and Viewing 25

4. Stories, Readers, and the World Beyond Books 27
   Renate Schulz

5. Reading *Ceremony*, Reading Ourselves 35
   Bruce Goebel

6. Reading Writers/Writing Readers 44
   Claudia Greenwood and Cynthia Walters

7. In Praise of Simple Things 51
   Carol Jago

8. Rainer Maria Rilke's *Song* Poems 53
   Leslie Richardson

9. The Perfect Novel for Creative Writing Assignments 58
   Kathryn Megyeri

10. What's the Big Idea? Linking Creative and Academic Writing in the Multigenre Research Paper 66
    Sheryl Lain

11. Writing toward Thoughtfulness through Logs 74
    Cynthia G. Kuhn

12. "You learn from within yourself" 87
    Helen Collins Sitler, Kelly A. Carameli, and Brandi J. Abbott

13. Connecting Letter Writing and "Real Life" in the College
    Writing Class ... 93
    Erika Scheurer

14. Living What You Read and Write ... 100
    Darrell g.h. Schramm

15. Searching for Words to Cross Cultures ... 106
    Susan Tchudi, Stephen Adkison, Jacob Blumner,
    Francis Fritz, and Maria Madruga

16. Media "Target Assignments" Invite Students to Tune In,
    Turn On, and Write ... 113
    Meta G. Carstarphen

17. Activating the Viewing Process ... 117
    Richard H. Fehlman

III. Reflecting and Connecting through Presentations, Projects, and Portfolios ... 123

18. Vietnam War Literature and the Arts ... 125
    Larry R. Johannessen

19. Crossing Borders with a Multicultural Poetry Project ... 132
    Dana Nevil

20. Investigation Waltz ... 140
    Daniel L. Kain

21. Distinguishing between the Myth and Reality of Self ... 146
    Ann Wheeler

22. The Project Method in the Literature Classroom ... 149
    David S. Miall

23. Reflection and Portfolios Across the Curriculum ... 156
    Barbara King-Shaver

24. The Resource and Professional Development Portfolio
    Projects ... 165
    Thomas Philion

25. Keeping the Candle Lit through the Fierce Winds:
    Encouraging Personal Mastery through Portfolios ... 171
    Patrick Monahan

IV. Time for Reflection — 181

26. Nourishing Independence through Self-Assessment — 183
    JoAnne P. Miller

27. How-Two: Learning about the Horizons of Our Teaching Selves — 190
    Linda Shadiow

Editors — 201

Contributors — 203

Introduction

This book is a collection of classroom-tested practices informed by a constructivist approach to learning. A constructivist approach to teaching and learning values the student's contribution to understanding. Teachers who use constructivist approaches realize that reflecting and connecting are two central processes for helping students to construct their understanding of the world and to become conscious of what and how they have learned.

The authors of the articles in this book know that classroom practices never occur in a vacuum. Whether or not we articulate them, everything that we do is informed by our beliefs about what learning is and how best to make it happen. The activities in this volume range through all of the language arts and across middle, secondary, and college classrooms, but they all share a common philosophy: learning must be active, constructive, and conscious.

For true learning to occur, students must reflect, thus gaining awareness and control of their learning processes. As Margaret Donaldson (1979) writes, "If the intellectual powers are to develop, the child must gain a measure of control over his own thinking and he cannot control it while he remains unaware of it" (129). Students must realize that they have learned something and feel a sense of accomplishment and self-renewal.

Connecting is also an essential learning process. Rosenblatt's transactional theory of the literary work (1938/1976) posits that the process of making connections is comprised of transactions wherein both reader and text contribute to the meaning that is constructed. Learners also make connections when they use modeling to write a poem, reexamine a story in light of what a critic says about it, or explore a topic from the perspectives of several disciplines.

Together, reflecting and connecting help learners make experiences meaningful. John Barell, in *Teaching for Thoughtfulness* (1991), cautions, "If one does not engage in reflection, the danger is that . . . actions and responses become an undifferentiated mass of information without significant relationships. Finding these relationships is one way of creating and disclosing to ourselves and others the 'meaning' of experiences and of determining the extent of our personal control of the situation" (10).

The teachers who authored the articles you are about to read have themselves engaged in reflection on their classroom practices. Some make that reflection evident in their chapters. Others do not reveal the process, but it is evident in the product.

We received more than one hundred manuscripts for this volume. From them, we selected the ones that best describe teachers and students using powerful approaches to learning in classrooms. In the first section, teachers describe how they set up instructional situations and tasks to provide opportunities for students to use their minds well. These teachers show that reflective thinking does not occur automatically or just by asking students questions about what they have learned.

Activities in the second and third sections require that students both reflect and connect. These sections, respectively, show students constructing their knowledge through reading, writing, and viewing, and through presentations, projects and portfolios. Although the practices in these sections are closely related, articles in the second section emphasize the processes, whereas those in the third section emphasize the products.

The last section deals with ways of encouraging self-assessment in students and ourselves. Teaching and learning are never finished, as the authors in this section remind us. We are exhorted not only to examine the emerging patterns of the "how-to" ideas for classroom practices that we gather from diverse sources (including this book), but also to become aware of what our instructional choices reveal about our own assumptions regarding what is worth knowing and how students learn.

The articles in this volume offer a variety of strategies to help students reflect on their work and, in so doing, make learning happen consciously, consistently, and constructively. We sincerely hope that, as you read these articles and try out these activities, learning will happen for you, too.

References

Barell, John. 1991. *Teaching for Thoughtfulness: Classroom Strategies to Enhance Intellectual Development*. New York: Longman.

Donaldson, Margaret. 1978. *Children's Minds*. New York: Norton.

Rosenblatt, Louise. 1976. *Literature as Exploration*. 1938. Reprint, New York: Noble and Noble.

I Establishing a Climate for Reflection

Learning is an active, constructive process, not a spectator sport. It is also hard work. In the first essay of this section, Dan Chabas quotes one of his students reacting in his journal to this active nature of reflecting and learning: "I hate reflection. It makes me think too much."

Despite this student's reservations, we believe that this is one of the major benefits of reflection: it makes students think! But, as you'll find from the authors in this section, teachers do not teach thinking directly; instead, they set up classroom instructional situations and tasks in such a way that thinking happens. Chabas talks about how to establish such an environment and make reflection an integral part of discussions, writing, and classroom culture.

Besides simply making students "think too much," reflection also helps students gain increased awareness and control of their language performance. This is the goal of Jeff Schwartz's use of reflective strategies, as described in the second essay in this section. Schwartz demonstrates the value of reflection by citing his students' descriptions of reflection as a valuable process of connecting ideas, discovering, analyzing, questioning, hypothesizing, and forming opinions.

Learning can be active and constructive for preservice teachers as well. Kathleen and James Strickland describe their use of dialogue journals, interviews, and self-evaluation techniques to help their English-methods students understand their own learning and "formulate their own philosophies of learning."

1 A Well of Mirrored Mirrors

Dan Chabas
Douglas County High School, Castle Rock, Colorado

Staring at Walls

In thinking about what I should say about reflecting, I started to remember that neat little effect you get when you combine several mirrors at right angles (or point the camcorder at the same TV you're using to monitor): that of an infinite well of the same picture within itself. It's an image that is to me as perplexing as anything Narcissus saw; I could waste away looking into it. That's what always happens to me when I start reflecting. My mother-in-law once confessed to my wife, "I don't know what he was doing. When we came in he was just staring at the wall." It is with empathy, then, that I remember a student from several years back. I'd been over-pushing the word *reflection*, apparently, because he said on his course evaluation, "I hate reflection. It makes me think too much."

Of course, the fact that he was thinking "too much" is exactly what I wanted to hear from him, given what I knew about him. He wasn't a person likely to say much in English class normally, and I'd gotten to know him through his reflective work. But the comment does remind me that reflection doesn't necessarily come naturally to anyone, and that I always will have a certain amount of selling to do in the form of "What did you learn?" questions.

Not Another Questionnaire

I overbalanced the scales, I think, one semester when I distributed yet another of my masterful questionnaires reviewing the unit we'd just covered. In love with print, I've been working at questionnaires the way a sculptor might keep trying to sculpt the perfect eyebrow: *I'll get it right the next time—I'm so close.* This last one was two-sided and contained every reflective question in my tool box. I included questions asking students to look back on their final performance, their process of creation, their plans for the future, their opinion of the assignment. . . . I'd blocked out a big chunk of time for them to work through the questions, but I looked up after seven minutes, and here came the first person finished, followed by the flood of her classmates. I think I said, "Are you *sure?"* to the first several and then gave up. Needless to say, none of them felt they needed to attach an extra sheet in case their answers spilled over the eighth of an inch I'd allowed.

I realized later, looking back myself, that they'd already done so many reflective activities during the unit that the answering of further questions was as wearisome for them to write as it was for me to read. Coming as it did when the activity was over (as so many things in education seem to do, e.g., tests, grades, evaluation, commentary, even encouragement), this particular questionnaire was not an organic part of the process. It was artificially wired onto the end. And both the students and I knew that.

The Act of Stopping

I think good reflection isn't usually a thing in itself but a characteristic of what John Barell (1995) might call a healthy classroom culture. It is grown with the rest of the environment from day one. I remember stopping that class at the end of a pretty engaging discussion early in the semester in order for each student to write an Exit Visa, a pretty traditional use of reflective writing: a short commentary that might expand on some aspect of the discussion, bring up new points, or say what the student wishes she'd gotten an opportunity to say.

It may not matter what the students actually write; what matters most, I think, is the act of stopping. *We're stopping. This must be important.* There's also a significant message about audience accountability in there, too. And the silence during the writing always grows deeper with the intensity of the discussion that preceded it. Every act contributes to the whole culture. I try to make as many of those acts as deliberate as I can, asking, for example, What do I do with the writings next? Of course, one hazard of reflective writing is that it adds to the paperwork load: Do I really want to assign a grade to it? Do I want to attach a comment? Should I comment instead in class the next day? Which papers do I comment on? Are there other ways of promoting reflection that do not involve writing?

So I think the best reflective activities—the ones that seem to get students to make their own meaning and think deeply—come as a result of their having been trained in reflective thought. I wouldn't have attempted the activity I'll discuss next at the beginning of the semester. I might have spent more time answering questions about my assignment than listening to interesting responses to it.

The Week of a Disaster

There's something a little disturbing in discussing the bombing of the federal building in Oklahoma City, even now. But tragedies happen all the time, it seems, and we are always faced with the question of what to do—or of *whether* to do anything—with student responses and discussion. One of the authentic purposes of reflection, I think, is to make sense of feelings and thoughts, to take a little of the randomness out of life and build something from it. So I offer the following situation as an archetype of a lesson that might help students process their own thoughts about a current event while at the same time dealing with the coursework.

Making Sense

My high school Literature of the American West class met every other day, so I had the advantage of seeing students two days after the bombing instead of the next day. I'm not sure I would have done anything formal had they not had the opportunity to talk about it for a while on their own.

I told them I wanted to do an experiment, and I wasn't sure how it would come out, so they were free to explore possible responses. They'd been reading *Black Elk Speaks* in class, so this was a change of pace for them. I started by showing them brief clips from two films: from *Dances with Wolves*, the scene toward the end in which Dunbar is being driven in chains in a wagon by U.S. troops, and the Lakota tribe he's lived with stages an ambush to rescue him; and, from *The Searchers*, the scene in which John Wayne's family is attacked in their ranch house by "hostile Indians" while he is away. Afterward, I put the following assignment on the board:

> What do these things have in common, both individually and as a group?
> - the clip from *Dances*
> - the clip from *The Searchers*
> - Chapter 2 from *Black Elk* (This chapter involves a story told by one of the elders of Black Elk's tribe about a decisive ambush of U.S. soldiers that the Lakota mounted when they felt they were threatened. We'd just read it the previous week.)
> - the Oklahoma City bombing

And I asked them to do some writing after they'd thought about it.

I modified the approach from work done by Rick VanDeWeghe at the University of Colorado at Denver, and by Irvin Hashimoto, whose book, *Thirteen Weeks: A Guide to Teaching College Writing* (1991), is full of similar assignments. The approach is interesting to me because, on the outside, it forces students to use what they know, or what they think they know, and, on the inside, it asks them to make personal connections, to survey their own emotions, opinions, and values. It is difficult, especially if the student didn't read or watch critically, but it allows the student flexibility and also the opportunity to go back and reexamine the texts (whether print or visual). In this case, I'd shown them *The Searchers* earlier in the semester, and most students had already seen *Dances with Wolves*, some of them several times, so I didn't get any requests to see the scenes over again. I did, however, see about half the students opening the novel and searching the chapter in question. When I chose the clips, I tried not to think too much about what I was choosing; I tried to pick clips that would "fit," but I didn't want to go into this with an answer of my own already worked out. I remember thinking that I liked the variety of perspectives that the film and book excerpts represented toward the Native Americans. It would be tough to see a clear good-guy/bad-guy relationship. I was curious what connections they might make.

> *Mary Beth:* Well I guess that all four scenes and situations focus on the loss of people and certain ways of living.
> In *The Searchers* I found myself relating it to the Holocaust in a very small way. The people were awaiting some sort of destruction from the Indians. In Europe during World War II the Jews found themselves awaiting destruction from the Nazis. . . .
> In *Black Elk Speaks*, I can relate the Sioux Indians feeling threatened and ambushing the white men to the Warsaw Ghetto Uprising of 1943. The Jews in this particular ghetto found their way of living being threatened by the Nazis.

Right away I'm interested in how she might tie in the bombing to this scenario: What "ways of living" might have been lost in Oklahoma? In our country, maybe? Are we seeing signs of an "uprising" here? Who's getting ambushed here? . . . Unfortunately, Mary Beth chose not to work the bombing into her writing. But she paved the way for some good follow-up questions, both for herself and for the class. Sometimes it's interesting to take a question suggested by someone's writing and pose it to the class, even if the student who wrote it doesn't have an answer. I could see what Mary Beth thinks, too, even if she doesn't have an answer in mind initially, by using hypothetical language: what *might* you be saying about Oklahoma here? I circulated and read a few writings to myself, then asked for volunteers. Sometimes they read their writing; more often they discussed what they'd written.

After the discussion that ensued on that first day, I collected the papers just to skim through them. The next day I gave them back and asked students to record any thoughts they'd had during the intervening time, or at least to revisit what they'd written and add a comment. Mary Beth now included *Dances with Wolves* in her scheme.

> *Mary Beth:* In *Dances with Wolves*—the young Indian lost his innocence when he killed the white man. He felt bad about this. I think the Jews, while fighting in the resistance, lost their innocence. Even though they were fighting for something they believed in (as was the young Indian in *Dances with Wolves*) they felt bad about it.

The Holocaust figured in several of the writings, and it turned out that those students were in the same history class. I like that interdisciplinary connection a lot. It shows me that the students who pursued it were reaching for material on their own out of their overall studies. For a moment, we weren't just English class. We were class.

> *Danielle:* In all three, there is killing, destruction and pain, but I don't think we can compare the one day bombing to the years of pain, torture the Indians had to under go. Although I think that each are about the evil side of human behavior. The evil experienced in *Dances* and *Black Elk* is different than in Oklahoma.

Danielle used the bombing as a base from which to discuss the course material; others employed the reverse tactic, using the course material in order to discuss the bombing. In the discussion that followed the writing, a lot of anger came out (as it did elsewhere, of course), and I heard for the first time in several years the word "Towelhead" to describe Arabs. Before the next class meeting, though, it came out that the FBI had long since ruled out foreign terrorists in the bombing, and this fact was reflected in Danielle's writing the next day.

> *Danielle:* During Oklahoma we quickly blamed the middle east terrorists, but we shouldn't be so quick to blame because we were wrong. The bomb caused us to

> feel violated but we caused the middle east americans to feel violated when we blamed their race. You would think we could learn from our mistakes, but we don't seam to. If one Indian tribe attacked white settlers the whites blamed all Indians, which was wrong, but we continue to blame a whole race when only one group does terrorist activities.

I think her opinion this second day of class is much more formed and articulated. She's used course material, outside events, and class discussion to frame her understanding. Danielle is a talkative, confident person as it is. I'm sure she spent time talking about the crisis with people outside of class.

But for some students (like Laurie below), who are opinionated yet quiet, I wonder what other forum exists in school to allow them to shape their opinions.

> *Laurie:* Some of the similarities I see within the Oklahoma Explosion, *Dances W/ Wolves, Searchers,* and *Black Elk Speaks* is that its a Man vs Man. Man killing man. Someone dies, someone wants revenge. Terrorists (we think) had something to do with the explosion. What do we want to do? Find them and give them the death penalty . . . [She gives examples from *Dances*.] There's innocent people dying and not-so-innocent people dying. The ironic part about it is that not-so-innocent people who are dying (or going to die) don't seem to think that they're "bad" people at all (I'm guessing). I just wonder what it'll take to end all this killing? Answering my own question. I don't think it'll ever end. It's been going on since the beginning of time, its going on now, and it'll continue into the future, long after we're all gone.

> *Laurie:* [The next day] I agree with Danielle in the fact that we were a little hasty in accusing someone else for the explosion. I understand why everyone (media, president) would think it was terrorists, I mean, what else are we supposed to think. What makes me sick is that it was Americans who killed all those people.

A good follow-up question for Laurie might have been to ask why we are supposed to think that terrorists did it. I might have asked her to explain more about what the difference is for her in the possibility that it was Americans as opposed to foreigners. She's presented lots to think about here.

When It Doesn't Work

> *Tony:* I don't think there is any connections between *Dances, Searchers,* and Oklahoma. The only similarity between them is violence and death. The movies were stories with a plot and Oklahoma was a simple, violent bombing.

Tony may have been one of those who said "Towelhead." He often sat in the back of the room, talking with several friends, resisting invitations to participate in class discussion. While the rest of the class was writing, I was working to get Tony and his friends to stop talking. When Tony took the time, though, he usually had plenty to say. His response suggested to me that, one, he probably hadn't read or understood the *Black Elk* segment; two, he really didn't want to discuss the bombing, for one reason or another; and three, he'd given up too soon. I hadn't given him the option of finding no connection. I may have communicated that poorly. There usually seems to be a big difference in response when I say, "What might be the similarities . . ." and "What are the similarities. . . ." In any case, Tony's response presents a great opportunity for follow-up questions. He needs to articulate his answer, and he needs to use the material in a way that demonstrates he's thought deeply about it. Right now those elements aren't evident. My job is to ask him questions in class that will draw him out or force him to go back to the text. That can be tough, of course, especially if I don't get a chance to read his work until later, or if I fail to get him involved in the discussion so that he has to begin forming his ideas and become more engaged.

Artwork

Lately I've been encouraging students to use alternative methods, if they're interested, in order to think about the coursework. What if, for instance, I asked them to draw an object that incorporated—that represented symbolically—the connections they saw among all four texts? What if I had them find an object in the room that came closest to representing those connections? What if I had them arrange the four items into "meaningful" groups and explain what they'd done? What if I asked them to arrange the items in terms of importance; which would be the second most important and why? What if I passed out some pipe cleaners or plastic building blocks or modeling clay and asked them to build something that represented the connected relationship? What if I played a song for them and then had them explain why the song might stand for all four items—or showed them a piece of artwork and asked the same question?

All of this is very complicated for me to talk and think about, although on the surface it seems like just another activity anyone can do. I am more and more in awe of the artful teacher who pulls together all the elements demanded by a successful classroom culture every day: maintaining a balance between individual meaning-making and group processing, between quiet thinkers and garrulous ones, between coursework and personal agendas. . . .

And that's probably why I find myself staring at walls so often.

References

Barell, John. 1995. *Teaching for Thoughtfulness: Classroom Strategies to Enhance Intellectual Development.* 2d ed. White Plains, NY: Longman.

Hashimoto, Irvin Y. 1991. *Thirteen Weeks: A Guide to Teaching College Writing.* Portsmouth, NH: Boynton/Cook.

2 Lightbulbs and Pandemonium: Thinking about Thinking

Jeff Schwartz
Greenwich Academy, Greenwich, Connecticut

For the last two years, I've been asking my juniors to think about thinking. They are used to reflecting on the elements of their reading and writing processes: they reflect on their reading via paper drafts, expressive writing, and classroom talk, and they reflect on both their own writing and that of their peers. So it makes sense for them to reflect on their reflections. They do this as part of an ongoing portfolio project, usually halfway through the year, after they have read a wide range of genres and time periods in American literature and after they have written extensively in a variety of forms.

By articulating their own sense of how they think, the students are capturing strategies that help them to become better readers and writers. When I collect and share excerpts from their reflections on thinking, students can see patterns. It's as if they have x-rayed an otherwise invisible process which they can now picture, and thus their chances of seeing or controlling it increase. This is probably even more helpful for the student who isn't a fluent writer and who doesn't read quickly or find interpretation an automatic process. When these students define thinking for themselves, it is sometimes quite visual. "My mind is a movie screen," Emily writes. "I weed through the notes in my books and think about what we've discussed in class and then map out in my mind how I'm going to go about answering the question and formulating it into an essay." From movies to weeds to maps, Emily grasps thinking by turning it into concrete and visual metaphors. "Thinking is like a tree," Ariana writes. "You start off with one major idea, or even just one simple word, and as you build on to your original thought, you branch out to explore and create 'sub thoughts.' And from these 'sub thoughts,' you break down even further into the most intricate, deepest thoughts. You philosophize, analyze, and reflect, proposing different solutions, different variations on a theme."

The words "explore" and "discover" keep reappearing in my students' reflections. They see themselves as explorers and discoverers of meaning. "I discovered things I hadn't before. I dug into each idea and made a clear base for myself," Adriana writes. How do they discover? They make choices, they connect, they ask good questions. Westy sees that "thinking is about making choices about what to believe, whether to go left or right, to eat this or that, or to follow a friend who has jumped off a bridge." For Elizabeth, "thinking, to me, means connecting things I read to events in my life or other poems, stories, etc." Thinking in English is an active process of inquiry. "That is what thinking is to me—it is understanding something and then questioning it," writes Tracy. "It is forming opinions about issues, even if these opinions are in conflict with those of the author."

Many of the students also address the metaphor of depth—probing an idea below the surface. Thinking for them is not superficial. While it may appear as natural as breathing, they also realize that the kind of thinking one needs to do to interpret Emily Dickinson's poetry and to write about it requires work and persistence. As Katie writes,

> Everyone thinks in some way or another: what to do today, what if he doesn't like me? I think it's going to rain, I'll think about it, I don't think that's fair, etc., etc. What is less obvious, and what I will focus on are the implications of thinking: the fact that because I can think, I am able to do things like analyze, plan, hypothesize, discover, describe, and form my own opinion.

These are acts of mind that we all do when we read, but we don't always articulate them. However, when students reflect on thinking, they articulate what it means to read for meaning. Sara writes:

> First as I read I automatically (involuntarily) create a running movie in my head. My mind creates a mental picture of everything I read and stores it. This enables me to remember precisely where and when something occurred in any particular book. As this goes on, I constantly evaluate what is said, why it is said, and any inconsistencies with past statements.

Sara and others recognize that reading cannot be passive. She evaluates as she reads and can store pages like a "running movie" in her head. But most readers can't do this. They must write as they read, and that process of annotation becomes one of the biggest breakthroughs for them as learners. As Bevan writes,

> When I am reading, I have to be able to write in the margins of the book, so that I can get my thoughts on the page. When I read,

many times I will have questions or if I understand what the author is trying to say, I know I won't remember later what it was he was trying to say. It is like a fleeting revelation that comes and goes, and if I don't write it down, it will be gone forever. Thinking, for me, is something that is always going on, with new thoughts going through my head every second; if I don't write down a thought, I will never remember it.

Annotation aids memory as the reader comments, questions, reacts, or simply marks central ideas in the margin with checks, stars, brackets, smiles, abbreviations, or other graphic symbols.

Writing response statements—frequent, informal writing in response to literature—is another way to think about reading. "When I've read a story or poem that I don't understand," writes Tyler, "the last thing that I think would help is to write a response. But it really does help to think out loud on paper. I know it sounds kind of weird, but it's true. I ask questions in the beginning of the response, and by the end I have pretty much figured it out for myself." Learning couldn't be clearer.

Andrew sees a response as an argument with himself:

> What I did was started to argue with myself as I wrote. I would put down what possible ways there were to look at the poem, then I argued them while I wrote, and it seemed to work rather well because by the end, after I had tidied up a little and explained the pandemonium, I had what I considered a rather good view of the poem.

The informal responses allow for and even encourage pandemonium. If, in the process of writing them, the student raises a good question and figures it out independently, then the response has succeeded. Thinking may be best without the teacher.

Students recognize how they think in drafting essays, too. In Courtney's reflection on thinking, she says,

> Writing a paper is one way in which I have to think a lot. When doing this, I first ask myself questions. What do I want this paper to say? What is my argument? How can I prove it? After having these and other questions out, I try to answer them. I look through my journal entries and free writing to try to establish what my opinion is. I look at the context, trying to find examples and ways to back up my opinion. I hypothesize, plan, and analyze the information I have gotten, so I can make a paper out of it. I try to make sense of all the jumbled up ideas and creations in my brain, as if I were trying to untangle a big knot.

Andra and many others recognize the value of thinking through their drafts:

> I am a long-winded thinker whose mind changes quite a bit before my final stand is taken on any given issue. It takes me a long time to be convinced of any one thing, as I usually debate all sides before I choose. Therefore, revision allows me to reorganize my thoughts and analyze them before I am held to my words.

In their reflections on thinking, students have recognized how important it is to explore, question, connect, choose, and persist. Thinking through pandemonium can be a frustrating struggle. It is almost always a pleasure, too. Branching out an idea, distilling a complicated point, exploring a deep question, discovering a new perspective, or making sense of a previously confusing poem is a joyful, satisfying process. To feel the brain's synapses fire—the light bulb flash—is the reward for the persistence and hard work of thinking. As Katie concludes,

> When I was first given [Dickinson's] "The Soul Selects Her Own Society" and told that I was to relate it to one of Whitman's poems, I gave the sheet of paper a look that said, "What, are you joking?" But as I began to read the poems more carefully and analyze each one, the little light bulb began to go off. I began to see more and more connections, one thing seemed to lead right to another. Before I knew it, my interpretation had gone from "I don't get it" to "they're both talking of making decisions" to "they say you should be yourself" to "they say that they both are resisting the influence and temptation of personal prestige/wealth." All this happened in forty minutes, through a miraculous process of human life, complex beyond imagination and referred to simply as thinking.

3 Responding, Reflecting, and Evaluating

Kathleen and James Strickland
Slippery Rock University of Pennsylvania

Practicing what we preach—involving students in authentic learning and meaningful, reflective activities—is the most difficult part of being a whole language teacher. Jim and I spend a great deal of time trying to keep our teaching authentic; we invite our students to read the experts, to reflect about their own learning experiences, and to begin to develop their own philosophies of teaching and learning, while we model the kinds of teaching and learning our students are examining.

The temptation always exists to tell them about student-centered classrooms with generative curricula and organic lesson plans. Many of you who teach at the elementary or secondary level can empathize with the excuse that some of us at the college level resort to when we backslide to teacher-directed instruction: "I only have fifteen weeks, two (maybe three) meetings a week; I *have* to give them information. There isn't time to let them discover, reflect, connect—I have to tell them what they need to know." It's easy to fall into the trap of lecturing about a whole language classroom and what it would look like if they were to find themselves in one. We really understand the frustration. There *is* little time to create community, and, as the weeks go by, we too worry about the progress of our classes. What if we don't "cover" everything we addressed last semester? What if too much time is spent asking questions? Will it come down to simply telling them the answers?

Teaching is always risk taking. It's much harder to create a classroom where students discuss what literacy is and how language can be used to think and discover across the curriculum—a classroom, that is, where students are responsible for their own learning. We never know from semester to semester just what the students in our classes will take with them as they leave to enter student teaching or begin their first teaching jobs. Our outcome-based assessment shouldn't center on a mythical body of knowledge that students should leave with; instead, we should worry about how well they understood their own learning and came to formulate their own philosophies of learning. We hope that in our major's courses we help prospective teachers learn about learning and, in the process, discover how to support such learning in their own classrooms.

Reflective Journal

In order to facilitate thinking about philosophy, we use various reflective practices in our courses. One practice that Jim and I have used for years is that of journaling. As part of my methods course, I assign many readings from professional journals, and the students themselves distribute readings to the class that they have found while researching their personal language interests. Students respond to these readings by writing entries in their journals, responses that are reflections about the theory and practices addressed in the readings (as distinct from summaries of the readings). But these journals are not solitary activities written by students to display knowledge for their teacher. These are dialogue journals, in which a dialogue takes place with classmates and with me. I ask students to leave a double margin on the left-hand side of the page when they write their initial responses, and then, for the first few minutes of each class, we share our journals and respond in the extrawide margin to one another's thoughts, perceptions, and opinions (see Figure 1). Students reflect on their own experiences as learners and as teachers and are free to question, argue, wonder, and often celebrate with their classmates. I participate as a member of the community and facilitate the discussion instead of directing it.

Jim often uses a sequential dialogue journal whose topics begin with responses to the reading but shift to reflective responses by the students to their own learning. His students write the first entry of the week in response to the reading assigned for the week, as my students do; the second entry, usually done in class, is written in response to a classmate's entry of the week (actually written in the classmate's journal following the writer's entry); after the journal is returned to the original writer, the third entry is made, a further reflection upon what was written in the journal by a classmate (or a reflection upon what has been learned in the class or a related class). The purpose of each week's entries is for students to reflect upon their growth as learners.

In Jim's Composition and Rhetoric class, a student who'd been out for a semester on probation began every week's journal entry in the early part of the semester with a statement like, "This was really boring, I kept falling asleep reading it." The classmate who traded journals with Scott for the second entry was often hard-pressed to find some-

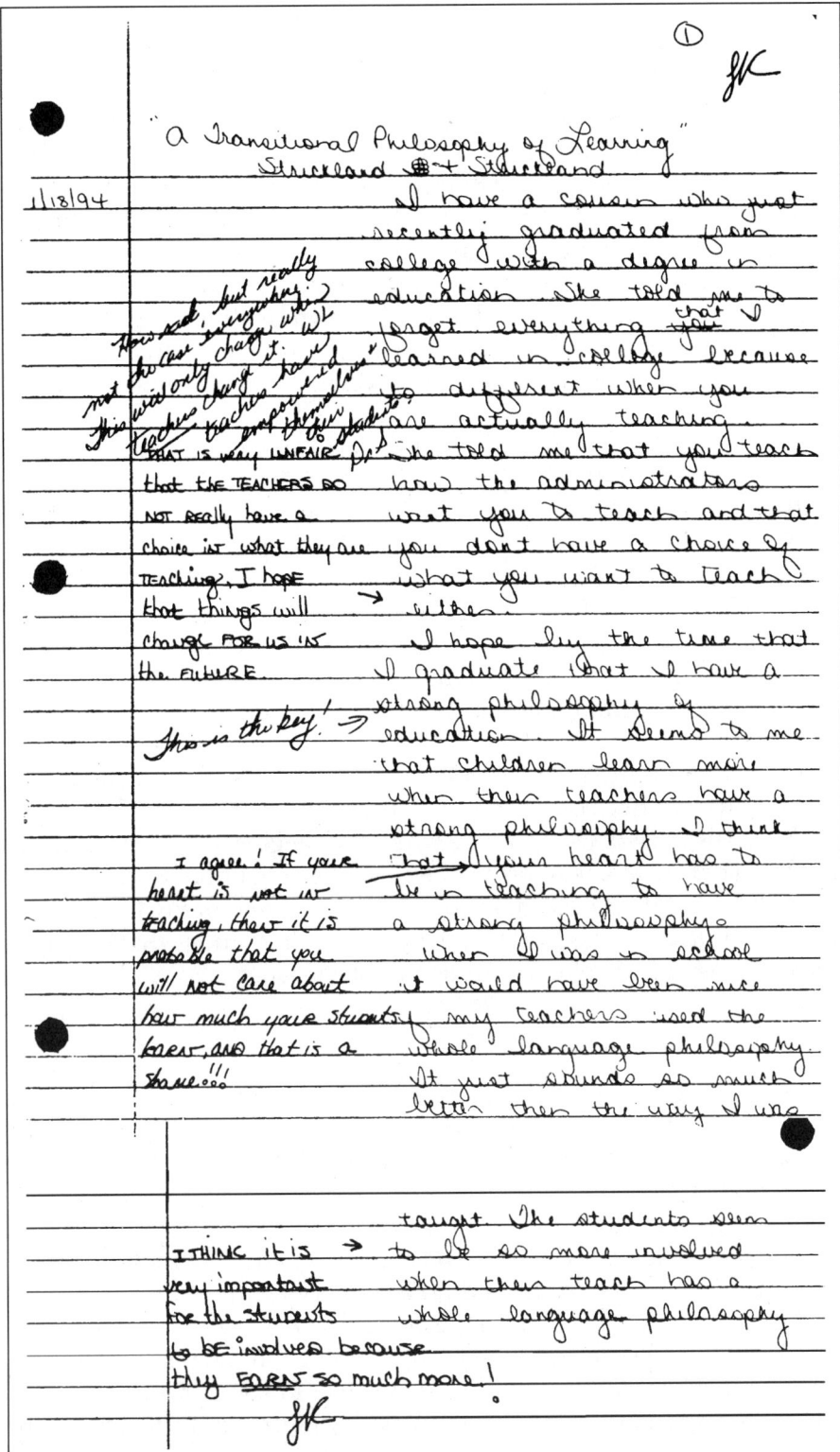

Figure 1. Sample pages from dialogue journal written by Jennifer Cowmeadow. Used with permission.

thing to respond to. His classmates would resort to responses such as, "yeah, I thought it was boring too. I had trouble understanding the part about..." The saving grace of the sequential journal was that when Scott traded his journal, he got one in return (and whatever that student wrote, it had to be more engaging than "this was really boring..."). So Scott was coerced into responding to a classmate's reflection about the reading, and, no matter how limited his own reading of the text was, he was thinking about someone else's reading and thereby learning something about both the assigned reading and his classmate's reflection upon it.

A colleague of ours in the English department, Cindy LaCom, uses a variation of the reflective journal that she calls the "team" journal, a collaborative journal kept in a central location, usually the reserve shelf of the university library. Cindy divides her class into four-person teams, and each member of the team reads and responds to the entries of the other members. The first person for the week to check out the journal from the reserve shelf begins the conversation; each succeeding member of the team reads the dialogue as it exists so far and continues by responding. Student opinion is divided as to whether it is easier to begin the conversation or to respond to what the others have put forth. The important thing is that students are engaged in reading and writing and in reflective consideration. No matter what approach to reflective journals is used, we find that, when class begins, students who have prepared not only by reading, but also by reflecting upon what they have read and what their classmates have thought, are more willing to participate in class discussions, which become deliberations that belong to the class instead of being controlled by the teacher.

Reflective Research

In Jim's Composition and Rhetoric course this semester, after the class read Maxine Hairston's "The Winds of Change" (1982) and Frank Smith's "Myths of Writing" (1981), Jim asked his students to design a series of interview questions to try to discover which side of the paradigm shift in viewing and teaching writing (to which Hairston refers) potential interviewees would fall on and what myths about writing they subscribed to. Students worked on the interview questions in groups and then volunteered their suggestions to the class as a whole. They discussed the relative merits of each question, what it was addressing, how it might be answered, and what they would know from the answer. The class made adjustments, friendly amendments, and revisions to the

> **Writing Survey**
> 1. Are there special qualities or characteristics that set a writer apart from everyone else?
> 2. What do you think is the proper sequence for writing a paper?
> 3. If a student turns in a paper that needs revision, do you let him or her revise? And if so, do you change the grade?
> 4. Can children learn to write without completing drills and exercises?
> 5. What is the secret to becoming good at writing?
> 6. Is it possible for a writing to be perfect the first time?
> 7. Do you believe in writer's block?
> 8. What environment is most conducive to writing? (Where do you write?)
> 9. Why do people write?

Figure 2. Student-generated interview questions regarding myths about writing.

questions. After they had agreed on ten or so questions, Jim took a copy handwritten by one of the students and typed it for distribution. The only change he made was in deciding the order in which the questions would appear (see Figure 2). Students then chose teachers they were curious about or felt comfortable enough to interview, negotiating choices so that no teachers were asked twice. Some chose to go back to their high school teachers, one wanted to interview a community college teacher, and one student interviewed her mother who was a high school teacher.

The students were given as much time as it required to complete the interview (some teachers were notoriously difficult to locate). Because the interview project was begun early in the semester, many of the students at that time actually subscribed to many of Smith's myths, arguing that was how they learned. Some felt that "writing involves transferring thoughts from mind to paper" and that "writing is speech plus handwriting, spelling, and punctuation" (Smith 1981, 793). Even more believed that writing is a "sedentary," "silent," and "solitary" activity (797–98). Smith believed that recognition of the myth was generally enough to avoid falling victim to it, but he was writing for teachers, not for undergraduates.

Jim's class became so involved in other projects during the semester that they did not return to the interview results until late in the second half of the semester. By that time the students were much more informed about the history and origins of what is considered the domain of English teachers, so much so that the writing survey took on additional significance. The week they examined the survey results, instead of having each student simply read the answers to the class, Jim began by having them share the responses in small groups. Then he asked the groups to decide which answers were interesting enough to share with the class as a whole and to comment about the responses. As a culmination to the survey, and as part of the library research they were doing about individual contemporary composition theorists they had selected to present to the class, Jim asked them to search the data banks for anything their interviewees had written. At the next class meeting, instead of presenting tallies and scores, the students simply commented upon any surprises they had found and on Smith's and Hairston's notion that teachers of writing must be writers themselves. This activity turned up in the reflective entries in their journals; some wondered about the advice given by people who don't practice what they preach and many affirmed that they would be writers who teach writing.

Reflective Self-Evaluation

As is the case at most universities, we are required to evaluate our students with the traditional letter grades of A, B, C, D, and F, according to criteria that, historically, have been set up by the instructor and that have imposed expectations which students must hope to measure up to. Over the past few years, I have involved students in their own evaluation, since the primary purpose of evaluation is to help the learner see strengths and areas of need, regardless of course or grade level. For every assignment, students are directly involved in drawing up the criteria by which the assignment will be evaluated, based on what they have read and discussed in class. In the beginning, it sometimes takes as long as two class periods to help the students develop appropriate rubrics or checklists for their assignments. Because the purpose of the assigned projects is to demonstrate what they have learned in the course, the assignments are open-ended, but all the projects are judged by the same criteria developed for that assignment.

For the last few semesters, one assignment asked students, working in pairs, to construct a thematic framework to demonstrate how they might use language across the curriculum to study a topic or theme (Weaver 1994, 429–35). Last semester the students developed an extensive rubric that addressed what they felt was important for this framework (see Figure 3). Under each category were found the components that the students felt should be reflected somewhere in the framework. For example, students felt that the teacher's role as facilitator, i.e., category seven, might be demonstrated by evidence of student choice,

Integrated Framework—Criteria for Evaluation	Much	Some	None
1. **Web** 　Connections between/among categories 　Categories relate to theme 　Variety of subjects			
2. **Transactional Objectives** 　Stated in transactional terms 　Goals, not activities 　Objectives appropriate to theme			
3. **Activities Appropriate to Objectives** 　Meaningful activities 　Activities relate to objectives 　Activities relate to theme			
4. **Schedule** 　Blocks of time/flexibility 　Daily reading/writing 　Minilessons/conference time			
5. **Reading and Writing Across the Curriculum** 　Writing to learn through research 　Journals and/or logs 　Reading and writing in content areas			
6. **Resources** 　Appropriate to theme 　Includes fiction and nonfiction 　Adequate for activities, choice 　Multimedia			
7. **Teacher as Facilitator** 　Student choice 　Cooperative learning 　Conferencing (tch/stu; stu/stu) 　Inquiry-based learning			
8. **Student-Centeredness** 　Choice 　Minilessons 　Student needs driving instruction 　Centers/environment			
9. **Culminating Activity** 　Appropriate and meaningful 　Puts closure on framework 　Students share with parents, etc.			
10. **Presentation** 　Organized 　Neat 　Bibliography			

Figure 3. Student-generated rubric for open-ended assignment.

cooperative learning, conferencing, and inquiry-based learning. The student-centeredness of the framework, category eight, might be demonstrated by evidence of choice, minilessons, instruction driven by student needs, and a student-centered environment. Each group completed a self-evaluation using this form and turned it in with the assignment. As the person ultimately responsible for assigning a grade, I used another copy of the same rubric to look for evidence of each element in the framework. I awarded points according to whether there was much evidence, some evidence, or no evidence and translated the sum into a grade, again according to a point spread previously decided by the class as a whole.

As a result of this type of reflective evaluation, the work turned in was, for the most part, very good, the product of time spent reflecting on the assignment itself without wondering about "what the teacher wants." Although I grade these assignments, I no longer lose sleep wondering if I've been fair; the students own their work—they make decisions about topics, purposes, and components of the assignment based on what they have learned in theory about teaching literacy across the curriculum. Students worry less about the grade and more about producing something that reflects what they know about thematic teaching. Instead of directing and making all the decisions, I have been able to facilitate this activity—what whole language teachers do.

Rubrics are designed for every graded assignment in our courses and many are simpler than the one my students developed for the thematic framework. Because students spend a great deal of time writing reflections in their journals, evaluating these writings is an important part of the class. Twice a semester Jim collects his students' journals, reads and comments on them, and gives the students credit for completing the minimum number and for the length of entries. Counting pages is admittedly the least successful aspect of the reflective journal, but he found that his students were slacking off on the third entry of the week—the hardest one—until they realized that it "counted." Such thinking is learned from years of school which have taught students that "serious" work is graded to prove its worth.

Nevertheless, we all feel unsatisfied with the number-crunching approach, so I asked my students to design a way to grade journals. They decided that points should be given for completion, since the actual commitment to writing is of itself beneficial. The students felt that content should also be evaluated, and decided that they would photocopy what they believed were their three best entries to be evaluated accord-

---

Criteria for Journal Evaluation

Number of Readings: 20 assigned (possible 2 pts.)
    18–20 completed = 2 pts.
    15–17 completed = 1 pt.
    less than 15 completed = 0 pts.   _____ pts.

Content: (2 pts. each; 6 pts. possible)
    Evidence of Theory   _____ pts.
    Connected to Actual Experience   _____ pts.
    Depth of Understanding   _____ pts.

                      Total   _____ pts.

    Scale: A 8 pts.
               A- 7 pts.
               B 6 pts.
               B- 5 pts.
               C 4 pts.
               C- 3 pts.

Figure 4. Student-generated approach for evaluating reading journals.

ing to evidence of understanding, theory, and connecting with actual experiences (see Figure 4). Because students choose what they feel reflects their best work, they are still part of the process of evaluation, and they understand that everything counts toward their grade, still an important consideration when students decide the relative worth of an assignment.

    As we have affirmed elsewhere, "teachers need to evaluate student performance, but . . . more honest, worthwhile, and humane ways exist to assess than have been employed in traditional classrooms" (Strickland and Strickland 1993, 135). And as Elliot Eisner (1992) says, "We need . . . to approach educational evaluation not simply as a way of scoring students, but as a way in which to find out how well we and our students are doing in order to do better what we do" (5). Each year we continue to help our students reflect on their learning and their own development as learners. Each year our students help us become better teachers.

References

Eisner, Elliot. 1992. "The Reality of Reform." *English Leadership Quarterly* (October): 2–5.

Hairston, Maxine. 1982. "The Winds of Change: Thomas Kuhn and the Revolution in the Teaching of Writing." *College Composition and Communication* 33: 76–88.

Smith, Frank. 1981. "Myths of Writing." *Language Arts* 58 (October): 792–98.

Strickland, Kathleen, and James Strickland. 1993. *UN-Covering the Curriculum: Whole Language in Secondary and Postsecondary Classrooms.* Portsmouth, NH: Boynton/Cook.

Weaver, Constance. 1994. *Reading Process and Practice: From Socio-Psycholinguistics to Whole Language.* 2d ed. Portsmouth, NH: Heinemann.

II Reflecting and Connecting through Reading, Writing, and Viewing

When we issued the call for manuscripts for this volume, we believed we would receive some chapters that could be categorized neatly under the term *reflecting* and others that could be categorized under *connecting*. It soon became clear in our reading of the manuscripts that such divisions were not going to be possible. The two thinking processes that we're focusing on here are intertwined in practice. While students may be asked to do more of one or the other in any given activity, they certainly reflect *and* connect as they use their language in meaningful ways for authentic purposes and audiences.

In some of the manuscripts we received, authors placed more emphasis on the processes that students used in their reading, writing, and viewing while in other manuscripts authors emphasized students' learning through the presentations, projects, and portfolios that they produced. In Part 2, you will read descriptions of successful classroom practices that encourage students to reflect and connect as they read, write, and view.

The section opens with a description of a middle school classroom. Renate Schulz relates her observations of a teacher helping students connect their own experiences with those in *Sadako and the Thousand Paper Cranes*. The processes of reading continue with two descriptions of classroom practices that help students cross boundaries in various ways. Bruce Goebel offers specific assignments and student comments to illustrate the advantages of rereading as a means of reflection. Claudia

Greenwood and Cynthia Walters explain how they paired high school students with preservice teachers to choose, read, and write about books together.

Writing and reading continue to be intertwined in the next three chapters. Carol Jago asks high school students to model their own poems on the odes of Pablo Neruda, and Leslie Richardson encourages middle school students to use the poems of Rainer Maria Rilke as models for their writing. Kathryn Megyeri describes several creative writing activities which grew from her students' reading of Paul Zindel's *The Pigman*.

The next seven chapters in Part 2 focus more on writing, encouraging students both to reflect and to connect. Sheryl Lain breaks down the traditional barriers between creative and academic writing as she tries a research assignment that many of her colleagues find unusual. Cynthia Kuhn demonstrates the power of thinking logs as tools for helping students develop thoughtfulness. Using dialogue journals in an introductory literature class was a powerful strategy for Helen Sitler, Kelly Carameli, and Brandi Abbott. Erika Scheurer uses "discussion letters" to help students employ writing to connect experiences and explore their thinking. Darrell g.h. Schramm offers a series of open-ended response questions that invite students to become more engaged in their reading and writing. The last article with a focus on writing presents reflections on and dramatic samples from a multicultural and cross-generational writing workshop led by Susan Tchudi, Stephen Adkison, Jacob Blumner, Francis Fritz, and Maria Madruga.

These articles are followed by two that emphasize viewing processes. As more and more of our students spend increasing amounts of time surrounded by film, television, and computer screens, we must be prepared to reimagine literacy to include an understanding of "reading" and "writing" visual images. Meta Carstarphen uses "target assignments" to challenge her students to investigate and critique a variety of popular media. Richard H. Fehlman demonstrates the ways in which viewing should also be regarded as a language process as he guides students in viewing a "Calvin and Hobbes" comic strip.

4 Stories, Readers, and the World Beyond Books

Renate Schulz
Winnipeg Education Centre, University of Manitoba, Canada

More and more, teachers are realizing the importance of teaching literature for its own sake and not just as a motivating way to teach and practice reading skills. And more and more, teachers are beginning to understand that the follow-up to reading a story or a novel has to be more than just a summary of the plot and a series of comprehension questions to be answered by students. Literature invites reaction and response, and Rosenblatt's transactional theory of reader response (1938/1976, 1978, 1988) has given classroom teachers a greater awareness of the ways in which readers experience texts, the ways in which readers bring meaning to texts, and the ways in which they take meaning from texts. Teachers of literature have come to understand that it is their task to focus on this transaction between the reader and the text and to deepen and extend this meaning-making literary experience for students.

Often, however, teachers themselves have had little experience in transacting with a text and are unsure of their own literary insights. As a result, after the reading of a story or novel, a discussion of comprehension questions seems safer, and literature study becomes, in Rosenblatt's terms (1978), an efferent, fact-accumulating process, rather than an aesthetic experience. In distinguishing between efferent and aesthetic reading, Rosenblatt reminds us that aesthetic reading is most often neglected in schools. In efferent reading, the reader looks for facts and information to draw from a text. An efferent reading stance is most frequently adopted for content-area reading, and follow-up questions that focus on comprehension are quite appropriate in conjunction with the reading of social studies textbooks, health textbooks, or reference books. In aesthetic reading, however, the focus is on what Rosenblatt

---

This chapter was published in 1992 in issue 25 (3) of *Insights into Open Education*, the journal of the North Dakota Council of Teachers of English, under the title "Reading Stories: Responding to Literature and Making Connections across the Curriculum." It is reprinted with permission of *Insights* editor Sara Hanhan.

(1976, 1978) refers to as a lived-through evocation of the text—or the process in which readers select ideas, sensations, feelings, and images from their past linguistic, literary, and life experiences and synthesize them into a new experience.

A good book can be very powerful and can deeply affect the life of its reader. What happens to all of us when we are impressed by a book is that we want to talk about it. We have undergone an experience and we want to discuss it in order to understand it more clearly. We want to share it with others. Children respond to stories in the same way. Their initial response to literature, and the questions they ask about literature, most often reflect an aesthetic reading stance. It is up to teachers, then, to nurture this natural response to stories, and to establish a classroom environment that invites an aesthetic reading of literature. Teachers can do this by the way in which literature is presented, by the kinds of questions they ask during story time, and by the types of discussion they encourage. David Bleich (1975), a reader-response theorist who is very interested in the classroom application of reading theories, has developed a basic set of questions, intended not to glean facts and information from a reading but, rather, to evoke feelings and encourage an affective transaction with the text. Using Bleich's approach, teachers might frame their questions for students in this way:

1. What details or features of the story stand out the most?
2. How does the story make you feel?
3. Does the story remind you of any experience you've had, or of any other work you've read?

It is evident from the nature of these questions that Bleich's technique can be applied equally well to any story and at any reading level. A variation of this approach is to ask students to close their eyes and picture the story or passage they have just heard or read. If the teacher then asks students to talk about which pictures from the story come most clearly into their minds, each child will have a different image and will speak of different things. The many different responses to these questions can then form the basis for group discussions, where students listen to the thoughts of others, learn from others, and reflect on their own initial responses to a story. As students gain confidence in their ability to respond to a story, the teacher continues to extend and deepen the students' interactions with the text by encouraging them to evaluate the story and the characters, to examine the author's style, to link their reading to other books and experiences, and to think critically about all they encounter in the pages of a text.

Judy Harapiak is a teacher who provides her middle-years students with many such opportunities to respond to stories in different ways, to reflect on their responses, and to link their reading to their own experiences as well as to other areas of the curriculum. Judy teaches a grade 4-5-6 class in the Elementary Alternative Education Program at Montrose School in Winnipeg, Canada. Montrose School houses several alternative classrooms, and Judy Harapiak and Diane Zack are the two teachers responsible for the grade 4-5-6 alternative program.

The Alternative Education Program is based on a belief in the value of a student-centered, activity-based, thematic approach to learning. In each classroom there are children with a grade span of three years, working collaboratively to investigate topics and to learn through discussion, research, and hands-on activities. Parents are involved in the day-to-day activities of the program and are welcomed in the classroom. Students are encouraged to become responsible for their own learning and to transact in meaningful ways with the real world around them and with the world of books before them.

It is in this classroom setting that Judy introduces her students to Eleanor Coerr's story, *Sadako and the Thousand Paper Cranes*. This is the story of Sadako Sasaki, who was only twelve years old when she died. She was two when an atom bomb was dropped on the city of Hiroshima where she lived. Ten years later she had leukemia as a result of radiation from the bomb. While in the hospital, Sadako began making a thousand paper cranes, hoping thereby to heal herself. In Japanese mythology the crane is the symbol of life, and to make a thousand cranes would mean that her wish would be granted and she would be well again. But Sadako could make only 644 cranes before she died. Her classmates then folded 356 cranes so that 1,000 could be buried with her. They also collected Sadako's letters and published them in a book, which is widely read in Japan. Sadako became a heroine to the children of Japan, and a statue of Sadako was erected in the Hiroshima Peace Park as a monument to her and to all children who were killed by the atom bomb. Sadako now stands on top of a granite mountain, holding a golden crane in outstretched hands. She represents all those children who lost their lives, and the inscription at the base of the statue speaks for all these children: "This is our cry, this is our prayer; peace in the world." Now, visitors from all over the world leave paper cranes at Sadako's memorial in the Hiroshima Peace Park, and every year on August 6, Peace Day, the children of Japan and children from all over the world honor Sadako and remember her wish by sending cranes to be placed beneath her statue.

In Canada, as in the United States, November 11 is designated as a day to remember those who died in war and to celebrate the hope of peace. Therefore, Judy chose the month of November to introduce *Sadako and the Thousand Paper Cranes* to her students. Through friends and through the generosity of the Japanese Consulate, she was able to accumulate an assortment of Japanese posters, pictures, calendars, fans, and even a kimono. After school one day, these were all arranged about the room, so that when the students arrived the next morning, the new decor immediately created a sense of anticipation. It conveyed a feeling of Japanese culture, generated excitement, and drew students into the activity of the new book about to be read. Eventually, as the literature study continued and extended into the other areas of the curriculum, the results of the children's own activities and investigations were also displayed. (See Figure 1 for an interdisciplinary planning web.) And soon the complexity of the classroom's decor reflected the complex interweavings of the theme of peace in Sadako's story with the students' new learnings about Japan, about peace efforts in other countries, about health, about science, geography, technology, art, drama, music, and physical education.

Judy begins the literature study by drawing her students' attention to the title of the book, pointing out that the selection of a title is a very important decision for an author, and asking students to think about the author's choice of a title for this short novel. Then students are asked to look at the cover illustration. Meaningful literature study generally moves from reading, to interpretation, to criticism, and the study of art follows similar stages. In order to understand and appreciate visual communication, Feldman (1970) suggests a procedure suitable for classroom discussions of art reproductions and illustrations. The first stage of the procedure is to have students describe everything they see in the work of art—all the colors, shapes, and objects. In Judy's class this means that students look carefully at every detail of the cover illustration of *Sadako and the Thousand Paper Cranes*. The next step is to analyze the relationships between the various parts of the illustration by answering questions such as, "Do certain shapes or colors seem to predominate?" or "Does any single object seem to be more important than others?" or "Are the figures looking at or touching each other?" In this way students begin to gain an understanding of how a mood or feeling is evoked through visual communication and how this knowledge might inform their predictions about the contents of the book. Because each student comes to the work with a different set of experiences, expectations, and associations, responses to the illustration vary.

Physical Education
Martial arts (Karate)
Judo
Sumo wrestling

Music
Singing or song writing
Listening for enjoyment

Language Arts
Vocabulary
Japanese words
Superstitions

Movement
Dramatic play
Puppetry

Role Playing
Dramatization
Diary
Log
Letters to Japanese students
Journals

Games
Card games
Board games
20 questions
Crossword puzzles

Discussion
Of cover (Feldman Approach)
Of student's questions
De Bono's hats
Small group
Interview (character)
Imaginary conversation
Reporter
- Newscaster
- Newspaper (obituary column)
Comparison to other books with same theme (death, war, courage)

Technology
Cars
Cameras
Electronics
- Computers
- Nintendo games
- Stereos
- Musical instruments

Customs
Did you know?
- Chopstick
- Kimono
- Shoes
- Hair
- Superstitions (beliefs)
- Holidays
- Calligraphy

Science
Atomic bomb
- Chemical reactions
- Radiation

Health
Leukemia
Radiation
Side effects

Math
Graph
- Weather
- Population

Food
Recipes
Cooking
Restaurants

Symbols
Peace
- Remembrance Day
- Christmas

Social Studies
Geography
Maps (Hiroshima)
Government (Emperor)
Time line (war)
Immigration to Canada
Comparisons to Canada

Sadako and the Thousand Paper Cranes

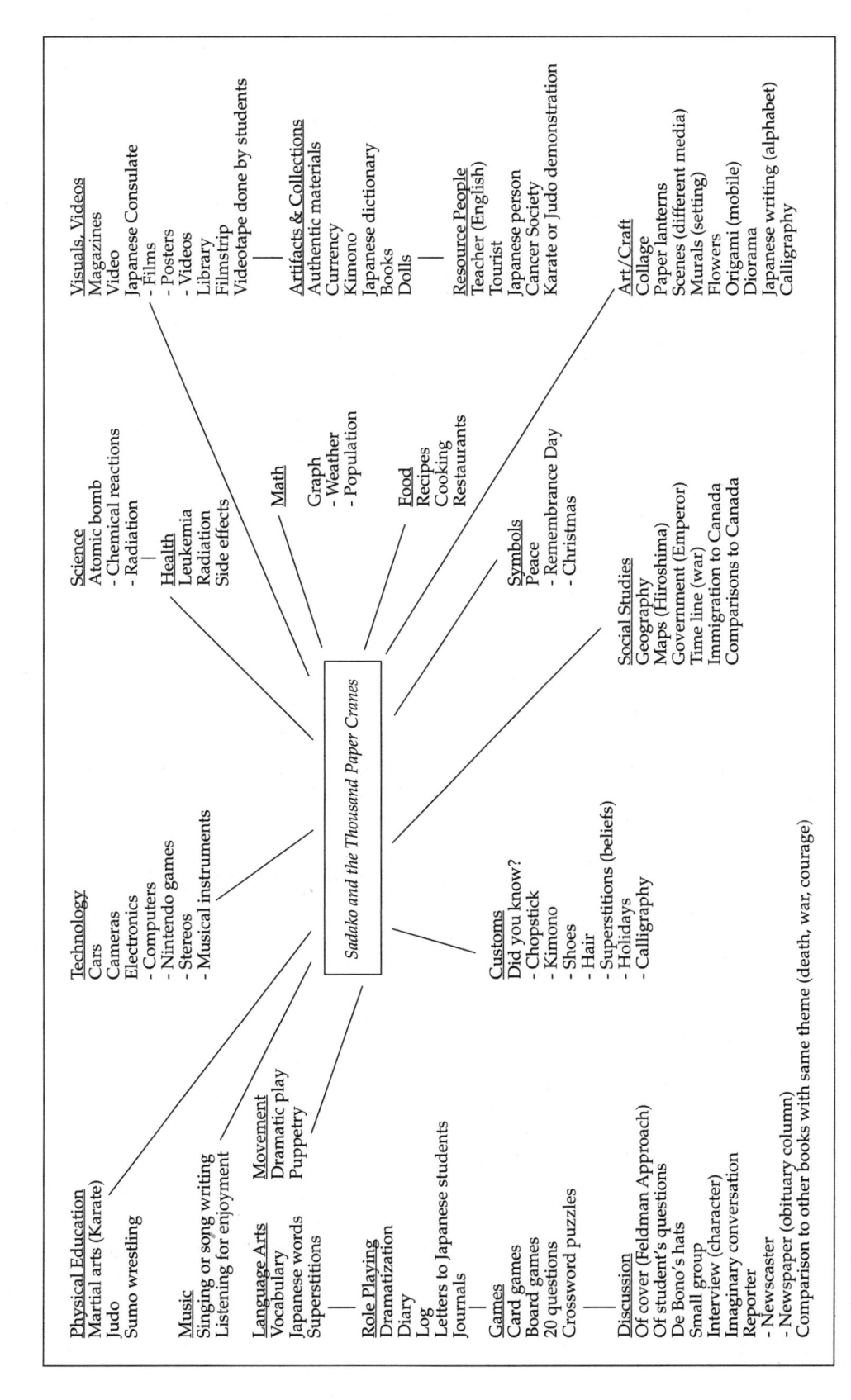

Visuals, Videos
Magazines
Video
Japanese Consulate
- Films
- Posters
- Videos
Library
Filmstrip
Videotape done by students

Artifacts & Collections
Authentic materials
Currency
Kimono
Japanese dictionary
Books
Dolls

Resource People
Teacher (English)
Tourist
Japanese person
Cancer Society
Karate or Judo demonstration

Art/Craft
Collage
Paper lanterns
Scenes (different media)
Murals (setting)
Flowers
Origami (mobile)
Diorama
Japanese writing (alphabet)
Calligraphy

Figure 1. Interdisciplinary planning web.

Generally, however, the only sense in which an interpretation could be considered incorrect is when it is completely inconsistent with the visual information presented. Just as Bleich (1975) and Rosenblatt (1976, 1978, 1988) encourage readers to bring their feelings and background knowledge to a text in order to make meaning of the printed marks on the page, the Feldman approach encourages a similar process in order to advance students' visual literacy.

The classroom decor, the title of the book (with its unusual words), the students' predictions based on their different interpretations of the cover illustration—all of these heighten their eagerness to begin reading. Judy reads the first chapter to the class, and then students go off to read on their own or in small groups. Reading groups sit at round tables to facilitate interaction, and conversational exchanges about the story are encouraged. Students comment on characters and events, offer their predictions, and share their interpretations.

Judy then helps her students extend their responses to the novel by drawing their attention to such elements of story as character and setting. During the reading of the first chapter, she directs her students to pay close attention to those descriptive phrases and sentences that might help them form a mental landscape of the story's setting. Then students draw pictures or create murals to show their understanding of the setting and to highlight what for them were its most vivid features. Art is used again when discussion turns to Sadako's character. The class as a whole brainstorms for words that would describe the kind of person Sadako is. Each student is drawn to different qualities of her character and each chooses a different method to convey what Sadako means to him or her. Some students choose to describe Sadako by cutting pictures and words from magazines to create a collage representative of her character. While some choose art as the medium for their response, others turn to poetry and write cinquains that describe Sadako. Still others choose to write letters to Sadako. They write about their feelings after having read the book. They share some of their own sad experiences with her and tell her of their thoughts about peace.

Besides many opportunities to extend and enrich their reading through art and writing, drama and role playing are also introduced as a way for students to enter imaginatively into the story. As a response to Chapter 4, where the secret of Sadako's illness is revealed, students are introduced to an activity based on De Bono's (1987) *Six Thinking Hats*. This activity gives students further opportunities to explore their emotional responses to the story, and to recognize that there can be many different yet authentic responses to a story, situation, or character. In this activity students wear colored paper hats to signal the role they are playing as they respond to the news of Sadako's illness. The student wearing a white hat is neutral in his or her report of Sadako's illness, presenting only facts and information to the group, offering no opinions, assumptions, or conclusions. The red hat is the counterpart to the white hat. The student in the red hat is emotional and subjective in his or her reporting, voicing impressions, hunches, and feelings. The green hat represents inventiveness and creative thinking, and the student wearing the green hat looks for alternative explanations when reporting on Sadako's illness. The green hat dares to think differently, to reverse the usual pattern of things, and to formulate new possibilities. The black hat represents the pessimist who points out in a very rational way, without being argumentative, the seriousness of Sadako's situation, the inevitability of her death, and the foolishness of those who hold out hope for her. The wearer of the yellow hat is positive in his or her perceptions and assessments, looking for ways of dealing with the problem, downplaying the bad news, generating concrete suggestions, counteracting criticisms and negative interpretations from black hats, and basing a generally positive outlook on facts rather than on the hunches and emotional responses of those wearing red hats.

As students work in groups to play the role demanded by their hat color, they become involved in reporting and defending their positions, and they enter into the story, move around inside it, and begin to realize that there is no one right response to literature. They begin to recognize that what they as readers bring to the story is as important as what the text contributes. The personal nature of the literary experience then becomes real for them.

Real connections are also made to a world beyond the pages of the book. A recent immigrant from Japan visits the class to teach students the art of origami, and students make cranes to honor Sadako's dream for peace. The visitor talks about Japan, students ask questions, and soon they are exploring elements of science, health, math, social studies, and physical education—all relating to Japan and evolving from Sadako's story. Mapping skills become important as Hiroshima is located. Some students investigate the science of the atomic bomb and radiation. A representative of the local cancer society visits the class to speak about leukemia and the side effects of radiation. Another visitor, recently returned from teaching in Japan, talks to the class about Japanese schools, and this prompts a comparative examination of Canada and Japan—their histories, landforms, people, customs, governments, and industries. Math activities enter the research as weather and population are graphed and relative living space in the two countries is calculated. Triumphs in technology are recorded as students investigate Japanese contributions to the automobile and electronics industries. Soon the room is filled with the results of the students' work: their maps, graphs, poems, letters, reports, models, and art creations. And when they leave their classroom to go to the gym, the connection to Japan continues, as a guest in the physical education class explains sumo wrestling and teaches students the rudiments of the martial arts.

The possible responses to a story, and the ways a story can be connected to different subject areas, are limited only by the children's imagination and the teacher's energy to support their ideas. Encouraging children to read aesthetically calls for a more reader-centered approach to literature study and suggests an emotionally and intellectually more active role for children as they read stories, respond to them, and explore beyond them, right across the curriculum. Through this active involvement in their own learning, students bring literature alive for themselves as they discover the interconnectedness of stories, readers, and the world beyond books.

References

Bleich, David. 1975. *Readings and Feelings: An Introduction to Subjective Criticism.* Urbana, IL: NCTE.

Coerr, Eleanor. 1979. *Sadako and the Thousand Paper Cranes.* New York: Putnam.

De Bono, Edward. 1987. *Six Thinking Hats.* London: Penguin.

Feldman, Edmund Burke. 1970. *Becoming Human through Art.* Englewood Cliffs, NJ: Prentice-Hall.

McConaghy, June. 1990. *Children Learning through Literature: A Teacher Researcher Study.* Portsmouth, NH: Heinemann.

Rosenblatt, Louise. 1976. *Literature as Exploration.* 1938. Reprint, New York: Noble and Noble.

Rosenblatt, Louise. 1978. *The Reader, the Text, the Poem.* Carbondale: Southern Illinois University Press.

Rosenblatt, Louise. 1988. *Writing and Reading: The Transactional Theory.* Technical Report No. 13. Berkeley: University of California Center for the Study of Writing.

Schulz, Renate. 1991. "Using Literary Theories in the Language Arts Classroom." *Reflections on Canadian Literacy* 9.1: 16–20.

5 Reading *Ceremony*, Reading Ourselves

Bruce Goebel
Western Washington University, Bellingham, Washington

Leslie Marmon Silko's *Ceremony* (1986) has proven to be one of the most successful cross-cultural novels in my classroom. The novel's form is an aesthetic point of convergence where prose narrative meets a Native American oral tradition resulting in a multivoiced text containing stories, myths, and ceremonial songs. *Ceremony* functions in form and content as a dynamic point of convergence between the predominantly white middle-class students in my classroom and the Laguna world Silko describes. Whenever I teach *Ceremony*, I try to do so in such a way that students approach an understanding of Silko's complex literary craft and her probable political intent. This novel presents for students the problem of unfamiliar social and historical context. Readers find themselves incapable of recognizing either the formal and stylistic techniques that Silko uses or the particular blueprint for survival that *Ceremony* offers to both Laguna and white societies. Students generally do not have the cross-cultural knowledge necessary to adequately read, interpret, and evaluate her novel in a way that would approximate her probable intent.

Their inability to interpret across cultures offers a wonderful teaching opportunity, one that not only helps them understand *Ceremony* more adequately, but also allows them to reflect upon how their own interpretive processes are embedded in cultural context. Toward this end, I designed a reading unit to lead them from a conscious recognition of their interpretive limits to a cross-cultural interpretive competency that would bring them to a closer approximation of Silko's intent. This unit asked students to follow a three-part sequence consisting of an *unassisted* reading of *Ceremony*; two weeks of reading and discussing myths, stories, and essays related to Laguna culture; and a second reading of *Ceremony* that would give them a chance to apply their newly acquired cultural knowledge and develop a sense of interpretive competency. I hoped that such an approach would increase their appreciation for Silko's craft and their understanding of her political project, as well as help them realize firsthand the function of cultural knowledge in any interpretive act.

On the first day of this unit, I asked my students to begin reading *Ceremony* and to keep a journal during the process. The journal is a crucial tool that can enable students to see and reflect upon their own progress in making sense of a text. I requested that they write split-page responses in which they divide the page into two vertical columns. On the left-hand side, they were to write out informal, personal responses to the plot, the characters' actions and motivations, symbols, themes, Silko's style, and whatever else moved them to respond. I hoped to discover, through their affective responses, which parts of the novel elicited an aesthetic experience and which parts failed to move them. I made it clear to them that any thoughtful response, negative or positive, was welcome. For example, one student wrote in her journal, "I don't like the little poems in between parts in the story because I can't find a way in which they make sense." This brief response proved valuable, first by confirming a concern I had about a potential area of interpretive difficulty, and later by revealing to her how her enjoyment and judgment of the quality of the novel relied upon a cultural knowledge of Laguna myth and its function in society.

In the right-hand column of the journal, the students wrote questions they had about the novel. They were to identify passages, themes, symbols, allusions, and stylistic techniques that proved particularly difficult for them to understand. I hoped that this part of the journal would increase their awareness of their own interpretive limitations and help me to further identify those parts of the novel that needed the most attention in class discussion. For example, when several students in my class echoed the feelings of one who wrote, "What I found confusing was when the author changed the setting and time . . . the story jumped around a lot and at times I did not know what or who the author was talking about," then I knew that a good part of class discussion would need to focus on Silko's use of flashback and magical realism.

When the students returned the following week after having completed their initial reading of *Ceremony*, we listed on the board all the questions that they had asked in their journals. They quickly realized that they shared many interpretive difficulties. Nearly everyone wanted to know:

> What is flashback, what is dream, and what is reality?
>
> What's the significance of the color blue?
>
> Is Ts'eh real?

What do the little stories in between mean?

Who are the people in Gallup?

We discussed why the individual members of an entire class would have nearly the same set of questions about the novel. While there were a couple of students who attributed their difficulties to "poor writing" on Silko's part, most students readily recognized that a kind of opaque wall or barrier of cultural difference between Laguna Indians and predominantly white, middle-class college students lay at the root of their repeated questions. Seeing through that barrier to discover answers to their questions required filling in some of the missing knowledge about Laguna culture.

So, I temporarily stopped our discussion of *Ceremony* at the conclusion of the question-listing session. Such a strategy was a bit disconcerting for many of them. Nevertheless, I told my students that I wanted them to make a list of the questions we had raised and to keep them in mind while we read a number of shorter texts that might fill in the gaps we had in our knowledge about Laguna culture. I asked them to read and interpret these shorter works as separate texts but also to look for possible connections with *Ceremony*.

In supplementary texts, I selected primarily myths, tales, and short stories which had helped me make sense of the novel, both in terms of information about Pueblo culture and in terms of Silko's personal aesthetic and political concerns. Students generally find it helpful to hear me reflect explicitly upon how I developed the cross-cultural competency necessary for interpreting a particular novel. By asking them to reenact my own reading, I hoped that they would be able to historically situate the literary and social adaptations and innovations that Silko illustrates in *Ceremony*.

I selected texts that would make more clear the often radical opposition between Native American and white mainstream perspectives, and that would help situate *Ceremony* in a broader debate about our democratic heritage (see the Resources list at the end of this chapter). The first supplementary text that we examined was the documentary video *Hopi: Songs of the Fourth World* (1983). Although this film is about a neighboring pueblo, it exposed students to visual representations of the New Mexico landscape that is so important to Laguna culture. This documentary also introduced some of the basic cultural symbols of Pueblo Indians: the four cardinal directions of north, west, south, and east, connected respectively to the four cardinal colors of yellow, blue, red, and white—the four colors of sacred corn. This particular information proved helpful later when a student raised the question, "What's the significance of the color blue?" Several other students recalled that the narrator of the documentary connected the color blue to the rain clouds that come out of the west. Subsequently, they were able to connect Ts'eh, Night Swan, and the Mexican Captive—who all wore blue—to water, the life source of the Laguna world. In addition to supplying cultural knowledge, *Hopi: Songs of the Fourth World* offered students positive images of contemporary Native Americans as human beings successfully bridging the cross-cultural gap between traditional Pueblo ways and the presence of mainstream white society.

On the second day of this reading unit, we read and discussed three versions of Pueblo emergence myths, two Laguna and one Acoma. While describing the same essential genesis of the Pueblo people, these three myths differ in some significant ways. Perhaps more true to its pre-Christian, matrilineal history, the Acoma version identifies the first two human beings as the sisters Nautsiti and Iatiku and focuses both on their human strengths as co-creators and nurturers of the world and on their human weaknesses, such as jealousy, laziness, and carelessness, which would also constitute the history of human beings. In contrast, the Laguna versions, both titled "The Emergence," identify the first two human beings as brother and sister or as husband and wife; place a greater emphasis on male authority; and introduce concepts of sin and guilt. By reading these three myths in combination, students were able to understand a number of important issues regarding Native American literature and culture and *Ceremony* in particular. First, as part of an oral literature, these myths are not fixed in a permanent printed form but vary to some degree from pueblo to pueblo and from storyteller to storyteller. There is no true version; rather, there are different versions tied to a textual spirit that is true to the people's ongoing experiences. Second, the myths reveal how storytellers adapted to the influence of Christianity, altering in some significant ways the Pueblo people's traditional sense of self. The storytellers, in this sense, keep the myths alive with relevance to the continually changing context of Laguna and Acoma experience. Third, because Silko begins her novel with reference to Ts'its'tsi'nako, Nau'ts'ity'i, and I'tcts'ity'i, I knew that students would need to be familiar with Pueblo emergence myths if they were to see how she is integrating her cultural history into a contemporary novel and situating herself within a Native American literary tradition.

For the third day, I asked them to read a Laguna legend, "Hummingbird," and a Hopi legend, "The Twins Visit Tawa." The former is quite similar to the tale of Hummingbird and Fly that Silko interweaves throughout *Ceremony*. This legend helped students answer the question, "What do the little stories in between mean?" This Hummingbird legend reveals how, after the people allow proper tribal relations with the land to wane by neglecting the corn, Nau'ts'ity'i shows her disfavor by taking the plants and grass away. The people turn to Hummingbird and Fly to intercede with Nau'ts'ity'i. They go to her to ask for forgiveness, and she asks that they perform a healing ceremony that requires much arduous travel. This is not a particularly difficult story for students when in an unfragmented form, and in my class they quickly connected Tayo, and sometimes Rocky, to the actions of Hummingbird and Fly. Such interconnections, the recognition of reenactments of old stories, is a central part of Silko's novel. Because they became familiar with the legend before they reread *Ceremony*—in which the legend is fragmented and spread throughout the novel—their concern for simply making some narrative sense out of it was replaced by an increased ability to connect it to Tayo's experiences.

I included "The Twins Visit Tawa" because it emphasizes the role of the quest as a part of the Pueblo definition of masculinity. This particular version of a Pueblo Hero Twins legend portrays the two young men completing a journey to find their father, Tawa, and confronting a series of dangerous characters on the way. Their grandmother has prepared them for the journey and protects them throughout. Once they arrive at their father's house, he places them in a burning oven to test whether they are his sons. They pass the test. The last lines of the story are of particular interest when compared to *Ceremony*:

> Not so easily could the Twins be destroyed, for Spider Woman had watched over her own. A radiant smile, brilliant as sunrise, swept over the anger-torn features of Tawa. He knew that of all created beings none but his sons could have endured this fiery test, and so he gathered them to him and acknowledged them as his own sons.

I hoped that the dual themes of this legend, the ever-present care of Spider Woman, and the familial acknowledgment that follows a completed quest would help students understand, in their reading of *Ceremony*, Tayo's need to find the spotted cattle and complete Betonie's ceremony as well as to recognize Spider-Woman/Thought-Woman as a part of the guiding feminine spirit that Ts'eh and Night Swan represent.

For the fourth day, students read "Yellow Woman and the Whirl-Wind Man" (a version recorded in 1919) and Silko's "Yellow Woman," which appears in her book *Storyteller* (1981). In part, I chose these stories because the event traditionally associated with Yellow Woman is a seduction/kidnapping which takes form in *Ceremony* in Tayo's mother's estrangement and pregnancy as well as (in an inverted form) in Night Swan's and Ts'eh's seduction of Tayo. I suspected that if my students were to understand the significance of the interwoven stories in *Ceremony*, they would need to see the characters in *Ceremony* as simultaneously playing a number of traditional roles. I also wanted them to compare Silko's "Yellow Woman" story with an older version. While staying true to the essential plot line of earlier Yellow Woman tales, Silko infuses hers with a Native American militancy. The katchina/Navajo man who seduces/kidnaps the Yellow Woman/Laguna woman refuses to surrender to the white rancher who accuses him of stealing beef and, instead, apparently shoots him in an act of reclaiming tribal sovereignty over the land. By reading the two stories together, students might be able to understand on a simpler scale how Silko alters a traditional story in order to empower it with contemporary political relevance, enacting in a few pages the larger project she carries out in *Ceremony*.

In order to give some historical context to the political struggle of Native Americans, I assigned for the fifth day the Northwest Ordinance of 1787, signed by George Washington, which, in an ironically idealistic policy toward Indians and westward expansion, states in part: "The utmost good faith will always be observed toward the Indians; their lands and property shall never be taken from them without their consent" (Article 3). For this same day's discussion, I also asked them to read a couple of short excerpts from Francis Parkman's *The Oregon Trail* (1849), excerpts in which Parkman reveals his dislike for Indians through gross caricatures of Native Americans as dirty, ignorant, violent savages and his implied disdain for the process of nature on the plains through his random and senseless killing of buffaloes. These two texts reveal the historic tension between the democratic values we hold to be true and the contradictory racist and violent attitudes and behaviors that white mainstream culture has perpetrated upon Native Americans and the American landscape. I hoped that the blatant discrepancy between the two texts would induce some reflection upon democratic values and offer students a chance to recognize instances where our government has failed to live up to its highest ideals.

For the last day prior to a return to our discussion of *Ceremony*, I asked students to read two essays that might help ground the novel in a contemporary social and political context. For this I chose Silko's "Landscape, History, and the Pueblo Imagination" (1987), which outlines some of the differences between mainstream white and Pueblo perspectives toward nature, history, and community. I hoped that Silko's explanation of how landscape often informs the psychological well-being of both the Native American individual and the community would help students see, at least in a general sense, the socially and spiritually symbolic importance of the detailed description of the Southwestern landscape that appears in *Ceremony*. For the second essay, I chose Peter Matthiessen's "Four Corners" (a chapter from *Indian Country*, 1984), which explores the recent history of government and corporate manipulation of mineral rights and Indian labor on tribal land, particularly in relation to uranium. Matthiessen's interweaving of personal histories of Native Americans suffering at the hands of government and corporate agents, along with statistical data regarding the value of mineral deposits and continuing tribal poverty, offers a strong contemporary justification for the anger that often drives *Ceremony*.

Upon our completion of reading and discussing these supplementary texts, I asked my students to reread *Ceremony*, once again keeping a detailed split-page journal of their responses. I instructed them to pay particular attention to those passages in the text that changed meaning for them in the second reading and document their assumptions about how our supplementary readings may have helped them make sense of the novel in a different way. By comparing these journal responses with their earlier responses, students were able to learn something about the process of cross-cultural interpretation and see how the acquisition of cultural knowledge radically altered their interpretive competency. I will cede the final word in this pedagogical discussion of *Ceremony* to a few excerpts from my students' journal responses to their second reading of the novel:

> Through Silko's writing technique of including Indian prose within the story, I do think she is educating me on Indian beliefs and ideas. But I feel she could be creating a sense of mystery, curiosity, and confusion by adding such sections. Perhaps she is trying to place the reader in Tayo's situation of trying to figure out what he believes. I know these passages made me reevaluate my thoughts and ideas about the world.

> The second reading took much of the confusion out of all the switching around. When the story switched I flowed with its pattern more readily. Furthermore, I feel that this helped the conclusion of the story because I could understand Betonie's teachings a little more. I felt I got a different message from the *Ceremony* which he performed. Moreover, the ending seemed to imply a different meaning, one which focused more on the world and man's role in this world.

By showing us Tayo's problem, his remedies, and eventual resolution, she has outlined a form of creation—the one Thought Woman was speaking. It is hard to understand due to my Christian background but when I keep in mind their beliefs I can see that she was referring to something, I think, quite different from our view of creation . . . It seems to imply that humans can only be created in such a way that a "good" world is something that has to be worked at. . . .

Things are definitely looking better this time around. I kind of wish we read the coursepak first! But then again I can see why you waited. I enjoy this unit. It's funny how some little things become clearer and explain a lot. I found the explanation of the flies (green-bottle) particularly interesting. It sounds like everything has a purpose and therefore deserves respect.

After rereading *Ceremony*, many things were understandable that were unclear after reading the story the first time. The several Indian articles on the myths and traditions of the Laguna people clarified several parts of *Ceremony* for me. Each character in this book represents a different direction in Tayo's journey. It is now clear that Tayo's purpose in this book is to complete his "ceremony" in order to discover who he really is. Each character that Tayo meets is symbolic of a character in the Laguna myths. For example, Tayo and Rocky represent the hero twins.

In general, after rereading *Ceremony* and reading the stories of Laguna life, many confusing parts of the book are clarified and make more sense. I don't think I would have understood the book any better the second time around if it was not for those articles.

References

"The Emergence" (as told by Ko'tye, 1919). 1974. In *Keresan Texts*. American Ethnological Society Publications 8. Edited by Franz Boas. 1928. Reprint, New York: AMS Press.

"The Emergence" (as told by Gyi'mi, 1919). 1974. In *Keresan Texts*. American Ethnological Society Publications 8. Edited by Franz Boas. 1928. Reprint, New York: AMS Press.

Hopi: Songs of the Fourth World. 1983. Pat Ferrero, producer. Ferrero Films/ New Day Films. The MacArthur Foundation/Library Video Project.

"The Hummingbird" (as told by Pedro Martin, 1919). 1974. In *Keresan Texts*. American Ethnological Society Publications 8. Edited by Franz Boas. 1928. Reprint, New York: AMS Press.

Matthiessen, Peter. 1984. *Indian Country*. New York: Viking.

The Northwest Ordinance, July 13, 1787. Web site last revised May 20, 1997. Cleveland Free-Net. Distributed by the Cybercasting Services Division of the National Telecomputing Network (NPTN). <http://www.let.rug.nl/~usa/D/1776-1800/ohio/norwes.htm>.

"The Origin Myth of Acoma." 1979. In *American Indian Literature: An Anthology*. Edited by Alan R. Velie. Norman: University of Oklahoma Press.

Parkman, Francis. 1988. *The Oregon Trail*. 1849. Reprint, New York: Penguin.

Silko, Leslie Marmon. 1986. *Ceremony*. New York: Viking Penguin.

Silko, Leslie Marmon. 1987. "Landscape, History, and the Pueblo Imagination: Nature, Landscape, and Natural History." In *On Nature*, edited by D. Halpern. San Francisco: North Point.

Silko, Leslie Marmon. 1981. "The Yellow Woman." In *Storyteller*. New York: Little, Brown.

"The Twins Visit Tawa: Legends of the Hopi Indians." 1979. In *Spider Woman Stories*, edited by G. M. Mullett. Tucson: University of Arizona Press.

"Yellow Woman and Whirl-Wind Man" (as told by Ko'tye, 1921). 1974. In *Keresan Texts*. American Ethnological Society Publications 8. Edited by Franz Boas. 1928. Reprint, New York: AMS Press.

6 Reading Writers/Writing Readers

Claudia Greenwood
Kent State University, Ashtabula, Ohio

Cynthia Walters
Ashtabula High School

R ose, that was a good connection you made between Edna's behavior and her father's. I didn't even think about that, but now that you have mentioned it, I agree. Often children pick up ways of life and behavior from their parents. Thanks, Rose!"

The foregoing journal entry demonstrates the generative potential we believed possible in a semester-long pairing of high school and college readers. It demonstrates, as well, the naturalness of shared reading and writing. As Witte and Flach (1994) assert, "The meaning-constructive processes of both writers and readers (and of course speakers and listeners) are collaborative and social, dialogic and interactive" (221). In the case cited above, two students, complete strangers separated by over thirty years in age, met in mid-September and selected Kate Chopin's *The Awakening* for their project. Six weeks later, their completed dialogue journal contained 174 pages! In the interim, the two readers, the text, and multiple contexts intersected regularly to produce increasingly rich responses both to the text and to each other.

Rose and her young partner, Holly, were one of twenty-two pairs of students to participate in the project that we will describe and evaluate in this article. Planning for the fall project began as soon as the public school dismissed for summer vacation. Our discussions were influenced not only by current reading theory but also by current realities in public education. As one of us was teaching a college class in adolescent literature for education majors, and the other was teaching a course in high school English, we articulated shared concerns in the planning process. We accepted the fact that even Advanced Placement students are not always motivated to engage in reading activities as we would wish. We agreed that preservice teachers are not sufficiently prepared for the challenge of recalcitrant students, as they are seldom afforded the opportunity to interact with such students in an informal, informative way.

To initiate the project, we jointly prepared a handout that stated our objectives, presented a thumbnail sketch of the theoretical framework (Applebee 1993; Beach 1993; McTeague 1992; Probst 1988; Witte and Flach 1994), and suggested a calendar of important dates for book selection, journal reviews by respective instructors, final project identification, and completion. Individually, we elaborated on those elements of the project with additional handouts.

Our instructions for the journal entries, both reaction and response, suggest the difficult logistics of pairing students across communities:

- Keep loose-leaf notebook paper in a pocket folder for the purpose of the project. Keep carbon paper in the pocket so that you can make a copy of each entry. One is for your partner.
- Date each entry and record inclusive page numbers.
- Read and react to chapters individually. If the book is not organized in chapters, then select a reasonable number of pages or a natural break in the text for each reaction.
- Record your personal reaction to aspects of character, plot, style, etc. React honestly. Make connections to other texts, to movies, to TV shows, or to real-life experiences. Make predictions. Ask each other questions that come to mind (be sure to include the page number so that your partner can find the reference).
- Share your journals with your reading partner regularly, as time permits. If you cannot meet to exchange journal entries, mail them weekly so that you will have the benefit of your partner's response as you continue to read.
- Respond to each other in writing. Reflect thoughtfully, complementing/supplementing each other's reading experience.

Our excitement about the project built as we approached the opening of school. Class rosters revealed a near-perfect match in student numbers. Students in the college class ranged in age from twenty to fifty-five; several were parents of teenagers. The initial reaction of both groups to the project was positive. The college students were intrigued by it and eager to make contact with their partners via a phone call of introduction and an invitation to meet for the purpose of book selection. Delays in this first step were inevitable as many of the high school students were involved in fall athletics and several had after-school jobs or other activities. For some of the pairs, making initial contact was the most frustrating aspect of the entire project. In fact, once this frustration became evident, we requested a progress report—specifically, a brief summary written independently by each of the partners. What a revelation! Although several weeks had passed, not all partners had yet exchanged journals. Some had not even begun to read. Several did not agree on the status of their progress. For instance, a disappointing contradiction was revealed in the following progress reports of two partners:

> *Julie:* We have exchanged twice through the mail and are working on the third. Things are coming along very good. Whenever we have questions we give each other a call. I am really enjoying this project.
>
> *Julie's college partner:* I have written Julie three times as journal entries. Each time I talk with her she says that she has mailed a journal to me. Thus far no response from her.

Some, on the other hand, were working very well, and their responses were more encouraging to us:

> *Lori:* We have met at the library and exchanged papers three times. I think it is coming along fine as we both pose questions to each other now.
>
> *Elisabeth:* My partner is Lori. There are thirty chapters in the book and we switch every five chapters. So far we have exchanged three times and will exchange our fourth on Monday. Everything is going well.

We have agreed that in future shared reading projects, we will begin to monitor the journal exchanges earlier and do so more frequently. We will, perhaps, orchestrate the weekly exchange ourselves.

As the semester progressed, the potential that we had envisioned when we charted the course began to manifest itself in both anticipated and unanticipated ways. Classroom conversation flourished among both groups of students about reading and writing partnerships, about diverse reader responses, about friendship, about discovery, about real audiences, about risking guesses and confirmation. Journal entries, our primary data source and only complete record of the students' reactions and responses, validated our initial optimism regarding the potential for scaffolding within the written dialogue.

For some students the project altered reading behaviors, encouraging careful attention to text.

> *Michelle (college partner):* It's been great fun writing to you! It was interesting. You remember what happens very well. Do you read a lot in your spare time? I don't, so I don't catch what I should. I'm not used to reading. But this project has made me feel differently.

It also provided the opportunity for scaffolding and confirmation of experience-based knowledge. These partners, who read *Little Women*, reacted to each other and to the text on several levels (analytical, critical, personal) and in many voices. The number of spontaneous interjections of opinion increased with the number of journal entries. In fact, what began as a rather formulaic recording of summary statements evolved into written dialogue on a very rich, personal level.

> *Casey (Michelle's partner):* I know what you mean when you say boys are aggressive. I have two brothers....
>
> *Michelle:* It's so exciting watching and knowing how these girls are growing up and to remember how it is to be free of worries and dream little dreams. Who is your favorite sister? I haven't decided which I like the best. Which reminds you of yourself? I think I am more like Beth.

A word of encouragement near the end of their dialogue suggests the motivating force of a reading partnership such as this.

> *Casey:* Hi! How are you? I am all right, but VERY busy. I wanted to tell you I think we are doing a good job reading!

Among the unanticipated but equally valuable lessons of such a project for future teachers was the necessity of developing a scheme for motivation. Frustrated by her young partner's lack of response and, we imagine, believing it necessary to protect her grade, one of the college students kept a record of her attempts to make contact, with the final entry dated on the day the final paper was due and addressed to her professor:

> *October 30:* Ready for Act II? I haven't gotten your latest installment yet, but will write off a few quick notes so we can get moving on this.
>
> *November 4:* Hope everything is going OK. Are we completely stressed out yet? I'm rapidly nearing that point myself with journals, papers, etc. I'll go on with Act II and hope to hear from you soon.
>
> *November 10:* I'll go on with Act III and look for your responses.
>
> *November 14:* Angela: I'll try to finish Act III now and await your exchange. Hope everything is OK.
>
> *December 6:* I received several pages from Angela. Only questions, a few observations. No attempt at interaction.

Reality check. Such failures will occur, of course. But all was not lost. This student and several others whose partners failed to hold up their end of the conversation learned valuable lessons about the challenges of the teaching profession. Each completed the project with a paper that included reflections on adolescents, commitment, and responsibility, as well as the connectedness of reading and writing.

Among the more unusual yet successful partnerships was that of an eighteen-year-old female student with a fifty-five-year-old male student. With their first shared entries a process of increasing familiarity and trust was initiated that ultimately encouraged the younger student to react very candidly to the text. Her reactions were often introduced by the informality of conversation: "I was curious to learn . . . I am really excited about . . . I am becoming impressed with . . . I feel sad that . . . I couldn't believe . . ." Curiously, although the adult read and responded directly to comments made by his "literary partner" (their agreed-upon salutation), he failed to notice that while his partner was reacting vigorously to the text she was ignoring his questions. Even so, both considered the project a complete success, collaborating on a final paper based on research that they designed and carried out together by seeking comparative data from their peers.

The journal of greatest interest to us as teachers of writing was that of a middle-aged woman and her partner. Decades of fear of writing preceded Marie's engagement in this project. Years of carefully constructed attitudes rubbed against the enthusiasm of her high school partner, Rebecca, who took the lead in text selection and suggested Robert Cormier's *After the First Death*. Initiative switched when Marie sent the first journal entry, a mere list of questions—but a start. Ensuing reactions/responses on both parts quickly lengthened. Questions were interspersed with reactions. Ultimately, barriers collapsed and Marie began to write freely: "I am confused—why does Ben refer to his father as the phantom?" Rebecca responded, "I get the impression . . .," and the conversation continued as both readers wrestled with increasingly complex and uncomfortable issues. Remarkably, Marie's journal entries became pages long, filled with evidence of interaction on every conceivable level not only with the text but also with her young partner. As the final paper approached, however, Marie's old fear of beginning a formal written assignment surfaced once again. This time, the dragon was slain quickly by the journal! Encouraged to look into it for questions and answers, she discovered a topic, a focus, and unprecedented enthusiasm for writing. If increased fluency for even one partner is an outcome of such a project, then its value is secured.

Ideally, however, benefits are jointly shared, as they were in the thoughtful reading and responding of two students much closer in age than any of the others. Having chosen Hawthorne's *Scarlet Letter*, the girls' reactions were consistent with the fact that they were separated from the text by nearly a century. They were not separated from the context, however, for the high school student's father was a minister. Her insights reflected important prior knowledge: "Usually, in society, ministers are scrutinized very closely and I was surprised that no one even challenged him about his life. Most churchgoers are very good at sensing whether their minister is practicing what he preaches. Some, even if there is nothing concrete, will make something up and even that didn't happen in this situation."

While these partners' journal entries were usually short, they were pithy. An important observation about the relevance of literature is found in the following: "Once again his reasoning is spelled out for us in the form of a human-nature lesson." Quite early in their own dialogue they assumed the role of readers in conversation with a writer: "I thought the 'A' in the sky was getting a little off the wall, though if they saw it I don't plan on disputing them. . . ."

Nor will *we* dispute the value of this shared reading project. Of course, as we plan to repeat it, we consider changes. Revising is, after all, second nature to those of us immersed in reading-writing processes. While we will make some changes in the overall structure of the project, e.g., limiting time and tightening oversight, we will in all likelihood concentrate on troubleshooting and problem-solving activities to assist foundering partners. We must, first of all, devise a way to accomplish closer to the 100 percent participation we envisioned at the outset.

Because we have learned that book selection influenced the success of the project, we will be prepared to suggest alternatives to early selections as a means of getting a dialogue journal on track. Because we have learned that age difference was a factor of concern before partners found their stride as readers and writers, and that early on some adults tended to be too directive ("My partner was too pushy!"), we will encourage patience on the part of the adult college students. But because we have read many evaluative comments such as the following by a high school reading partner, we will continue to support the concept of reading and writing across multiple boundaries: "My mom said this was a very good experience. You have to learn to interact with different people in society. It is something that certainly is demanded in the workforce. Besides, I got to make a new friend!"

References

Applebee, Arthur N. 1993. *Literature in the Secondary School: Studies of Curriculum and Instruction in the United States.* Urbana, IL: NCTE.

Beach, Richard. 1993. *A Teacher's Introduction to Reader-Response Theories.* Urbana, IL: NCTE.

McTeague, Frank. 1992. *Shared Reading in the Middle and High School Years.* Portsmouth, NH: Heinemann.

Probst, Robert E. 1988. *Response and Analysis: Teaching Literature in Junior and Senior High School.* Portsmouth, NH: Boynton/Cook.

Witte, Stephen P., and Jennifer Flach. 1994. "Notes Toward an Assessment of Advanced Ability to Communicate." *Assessing Writing* 1: 207–46.

7 In Praise of Simple Things

Carol Jago
Santa Monica High School, California

Chilean poet Pablo Neruda breathed new life into the traditional ode. His odes conformed to the traditional definition—long and lyrical, dignified, and exalted in feeling, style, and subject—in every way except the last, the subject. Rather than praising mountaintops or great men, Neruda chose to sing of the simple things in life.

Neruda's odes glorify the ordinary and everyday—the tomato, bicycles, the dictionary. I thought they would be ideal models for students to imitate because, while simple in form, they encourage a celebration of familiar, often overlooked objects. (Many of Neruda's odes can be found in general literature anthologies or in collections such as *Odas Elementales* [1954], *Pablo Neruda: Selected Poems* [1990], and *Selected Odes of Pablo Neruda* [1990]. For further reference, see *Neighborhood Odes* [1992] by Gary Soto.)

After reading several of Neruda's odes, Andy Lebowitz wrote one to his pockets:

> What would I do
> without their luxury?
> My hands would be full,
> occupied all the time.
> These two crevices
> are here for my belongings
> my comfort
> my boredom.

I had asked students to cast about for an object that is unappreciated, unsung in the world, and to itemize its virtues. I urged them to describe features that less critical eyes might miss. Dan Corbett chose a spatula.

> Oh unsung hero!
> Standing tall
> on the counter top.
> You save the egg before it is scorched
> and dance with flapjacks.

What impressed me was the ease with which students took to the form, almost as though writing poetry was the most natural thing in the world for seventeen-year-olds to be doing at 10:30 on a Wednesday morning. Unlike other assignments which they dutifully complete, this seemed an invitation that they were eager to accept. And like the onion that Neruda praises as a "fairy godmother in delicate paper," their emerging poems revealed multiple layers of understanding about their world. Frankie Cornejo wrote "Ode to My Hood":

> 17th and Delaware
> you are home to me,
> market to drug dealers,
> and once a firing range.
> I know you well.
> Well enough to know
> you have let bullets
> hit the wrong people
> for no reason at all!

Such candor transforms the act of writing from a task for a teacher, a task completed for the reward or punishment of a grade, into a genuinely creative act. Students looked at their work and knew it was good.

I was so impressed by their output that we published the odes in a class booklet called *In Praise of Simple Things*. The brief lines, which left more white space than print on the page, provided inspiration for the artists in the class. And, like *Odas Elementales*, the latest edition of Neruda's odes, the text was illustrated. Is this rigorous education? Is this preparation for college? Is this training for a literate life? I think so.

References

Neruda, Pablo. 1988. *Odas Elementales*. 3d ed. 1954. Reprint, New York: French and European Publications.

Neruda, Pablo. 1990. *Pablo Neruda: Selected Poems*. Edited by Nathaniel Tarn. 1970. Reprint, New York: Houghton Mifflin.

Neruda, Pablo. 1990. *Selected Odes of Pablo Neruda*. Translated by Margaret Sayers Peden. Berkeley: University of California Press.

Soto, Gary. 1992. *Neighborhood Odes*. San Diego: Harcourt Brace.

8 Rainer Maria Rilke's *Song* Poems

Leslie Richardson
University of Houston, Texas

I begin the exercise by handing out copies of some of Rainer Maria Rilke's "Song" poems, such as "The Song the Orphan Sings" and "The Song the Leper Sings." The "Leper" poem, for one, usually stirs up a lot of interest. Some of the middle school students who have never heard of leprosy are concerned with logistical problems lepers face, such as how a leper gets food. It seems incredible that a person couldn't go into a bakery and buy a loaf of bread, the students say. As the students reread Rilke's poem, which focuses on the loneliness the leper feels, they talk about what it would be like to carry around a clapper that warns people you are coming and frightens away animals.

During the time that we spend discussing Rilke's poems, the students come to understand (along with the just plain "what is going on in this poem") what it is like to be someone else—to carry a different set of concerns. The students connect with Rilke's poems and understand the concept of speaking from another point of view. The insightful poems they write are proof.

While I was teaching writing in Houston public schools as part of the Writers in the Schools program, I discovered that many students, young and old alike, find that Rilke's work is unlike any poetry they have read before. Rilke's poems are not cute, didactic, or pat—they do not suppose they have all the answers. Instead, they are suggestive, compelling, and complex. The lives of Rilke's "singers" are not easily summed up or understood, and students appreciate Rilke's respect for that open-endedness, because they know that their own lives are complex as well.

The first step of the second part of this project (the writing part) is to have the students choose a person (usually not a particular person, and especially not a fellow classmate) whose song they will write. All of the poems should be written in first person, so that the student must speak in his or her subject's voice. If the students are a bit overwhelmed by the possibilities, I encourage them to choose a kind of person they encounter in their lives, such as a cashier. Once a student has decided on a person, he or she can begin to overcome the tyranny of the blank page by writing his or her title, "The Song the_____ Sings."

At this point, if the students are still hesitant and don't know where to begin, or if they want a definite structure to follow so that they know they are doing the assignment "right," I encourage them to look over their copies of Rilke's poems. I tell the students they can use the first words of his sentences to start the lines of their own poems. For instance, "The Song the Beggar Sings" begins, "I go all the time from door to door" (Rilke, ed. by Bly, 1981, 113). I have told students to think of something their person does a lot, and begin that way. Or a student may want to use as a template "The Song the Orphan Sings," which begins "I am nobody, and I will be nobody too" (125). The student may think of what his or her person feels he or she is (perhaps the student will use a metaphor here) and what he or she may become.

The poems my students wrote ranged from humorous to solemn. I like this project because it gives students the freedom to write about what they want and to express themselves in a way that is somewhat safe because they have chosen another person through which to speak. For this reason, I find it antithetical to put letter grades on the poems. This exercise also helps students make connections between the literature they read and the lives they lead. Rilke became a fast favorite in my classrooms because the students appreciated the emotions and subjects he treats. This reading and writing project also helps students observe, listen, and ruminate. When the students write from a different point of view, they may also discover certain traits of themselves that are similar to those of the person whose song they sing. In this way, students reflect and connect to others and to literature.

Examples of Poems by Middle School Students

The Song the Blind Girl Sings

I am a blind girl
never doing anything but sleeping
because I'm always in darkness,
and have no life.
People always are catching me
daydreaming or using my imagination.
I can only pick up, feel, and eat,
because I have no eyes.
Nobody—I have no friends to play with,
not even to tuck me in at night.
Useless I am, for I am always sad
or feeling sorry for myself.
Sometimes I wish I wasn't burned
blind, for now my parents don't want, nor
need me anymore.

Nobody wants a blind friend.
All I have is a dog to escort me.
I have no home, no friend or parents.
Just a blind girl with an escort dog.

Casonder

The Song the Dentist Sings

I am someone everybody knows
I am someone every little kid fears
I drill teeth when you have a cavity
or when you have braces I pull them tighter
I could clean teeth until they bleed
but if you are a new guy and are a
beginner you'll get used to it

Edgar

The Song the Poor Boy Sings

I see the kids playing—
without me.
I see their eyes wandering towards the school.
I hear the girls giggling
about a secret that was told.
I hear the shrieks and laughs
of all of them.
Laughing and shouting—without
me.
I see them happily running and chasing each other.
They laugh through their whole childhoods—without
me.
They have left me behind.
Not caring or noticing.
They leave me because
my pants are too big,
my shoes too small.
They leave me—
and continue with
their childhood.

Cynthia

The Song the Listener Sings

I feel senseless.
The whispers run in and out,
non stop. I don't comprehend
any of them.
The curiosity of my partner's eyes
rouses as people pass by.
I stand there speechless, cold

wind blowing up my skirt.
The smell of freshness
blows from the hair of
the others. The sound
of a crinkling bag.

    Adrienne

The Song the Parents Sing

Little child don't eat at all.
Please do not grow up.
If you do you will
run over us and
make us feel worthless.
We will clothe you
feed you and shelter
you and you will greedily
accept it all.
We can taste the bitterness
you will give us
through the years
and all the words
will lash us like spears.
We can hear
you driving
away to be
with those who
will hurt you
and you will
not care.
We can feel the
pain you will
give us day by day
but for some reason
we will let you stay.
We can see the cops
coming through the
door only to
tell us you are not
coming back no more.
We will try to forgive
you because
you are gone
but we will
still sing our
sad song.

    Jennifer

Reference

Rilke, Rainer Maria. 1981. *Selected Poems of Rainer Maria Rilke.* Edited by Robert Bly. New York: HarperCollins.

9 The Perfect Novel for Creative Writing Assignments

Kathryn Megyeri
Sherwood High School, Sandy Spring, Maryland

"It's the only book I've ever read all the way through," proudly admits one of my ninth graders. Another writes on his year-end evaluation: "That book is probably the only thing I'll remember about this class."

"That book" is Paul Zindel's near-classic and his first famous book, *The Pigman*. A science teacher at the time, Zindel wrote the novel in 1968, but it's timeless. It talks to teenagers, and they respond because the emotions are real, the plot is plausible, and the message comes through without preaching. The book's remarkable strength is that it stimulates readers to reflect on their own experiences, which they write about and then share by reading the papers aloud, truly a remarkable feat given the numbers of teenagers who, in their own words, "hate" to read and even more who "hate to write."

Zindel profiles a bonding between generations—a lonely widower, Angelo Pignati, and two high school sophomores, John and Lorraine. The tragic consequences of thoughtless actions sober both teens into the realization that, as John says, "There was no one else to blame anymore—no place to hide. Our life would be what we made of it—nothing more, nothing less" (148). Thus, it tells teens that they must take responsibility for their own actions.

Similar to Franklin High School depicted in the book, my suburban high school enrolls almost 1,700 students with 250 ESOL (English for Speakers of Other Languages) students and a separate wing to house the severely and profoundly handicapped, who attend in wheelchairs and who are afflicted with cerebral palsy and multiple limitations. In our search for the one book that all ninth graders could read regardless of ability groupings and backgrounds, we selected *The Pigman* a number of years ago because of its broad appeal and its ability to initiate a number of excellent writing assignments.

Letters to the Author

Paul Zindel is unique in that, at the end of his book, he includes an addendum in which he invites responses from his readers, provides an address to which students can write, and promises to try to reply.

> I urge kids who feel like writing me to please be very free and open and don't worry about your spelling or grammar and things like that. I'm most interested in your ideas, but I also love hearing about your dreams and just about anything you care to tell me straight from your heart. (154)

Zindel also answers frequently asked questions concerning his creation of the story and shares some of his favorite letters. Thus, he uses the addendum to establish a personal relationship with his readers. He makes students feel their responses to his book are important, and, after they've shared their musings with him, they feel more comfortable writing about the loss of childhood, telephone conversations they've had, and older persons who have affected their lives. For those less able students who need guidance and structure, we still assign the inevitable study guide questions.

The downside to the unit is that some of the book seems dated to today's teens—i.e., John's unfamiliarity with credit cards, the Pigman's gift of roller skates instead of roller blades, and the price of a six-pack of beer that in 1968 cost $1.19. However, the main characters, John and Lorraine, are no different from today's sophomores who have difficulty communicating with their parents, who want to be treated well by someone who's older, and who realize that life isn't filled with happy endings. Teens lose those they care for, death is a reality, and they realize at this age that their childhoods are ending. This book speaks in a way no teacher can, and students respond in such positive ways that at the end of the unit each year, I write Zindel a letter of appreciation.

Perhaps it is not surprising that pupils write more personal letters to Zindel than most families exchange with each other (see example below). At this time, we review proper business letter form, the use of transitions, and the four paragraphs they are to include: introduction, questions they wish to ask, suggestions for Zindel's next book, and a closing. In order to eliminate total dependence on simple sentences, we encourage using complex sentences and transitions.

17321 Buehler Road
Olney, MD 20832
June 5, 1994

Mr. Paul Zindel
c/o Agent Curtis Brown Ltd.
Ten Astor Place
New York, NY 10003

Dear Mr. Zindel:

Our class just finished reading THE PIGMAN. When my teacher told us that we would be reading this book, my first thought was, "Darn, another novel!" I really like to read, but I don't usually like the books that we're forced to read in school. Surprisingly, I liked THE PIGMAN. Right away, I was intrigued by "The Oath," because it was an interesting way to tell what the book was about, and I really enjoyed John's first entry. He sounded like someone I'd like to meet. His entries were funny at times and sad at others. I also enjoyed Lorraine's entries because they were so detailed. She also included how she felt about the events that were happening in her life, so I got a better idea of how she was affected.

I've never written a letter to an author before. First, in the back of the book, you explained how you came up with John's character, but you never said how you thought of Lorraine. Also, why did you make John's mother so obsessive? Actually, I liked reading about his mother because she was such an odd and unusual character. Something else that I was wondering was why Mr. Pignati lied about his wife's death at first? Was he denying her death to himself or to Lorraine and John? The book interested me so much because it wasn't just one person narrating it. Two people narrated it, and they were of the opposite sex. To top it off, they were total opposites in the personality department! I haven't read any of your other books, but the titles are catchy, so I'm going to check some out of the library. Can you also recommend some other teen books that you think might be interesting?

I have some suggestions for you for your next book. If you make any changes or updates for the next edition, don't have John drinking like his father who is an alcoholic. Kids are already drinking too much, especially at my high school. If you are planning to write another book, why don't you write about your childhood and how you lived? Or, you could write an autobiography. Each person in our English class had to write one.

I'm planning on writing you again after I read another of your books. In fact, I'm planning on reading all the books that you've written. My brother will probably read them too. I think your books are so popular around the world because of your characters, and teens like to read about other teenagers. Thank you for reading my letter and have a joyful summer. Don't forget to spend some time with your own kids.

Sincerely yours,
Karen Randes

P.S. Your zip code is soooo cool.
P.P.S. My friend's mother was a student in Totkinville High School on Staten Island where you once taught science. Small world, isn't it?

Students are amazed that an author is not only real and alive, but that he cares about fostering a relationship with his readers. As one student wrote:

I'm amazed that you're even reading this letter. Most authors don't even read their fan mail, and you actually read it and reply! I think your next book should be from a high school teacher's point of view to show what they go through every day. I think teens might be interested in reading this because they don't always realize that their teachers have lives outside the classroom.

In reply to letters from one of my classes, Zindel thanked the students for sharing their thoughts and questions. He told us of his latest playwriting efforts and closed by saying, "I promise one way or the other, I'll send all the energy you've given me back out into the world in ways that will make you proud" (May 25, 1988).

A Relationship with an Older Person

As another class assignment, I ask each student to write about a relationship with an older person, the features that make it memorable, and its evolution. The resulting essays are among the best and most sensitive my students write, and we share them with the adults who have been their mentors, teachers, counselors, and substitute parents but who often do not realize their profound impact on today's youth.

I met a caring individual when I was about seven years old. It was summertime, and my family was spending two weeks at the beach in Ocean City. My parents were on the beach relaxing, and my sister and I were building huge sand castles.

All of a sudden, an old lady started walking toward us. I was aware of her presence and just continued to play. But when she walked over and commented on my castle, I saw that she was a woman of about 60, and she had snow-white hair. In fact, she looked exactly like Jessica Tandy in the movie *Cocoon*.

She rolled up her sleeves and pant legs and started to help. She said her name was Mary, and we talked while we worked. In no time, we had finished building the castle and started another. After that, my family decided to go back to the condo. We agreed to meet Mary on the beach at the same time the next day to build another castle.

We built castles for the rest of the week and really had fun. I used to think senior citizens were dull and unexciting, but Mary taught me to look past the stereotype and judge one person at a time. From that point on, I looked at older people in a way that I never had before, and it felt good.

The older person who affected my life was an old lady who lived down the street. I was in third grade, and lived in Washington state. Every kid my age was terrified of her. On the Fourth of July, we would shoot off our bottle rockets at her house. The next day, her yard was covered with sticks and charred paper. One year, my parents bought me a compound bow. For the first few weeks, I was content with shooting at a target, but then I decided to see how far I could shoot. I pulled the string back, notched an arrow and let it fly. It was a beautiful shot, straight and even, right into the roof of the lady's house.

I ran to the house and peered into the window. It looked like no one was home. So I propped my ladder up against her roof and crawled up. I pulled my arrow out of her roof and proceeded back to my ladder. When I reached the ladder and looked down, there she was looking at me.

I hastily explained what I was doing on her roof, while at the same time, I was waving the arrow at her. I climbed down off her roof, and she helped me carry the ladder back to my house. She never said a word to me. She just looked at me with a puzzled look on her face.

That night, she phoned my house and told my parents what had happened. But the strange thing was that she was not angry. She found it funny that I had shot an arrow into her roof and was amazed that I had carried the ladder to her house.

She wasn't as mean as everyone thought. The next Fourth of July, I did not shoot a single bottle rocket at her house.

With the growth of senior citizens' publications, we have very good luck getting such essays published, and, in fact, some students have even received small royalty checks for their submissions which shows them that there is indeed a marketplace for their works outside of school publications and community newspapers. As authors, they find that their pieces are valued. *Senior Edition USA Colorado* published a series of these essays, and editor Allison St. Clair prefaced the series with this message:

> A thick packet of material crossed my desk a few weeks ago, sent by a high school teacher in Sandy Spring, Md. The enclosed essays, Kathy Megyeri wrote, were ones her students had written about older people who affected their lives. I used to teach school

nearby so I thought I'd flip through the essays as a nostalgic exercise—and to see what kids have to say these days.

Frankly, I didn't expect much. But several minutes of foggy glasses later, I was delighted to change my mind. These were some strong, poignant statements about the connections between generations. "Senior Edition" would like to share some of these with you in this column—and please let us know if you'd like to read more in the coming months. (1990, 8)

A Pigman in Our Lives

I also ask students to examine a "Pigman" in their lives. Lorraine says, "A Pigman is anybody who comes into your life and causes a voice inside of you to say, 'O.K. Buster, the jig's up. There's no more Santa Claus. There's no more blaming Mother or Daddy or your teachers or your brothers. And the day your childhood dies is probably the first day you really know what guilt is. Even if it's a divorce, if your father or mother walks out, that can make you feel like you've met a Pigman'" (Zindel 1980, 13). Students write about an experience that made them realize their childhood was gone—the time they lost their Pigman. On more than one occasion, these poignant pieces have gone on to win literary awards for their authors.

> The day I lost my childhood happened when I was five. My parents and I went to Disney World in Florida for our summer vacation. It was a very hot day, if I remember right. We had just gotten off the plane, so my mom and dad said we'd go to Disney World the next day to see my "idol," Mickey Mouse. When we were there, we went to see almost everything from Space Mountain to Epcot Center. I was getting tired and had to use the bathroom, and that's where I saw him, Mickey, or the so-called Mickey. He was standing a little behind the lavatory building. I could see his ears sticking out from behind the building, so I ran to see him and peeked from the side. What I saw I will never forget in a hundred years. It was Mickey taking his head off to make out with Snow White. I ran in horror to my mom and dad, never to tell what I saw.

> I remember an event which hurt me very badly, and I cried. It happened just two weeks ago. See, every year my father goes to Miami for the International Boat Show. Well, all of last year, he promised that he would take me with him. At this point, my parents were divorced, and so that made it a big deal to me, because it would just be the two of us, him and me. Then, about a week before the boat show, my dad called me up and said that he wasn't going to be able to take me. It wouldn't have been so bad except for the fact that my sister, who goes to school in Miami, called

and said that she saw my dad there, and he was with his girlfriend. His girlfriend is not much older than my sister. I was so mad that I don't think I'll ever forget that day.

Writing Dialogue

In order to teach the skills of punctuating dialogue and changing paragraphs when speakers change, I ask each student to narrate a page or more of telephone conversation in which they pretend they are either John or Lorraine soliciting funds for the L and J Philanthropy Fund, just as the characters in the book play their telephone game. Students must format the start of the conversation, the continuation of it for at least one page, and an end to the conversation. They enjoy the assignment because it allows them to assume the persona of one of the book's characters and to write a realistic telephone solicitation. Some prefer to alter the assignment by writing about a telephone prank they have pulled in real life, and I accept that as long as they remember to use quotation marks correctly and to change paragraphs when they change speakers.

A Telephone Prank

One day after school, John, Lorraine, Norton, the kids from our class, and I were again playing the telephone call game. It was my turn, and I picked a number and dialed. A long drawn-out man's voice answered, "Hello."

"Good afternoon, sir, I'm calling from the L and J Fund. We collect money for the people who never got out of high school and really need a job. Would you like to make a donation?"

"What did you say, lay foundation? Wait a minute while I turn up my Miracle Ear. Now, what did you say?"

"Sir, I said that I am representing a company that is collecting money for people who never got out of high school and really need a job. Would you like to donate any money?"

"What do you mean I look funny? Back in World War II, I would have snapped a man's neck if he called me funny. I ought to spank you, you young whippersnapper. Now, you had better apologize."

"But, sir, please listen to me; that is not what I said."

"Fill me full of lead; just try it. You wouldn't even get past the mines in the front yard, not to mention the trip wire in the yard. So, if you don't apologize, I will turn on my Caller ID. Then, I will cross-reference your number with the phone company and get your address. Then, I'll come to your house and talk to your parents. Then, I'll file phone harassment charges with the police. . . ." By this time, he was practically screaming.

"I'd like to see you try, you old geezer," I thought to myself. By this time, I was just trying to keep him on the line to win the telephone marathon game.

"Wait till you wake up tomorrow morning. You will see who is bluffing."

I was beginning to believe him.

"O.K., sir, I think it's time to take your medicine."

"No, I am not a Methodist. What kind of sick, twisted person are you?"

"Well, it's been fun, but I have to go." I hung up the phone. That had to be one of the strangest calls I have ever made. But I did end up the weekly winner. I kept him on the phone for two and a half minutes. So, thank you, Mr. Miracle Ear.

With all the writing that *The Pigman* elicits, I marvel that Zindel can capture the hearts and minds of teens that I never reach and can motivate them to check out from the library *My Darling, My Hamburger; Confessions of a Teenage Baboon;* or the Pulitzer Prize–winning play, *The Effect of Gamma Rays on Man-in-the Moon Marigolds*. He sustains his output and is simultaneously a playwright, novelist, teacher, and wordsmith. The last I read of Zindel was an article in *The New York Times* (April 2, 1989) in which he admitted that what he loved "doing best is telling stories in the theater." At that time, he was producing his play, *Amulets Against the Dragon Forces*, on an off-Broadway stage, but I haven't heard of its success or closing.

After *The Chocolate War* by Robert Cormier and *The Outsiders* by S. E. Hinton, *The Pigman* ranks third among adolescent novels deemed most teachable by the Assembly on Literature for Adolescents of the National Council of Teachers of English (Colby 1978, 3). Because of all the good writing he inspires in my classroom, Zindel gets my vote every year. And because he talks to teens so well, I recommend using his book to write creatively.

References

Colby, Curtis. 1978. *Discussion Guide for the Novel* The Pigman *by Paul Zindel*. Wilton, CT: Center for Literary Review, Current Affairs Films and Mark Twain Media.

St. Clair, Allison. 1990. "Listen to the Children." *Senior Edition USA Colorado:* 8 (June issue), 10 (July issue).

Zindel, Paul. 1968. *The Pigman*. New York: Bantam.

Zindel, Paul. 1981. *Pigman's Legacy*. New York: Bantam.

10 What's the Big Idea? Linking Creative and Academic Writing in the Multigenre Research Paper

Sheryl Lain
Wyoming Writing Project Director, Cheyenne, Wyoming

I have a friend—published poet and novelist, ex-teacher. Before she took early retirement, she moved from the junior high, where she was famous as a writing teacher, to the high school. On her first day, she came to school wearing one brown shoe and one black one. She was like that, not paying attention to ordinary things. Teaching school, tending minute by minute to the ordinary, was hard on her.

She was assigned to teach what no one else wanted, in this case Vocational English. That's always how it goes: new teacher, low man on the totem pole. Assignment: Blockheads.

In spite of her bright orange imagination, she had to teach a gray, set-in-stone curriculum. Which was fine with her—up to a point. But, the curriculum was chopped, pureed, canned, boxed, and labeled. No teacher dared veer off the daily diet of raw grammar, the unblinking focus on "basic skills" interpreted as memo writing, phone answering, and business letter punctuating. Literature? Nah! No practical function for it. Personal writing journals? Nah! Not useful on the job. What does a secretary do with "two roads diverged in a yellow wood." Why does a welder need "some say the world will end in fire." The school's "products" (the vernacular for flesh and blood students) do not need literature.

My two-shoed friend couldn't help herself. Her own need for beauty, pungency, texture made her do it: She taught a poem. In Vocational English.

The walls of this state-of-the-art school are hollow. The walls listen. A fellow English teacher burst in on Two Shoes. "I heard you teach a poem. You aren't allowed poetry in your curriculum." Finally the principal came down to remind Two Shoes she was hired to follow the curriculum.

Shortly after, Two Shoes took a year's leave to learn to breathe again. Obviously she was unsuited for the teaching profession, at least in that school, sensitive as she was to words and people's hearts.

But her kids! The other day the beautician cutting my hair asked me what I do for a living. "Teach." I thought the monosyllable would be a conversation stopper.

"Teach what?" she persisted.

"English."

Her enthusiasm surprised me. "My favorite teacher was my high school English teacher. She really turned me on to poetry. I still read poetry."

"The English teacher?" I asked. She told me. It was my friend, Two Shoes.

Way leads on to way, and I find myself teaching in Two Shoes' alma mater of heartbreak in a room with hollow walls. My assignment is to teach a composition class to college bounders. The vocational counselor gatekeepers already culled out the future secretaries and plumbers. Thumbs up, you go to Comp. Thumbs down, you go to Applied Communication, the new name for Vocational English, where, in spite of the name change, the future laborers—Deltas and Gammas every one—learn their basic skills.

At the so-called other end of the spectrum sits Comp, touted as a surefire passport to collegiate success. But Comp, I discover, is also a canned course with no creative writing allowed. The prescribed curriculum for Comp requires literary analyses, a research paper, and structured essays, five-paragraph ones with the thesis sentences planted precisely at the end of the introductory paragraphs. No poem and story writing allowed. Creative writing belongs to the creative writing teacher. Period.

At first, I follow the prescribed curriculum. But in my classroom the first year, I observe some disturbing trends. Why is the writing in the first essay of the semester—a freewheeling piece that I assign in order to get to know the kids—more alive, more fluent than subsequent pieces? Why do my students become increasingly dependent upon me—to prescribe the piece and to comment profusely on each, comments they blithely ignore on subsequent pieces? Why do I feel I'm doing more work than my students, what with all that tight control and, later, all the blood-red evaluation? Why are certain students, right-brainers maybe, always at a disadvantage with the outline-first formula? "How can I know what I mean till I see what I say?" Their drooping body language speaks volumes.

Then, in the spring of 1993, I hear Tom Romano present at the Northwest Regional NCTE Conference in Boise. He uses a multigenre research paper with his college English students. He has the department head's blessing. Romano's multigenre paper moves students up one click on Bloom's taxonomy—from analysis to synthesis (Bloom and Krathwohl 1984). Students create meaning from their study, writing their own stories and poems from the ideas and facts gathered through research.

Simultaneously, I read Linda Rief's *Seeking Diversity* (1992). In her secondary English classes, Rief uses a theme, such as the elderly in our society, and around this theme she arranges reading, writing, thinking, and discussing activities.

I also note in the September 1993 *Educational Leadership* that the "big idea" as a schoolwide theme is tried in particular Los Angeles schools where the drop-out rate is high and attendance is abominable (Anstead 1993). The research on these schools using Humanitas, an interdisciplinary humanities project, reveals that kids come to school and stay if they get to study, discuss, research, and write about big issues and concerns—prejudice, violence, equity.

After two years of teaching composition via grammar texts at my hollow-walled school, I veer off the well-traveled road. I take the plunge, armed as I am with Romano, Rief, and Humanitas.

"Our research paper will be different this year. You are the guinea pigs. I will become a student in this class with you." We start with big ideas. "What issues do you discuss around your dinner table? What do you wonder? What do you believe? What do you wish you could change about the world, the society? What do you like to study? What do you wish you could become in the future?" I ask lots of such questions in a rambling, self-interest survey I conduct orally. I ask the questions out loud; the kids answer in their journals. It takes all period.

I collect the journals and read them at night. It occurs to me that I need to keep track of each kid's first thoughts. I find some notebook paper and assign each student a page. I jot down the student's interests, ideas. Under the jot list, I draw a line. I spend some time brainstorming, scribbling down researchable topics for each kid to consider.

After a while, I notice that the interest areas tend to cluster. Great! We'll have groups based on Big Ideas. All the family issues cluster in one group. All the spiritual issues cluster. All the violence issues cluster, and so on. And within each group, each researcher has her own customized approach to the topic. She can bounce her ideas off the others, she can share sources, she can listen to her partners' writing.

The next day, I hand each student her piece of notebook paper filled with my musings. I say, "Draw a line under my brainstorming and offer your own ideas for topics."

We exchange notes for two days, notes rich with ideas, like love of animals, family problems, schizophrenia, yin/yang, totalitarianism, human fascination with horror, spirituality of the Sioux Indians, utopias, Christ symbols in art. Everyone has at least a vague idea for a Big Idea, and everyone belongs to a group. Then, we head to the library. Kids in the same idea groups park their backpacks at the same table. The search begins. I move from table to table brainstorming with first one and then the other as they make their way through their thoughts and the research. Table partners eavesdrop, gain insight, offer suggestions.

Back in class, we doodle in our journals.

At the NCTE Annual Convention in 1991, I heard Gabriele Rico talk about drawing in English class. After her college students work through a difficult text, they create what Rico calls a "one-pager." Using line, shape, form, color, they create symbols which express the theme of the work. Louann Reid presented her version of the one-pager at a national NCTE conference (1991). Reinforcing their work are Elliot Eisner (1991) and Howard Gardner (1993), who talk about envisioning and connecting, using various learning modes.

So, we doodle. "What's your favorite doodle?" They doodle. "Now, switch your pencil to the other hand." I turn on music. "Fill up the whole page with shapes." They lean back, legs stretched out, brows unfurrowed. They scribble. After a while I say, "Take a look at your scribbles. Look at line, shape, form. What do you notice. Write down, right over the top of your drawings if you want, words which describe what you notice. What does your work remind you of? Wind? Kaleidoscopes?" After the doodling, I give each person paper, markers, magazines, scissors, glue. I say, "Create some shapes that mirror your Big Ideas. Into the shapes, fit pictures and words you find in the magazines."

"Ohhhh," says Christie, stepping into the room second hour, "it smells like kindergarten in here." The whole day is yellow sunshine.

I ask each student to explain to her table partners how the one-pager, a sort of shaped collage, represents her Big Idea. I hope members of the group bond a little. I hope each student makes the connection between her idea and the representation of the idea. I hope links are forged among ideas in the group. I hope we get our hands dirty messing with metaphor, enriching the thin topsoil of class.

Later yet, we play mural mania. I drape each table with paper. Each student picks a spot and, using paint and brushes borrowed from the art room, he doodles lines, shapes, forms, and colors representing his Big Idea. Then I say, "Because you are one group, see if you can form the individual doodles into a whole." The finished murals are hung about the room, and each group explains to the whole class the meaning of the symbols. From the first, we all know each other's Big Ideas.

Meanwhile, the students chronicle their searching, thinking, reading, and reflecting processes in their journals. I tell them that I will give as much credit for the process as for the product. The tools to use for the process, besides the traditional note and source cards, are the journal and the portfolio. I suggest they buy an accordion folder to hold all their process artifacts.

Borrowing Sheila Sunstein's "windows" idea, which she shared at Shoptalk, a statewide Wyoming Writing Project conference in 1994, I ask students to use yellow self-stick notes as a road map through their journals, chronicling their journey. They write: "Here I changed my mind and decided to use Bradbury as my author instead of Vonnegut." Or, "Here I decided to interview Mr. Baird about Vietnam." Or, "Here is where I veered off my original idea and found my real topic." Or, "Here is my reader/response piece on *Brave New World*."

From the ruminating, reading, researching, drawing, and talking about the Big Idea, I move the students toward an author. After all, the curriculum calls for an in-depth study of an author and his writings. "What books do you like to read, on what topics," I ask. "Do you have a favorite writer on the best-sellers list? Do you like any gray-bearded author from the canon? What was the last book you enjoyed reading?" While each student researches her Big Idea, I have time to conference one-on-one about authors and books. I hear about Harlequin romances, Tom Clancy, Michael Crichton, Stephen King, Pat McManus, L. M. Montgomery.

I learn the reading fluency and preference of each student, and together we talk about what author connects with the Big Idea. Paul, who is fascinated with the criminal mind and who reads well, lands upon Truman Capote's *In Cold Blood*. Angie, who doesn't like to read and who wants to explore issues of adoption since she was adopted, decides upon L. M. Montgomery's Anne of Green Gables books. Melissa, pregnant and rethinking social values, decides to read and research two stacks of books—one is all the children's books she loves, and the other is the work of Madeleine L'Engle. From the children's books, she charts the morals of the stories, the values children learn through literature. She'll compare these values with L'Engle's adolescent and adult works. Christ is on Sarah's mind; she's taking classes to become confirmed in her church. The idea of Christ symbols in literature appeals to her, and she's liked Steinbeck since junior high when her class read *Of Mice and Men*. She'll examine Christ from the Biblical perspective as well as Christ symbols in Steinbeck's work. David, interested in social order and governmental control, hits on Huxley and Orwell. The *Dragonlance* fanatic decides to read Tolkien's trilogy.

Some students have one author, and some have several. Some use a stack of books from their own personal canons coupled with one "classic" dude. We link Pat McManus with Twain or Thurber. We link King with Poe. We don't restrict ourselves to authors stuck between the thick covers of the American literature or British literature texts. One girl reads Ntozake Shange, another Sandra Cisneros.

Because each student's study is customized, I periodically assign Status of the Study updates—a two-minute oral talk to the whole class on "what I'm studying and where I am now." They collaborate. Trish calls across the room, waving a book: "Here, Paul. Here's something on serial murderers for you."

During the three months or so while students research their topics and read at least four books by their authors, I teach minilessons demonstrating how to make bibliography cards, how to use the Modern Language Association handbook, how to access resources in the library, how to make note cards. I explain that they will be graded both on the process portfolio (containing drafts, notes, journal, logs, reflections), and on the paper itself, i.e., the product. The product will really be a collection, which might include a research-based expository essay, a literary analysis, a vignette, a poem. One student might include in the collection a letter to a congressman. One might write a letter to her natural mother, a person she has never met. One might include a contrast essay, showing the difference between Harlequin romances and *Jane Eyre*. I ask for a variety of pieces—prose and poetry, fiction and nonfiction. I ask that at least one paper in the bunch be research-based with work cited and that at least one paper be an original story or poem.

Along the way, each student writes three reflections which she includes in her final collection. The reflections answer such questions as: "What kind of learner are you?" "What did you learn and how do you learn best?" "Why are you fascinated with this or that portion of your study?" "Why did you select your subject, your author(s), your genres?" "How does your study connect with the whole of your life, your future plans, your favorite classes?"

In the last month of the year, after we are finished with both the research and the rough drafts and while we help each other edit and polish final drafts, students take over teaching the class. Each student has one period to teach us his study. His plans need to be out of the ordinary—a field trip, a film, an art experience, a music experience, a guest speaker. We write poetry in the Botanic Gardens. We hear a social worker talk about the inner workings of The Casey Family Program. We pet Rusty, the Seeing Eye dog and constant companion of a visually impaired guest speaker, who talks about the healing bond between himself and his animal friend.

I like the presentations. I like the intense reading and writing I see. I like the interaction among students. I like to read the papers. David, who loathes external control, researches totalitarianism and reads Orwell. I get a kick out of his vignette, a scenario he writes featuring Winston from *1984* and Napoleon from *Animal Farm*. The two are riding along in a limo—Winston the driver, Napoleon in tux and tails smoking his huge cigar in the back. "Turn right here!" Napoleon orders. Winston fails to negotiate the turn and thus disobeys the command issued too late. Thump! Napoleon raps Winston on the head with his cane. "Pull over!" Napoleon squeals. Winston obeys. "Get out!" Napoleon orders. Winston obeys. Napoleon proceeds to beat Winston to death. His anger spent, Napoleon trots back to the car, leaving the body in the borrow pit, its blood seeping into the roadside sand. At the wheel, Napoleon realizes too late that he doesn't know how to drive.

My department holds its breath when the news leaks out. "Lain's kids veer off the clearly marked road through Comp. Lain's kids write poetry in Comp." But Romano, Rief, Rico, Gardner, Eisner, and the Humanitas project carry authority. The multigenre research paper receives a stay of execution.

We still segregate kids in my high school. We still have long halls for English and other long halls for social studies, segregating subject areas. We still have too many kids in our high school. We still focus our educational aim too low—labeling kids as "products" to fuel our economy.

But in the classroom, at the grassroots level where it matters most, some innovations help make a difference. As a tribute to my two-shoed friend, my students will write poetry and stories in Comp. Maybe some students who ho-hum their way through the disconnectedness of modern high schools will see how Big Ideas connect with creativity. Maybe some day the learning environment, even in high school, can encourage a sense of community where learners reflect on and center themselves. Maybe future schools, as James Moffett envisions in *The Universal Schoolhouse* (1994), will foster wholeness.

References

Anstead, Neil. 1993. "Hooking Kids with Humanities." *Educational Leadership* 51 (September): 84–86.

Bloom, Benjamin S., and David R. Krathwohl. 1984. *Taxonomy of Educational Objectives: Handbook 1: Cognitive Domain*. White Plains, NY: Longman.

Eisner, Elliott. 1991. Presentation at the CEL Conference held in conjunction with the NCTE Annual Convention in Seattle.

Gardner, Howard. 1993. *Frames of Mind: The Theory of Multiple Intelligences*. New York: Basic.

Moffett, James. 1994. *The Universal Schoolhouse*. San Francisco: Jossey-Bass.

Reid, Louann. 1991. "Of Cows' Eyes and Shakespeare: Making Metaphors with Adolescents." Presentation at the NCTE Annual Convention in Seattle.

Rico, Gabriele. 1991. "Brain Research and Learning." Keynote address at the CEL Luncheon of the NCTE Annual Convention in Seattle.

Rief, Linda. 1992. *Seeking Diversity: Language Arts with Adolescents*. Portsmouth, NH: Heinemann.

Romano, Tom. 1993. "The Multigenre Research Paper." Presentation at the Northwest Regional NCTE Spring Conference in Boise.

Sunstein, Sheila. 1993. "Portfolio Assessment." Presentation at the Wyoming Writing Project Conference in Casper.

11 Writing toward Thoughtfulness through Logs

Cynthia G. Kuhn
University of Denver, Colorado

The neatly typed pages lie between us on the table. The student stares at them, then at me, then back at the paper. "I just don't know what to do with it now," he growls. "It was all I could do to get *this* cranked out."

As a tutor in the university writing center, I often meet students who confide that they are stuck, that they rely on last-minute paper generation, that they don't understand *how* to work toward completion of the assignments looming over their heads in a red haze of deadline. Their frustration reveals that they don't feel in control of their writing processes. Such encounters have made an impact upon me as a composition instructor. I have realized that, if we want to prepare students for future writing challenges, we need to promote ownership of thinking processes. In *Teaching for Thoughtfulness*, John Barell describes an important pedagogical goal as "help[ing] students recognize the attitudes they have toward themselves as thinkers . . . and their attitudes toward others" (1995, 6). Thoughtfulness (or critical thinking) combines the cognitive and affective dimensions of our lives (Barell 1995, 6; McPeck 1981, 17; Paul 1990, 305) in the process of exploring a complex issue or problem. To be thoughtful, we must be metacognitive, context-sensitive, inquisitive, willing to suspend judgment, and investigative of multiple viewpoints in order to arrive at a place of knowing; a thoughtful pedagogy encourages reflection as a catalyst for self-directed action.

The culture of a writing class seems a natural place to promote thoughtfulness; many writing issues, like problems in life, are messy and complex—without distinct answers—and they involve a process. Yet many students come to composition classes with the belief that writing is something to be done "right" the first time. Rexford Brown explains a potential reason:

> Observational studies of schools suggest that in many of them very little reading for comprehension goes on, that very little significant writing is done, that very little discussion occurs, and that very little meaningful questioning or Socratic dialogue takes place. Most people would agree that all these activities could be called thought-inducing. (1987, 50)

Without critical reading, writing, discussing, or questioning, how can students do something meaningful with the material? Furthermore, if we make meaning by interacting with the text (Rosenblatt 1978, 75) and with others (Moffett 1968, 11–12), then students deprived of such negotiation may equate thinking with recall, rather than with a process. Their schemas for writing may be similarly linear. After years of having had one-shot writing activities such as essay tests, students tend to focus on correctness upon first try. The one-shot approach makes it difficult for students to develop the ability to "re-see" their thinking (and revise the written presentation); as Nancy Sommers explains, a "recursive" stance is key for revision (1980, 127).

Our job, then, as composition instructors, begins at a place of invitation. When we are confronted with formulaic writing by students, this may be a sign of the students' rigid habits of thought. Since "learning to write . . . can be seen as a process of learning to think about one's own thinking" (Bizzell 1992, 162), students need to be given the opportunity to develop their own thoughtful habits of mind through enculturation in a reflective writing environment.

An Exploration

In my introductory college composition class, assignments such as essays and logs ask students to utilize what Chet Myers calls "a framework for disciplinary analysis—a structure for making sense of the materials, issues, and methodologies of the discipline being taught" (1988, 6). The class framework for analysis is rhetorical; that is to say, students explore how everything in writing (content, format, tone, language, grammar, and so forth) operates within the rhetorical situation and determines the effectiveness of a piece of writing given the audience and purpose of the situation.

Awareness of the rhetorical situation promotes thoughtfulness in meaningful ways. To read with a rhetorical eye allows students to discover that authors do things for specific reasons—that writers make choices related to the audience and purpose of the piece—and that careful exploration of a text can reveal examples which inform the ways we respond as readers. To write within a rhetorical framework requires transforming writer-based prose to reader-based prose, and it marks a movement from egocentric behavior ("What do I want to say?") to allocentric behavior ("What does my audience need in order to understand what I'm saying?"); projecting into the role of audience encourages the consideration of alternative viewpoints. As James Moffett explains, "learning is a matter of 'decentering'" (1968, 148), and developing allocentric perspectives is important for growth.

One activity which supports the development of thoughtfulness is having students write regularly in logs (see Figure 1 for a sequence). I ask students to write reading logs (one-page responses to readings—see Figure 2) and three kinds of writing logs (draft, workshop, and process logs—discussed next). The structure for logs is informal: students must write at least one full page in response to prompts, the logs can be handwritten, and the logs are not graded (although the students do receive points for completing them).

Reacting to readings in reading logs throughout the semester contributes to the development of rhetorical awareness and emphasizes personal interaction with texts. Writing logs, however, have proven to be especially valuable in helping students think themselves through their *own* writing processes. The rationale for and results of using writing logs are discussed below.[1]

Writing Logs

Writing logs are not new; many instructors use process logs or essay histories to ask students to be reflective about their writing experiences. Yet thinking about the experience only in retrospect may not be the most beneficial method of encouraging thoughtfulness—the chance for students to use their realizations has passed, at least for that writing project—and it does not take advantage of one of the most important critical thinking elements: metacognition. Metacognition essentially involves three stages: "planning, monitoring, and evaluating our thinking" (Barell 1995, 249); the three logs I have students write (draft, workshop, and process) incorporate these stages in overlapping, cyclical activities that ask students to be metacognitive during the entire writing process. In addition, the logs emphasize the importance of "posing questions to ourselves as we are planning, monitoring, and evaluating" (Barell 1995, 249). Writing logs are freewrites; the expressive writing allows what James Britton et al. call "immediate preoccupations . . . of

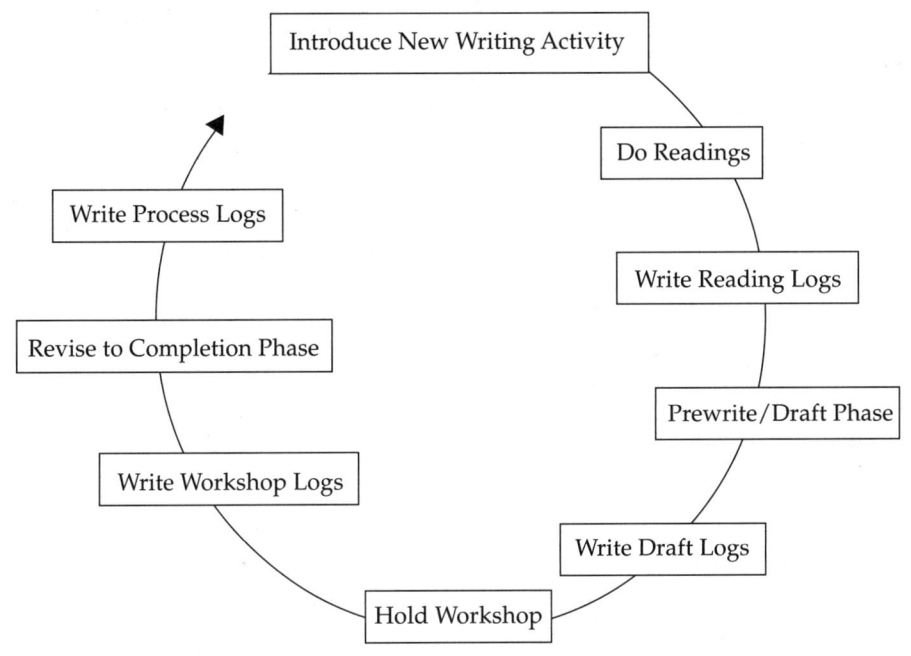

Figure 1. Sequence for logs.

the moment" (1975, 82) to emerge. Students can prioritize the impressions and needs of the present, bringing to the surface the elements about which they feel confident, as well as the issues needing attention, in their drafts; they are immersed in articulating new writing goals or problems and proposing strategies and resolutions.

The practice of integrating metacognitive activities throughout the process creates a framework for thoughtful interaction between students and their texts-in-progress; it provides opportunities for students to examine where they are in the process and to speculate about and explore how they might meet their goals. The following discussion of draft, workshop, and process logs will illustrate how using logs can shift the focus from going routinely through the writing process to *thinking* through the process.

Draft Logs

Draft logs are written when students have a first draft and are beginning the revision process. The questions address the status of students' essays-in-progress in order to set project goals and define writing prob-

Reading logs are introduced on the syllabus as places "to write about your intellectual journey, exploring your own thinking about a particular reading." The fact that they are not summaries is stressed; I give students questions at the beginning of the semester as options but encourage them to focus on the issue(s) burning brightest in their minds regarding the topic. Questions/prompts, with intended cognitive activities, are presented in the following chart.

Reading Log Question	Cognitive Activity
What is your response as a reader to the piece and why?	Articulating reader response/supporting
What did it make you think about regarding your writing experiences (for this class or others) or your life?	Activating previous knowledge or experience/making connections
What made the most impact upon you and why?	Focusing and exploring ideas
What didn't you understand or what questions does it raise for you?	Defining problems to reconcile

Anthony Petrosky maintains that we should "give students the opportunity to come to their own understandings of the subject by placing the responsibilities for making sense of the readings and writings on the students" (1983, 4). Reading logs are essentially opportunities for students to be immersed in the interpretive act on a regular basis and are intended to make students authorities by providing opportunities for open-ended transactions with texts.

Reading logs allow me to respond to ideas each time the students turn in logs (logs are collected the day a reading is due, after the reading is discussed in class); they create ongoing contact points between teacher and student throughout the semester. In addition—and more important—students use logs in small-group work, sharing their ideas about the effectiveness of the assigned text and developing a presentation to introduce the results of group discussion to the rest of the class.

When students use their own reactions to readings as a starting point for negotiating meaning with other group members, they are confronted with multiple viewpoints, which can put them in the position of explaining and examining their ideas while considering the validity of perspectives generated by others. As a benefit, full-class discussions improve because students, having worked through their ideas, are more invested in the outcome.

Figure 2. Rationale for reading logs.

lems; Barell believes that we must encourage students to set, monitor, and evaluate their own goals if we want them to "take control of their own learning" (1995, 79). Draft logs create an important opportunity for students to take control of the writing project (after having done some exploratory writing) by setting their own courses of action. Prompts for draft logs, with intended metacognitive activities, are listed below.

Draft Log Question	Metacognitive Activity
What are my goals for this essay?	Set goals
What is the status of my draft now?	Monitor
What questions do I have?	Monitor/wonder
What kind of feedback do I want/need?	Set goals

Identification of individual goals, as well as problems or issues to be considered in the writing process, provides a foundation for movement forward. John E. McPeck explains, "In part, critical thinking involves seeing when a certain common procedure is fruitless by entertaining alternatives to it" (1981, 6). After articulating a goal or concern in a log—and generating propositions or solutions to it themselves or taking it to a workshop for feedback—students can investigate alternatives and design a strategy for action. In the following log excerpts, students determine problems and goals while establishing the status of their drafts. In the first example, the writer pinpoints a lack of development in the draft and decides to research others' approaches to the essay as a way of resolving her uncertainty about how to proceed:

> I believe my draft is really just the basic idea—the story in its skeletal form. I want to bring all the color, intensity, visual and emotive imagery to flesh it out, make it far more of an experience for the reader. Now it's basically how I feel, basically it's like a news item, or a quite distant or distancing account of an event, rather than the 3-dimensional full-color version of senses colliding that I have in my mind's eye and ear. I have kept to the minimum up to this point—I guess I feel intimidated about where to start with words.... I feel my draft like an empty concrete parking structure—it's missing teeth. Goal: I'd like to be exposed to others' expressions of experiences so I can see how I could string mine together without it becoming a freewrite of senses like often happens in my writing.

In the next excerpt, another student also discusses the need for development and organization, then wonders about the strength of the main idea:

> My draft is only 4 pages—I know there's more to develop. I'm not sure, however, how clear my point-by-point structure will be received because it is rather muddled—organized in terms of chronology of the experience, rather than on points. There are more similarities than differences and I feel that while my point/point structure may be muddled, if I separate the two issues into whole-subject-by-whole-subject, it will weaken the analogy. I'm having fun with the idea though, so it is probably so clear to me... since I thought of it that I don't adequately convince the reader. Goals:

> To convince the reader my analogy works. Get reader response to see how clear/muddled I am.

She senses that the content may be affecting the organization, but her goals reflect a commitment to the topic; she decides to solicit reader input to test the clarity.

Another goal of draft logs is to encourage a wondering attitude, an essential dynamic in thoughtful classrooms. Richard Paul tells us that "critical thinkers are nothing, if not questioners" (1990, 338). Like goal setting, student-generated questions allow students to target issues or concerns about which they want input. A genuine desire to resolve students' own questions is very different from the motivation occurring when an instructor gives out whole-class directives, and, when students ask questions, they can realize a desire for feedback in specific areas, as the following excerpt illustrates:

> I'm now realizing that my draft isn't where I want it to be. I haven't established ethos and my pathos needs some more umph! I want to add at least one more claim of trickle-down economics, but I completely forgot about it when writing my paper. I have supported a lot of evidence which I am proud of, but feel that my own observations need to be stronger and less ambiguous. For this workshop, I'd like to get more ideas of how better to support my thesis. I guess I'm looking for claims from another perspective besides my own to make sure that I have covered all the bases in convincing my opposition to support pure capitalism. I also want to know if they think that I have put the piece together in a thoughtful, comprehensive way, or if I'm just babbling with no real reason. My goal for this essay is to have a convincing argument in favor of pure capitalism. I want to touch a trigger inside my reader that persuades them that capitalism works. I also am searching for a title that captures what I am saying because so far I haven't been able to think of one. Questions: Am I relating to the audience? Do I need to put personal experience (viewpoints) in it? Do I need to elaborate on my examples?

After clarifying their questions and the types of specific feedback they want, students meet with their workshop groups and negotiate a "contract" (see Figure 3 for examples) that outlines expectations for the presentation of feedback. Students then take each others' essays home to read before coming together later in the week for a workshop; the contract guides their reading and responding.[2]

Workshop Logs

Workshop logs promote responsibility and ownership through reflection on specific results of workshops. Students write workshop logs after

> **Contract A**
>
> 1. [Give] positive and negative responses.
> 2. [Be] honest, tell what doesn't work and why.
> 3. Use an example of why it doesn't work—be specific.
> 4. End comments are for general response.
> 5. [Present] ideas for improvement.
> 6. Realize that this is not a finished piece.
> 7. [Question to answer:] Does this need more development?
>
> Read a minimum of one time all the way through without making comments. Then go back and comment in the margins. Read a minimum of twice altogether.
>
> **Contract B**
>
> We agree to read each essay a minimum of three times.
>
> We agree not to hold back on either positive or negative criticisms.
>
> We agree to provide a page of comments in addition to comments throughout the essay.
>
> We agree to offer a minimum of two hooks for use as inspiration to the introduction.
>
> We agree to pay strong attention to the structure and flow of the essay, offering suggestions for transitional sentences.

Figure 3. Sample contracts for presenting feedback.

they meet with peers to workshop their essays and thus are ready to revise again. Asking students to write a log at this stage gives them a chance to reflect upon the workshop experience, examine the specific results of group work, and speculate about future experiences. Questions for workshop logs follow.

Workshop Log Question	Metacognitive Activity
How effective was the workshop?	Evaluate
How well did we meet our contract goals?	Evaluate
What did I do well?	Evaluate
How do I know my contributions were effective?	Evaluate
Did I get the feedback I needed? (Why, or why not?)	Monitor/evaluate
What did I learn, listening to others? (Or, What was I surprised to discover?)	Monitor

What might I try differently next time?	Evaluate/set goals
What is my plan for revision?	Monitor/set goals

The first seven questions are intended to help students evaluate the workshop experience and monitor their reactions to feedback received; if a workshop did not meet expectations, students can also identify potential reasons and suggest ideas for improvement.

Workshop logs provide evidence of students demonstrating ownership, displaying empathy or appreciation of others, and gaining an awareness of the benefits of feedback. Students are insightful about their own participation and exhibit a willingness to change for future experiences; after an early workshop, one student writes about the value of listening and the importance of questioning:

> One of the things I think I contributed in the workshop is honesty. . . . Another thing I did was give suggestions . . . for the student to think about. I was telling my true thoughts. I learned a few things in the workshop. I learned that there will always be different feedbacks from different people. For example, what may not be confusing for one person may be confusing for another. No matter how good you think your paper is, there will always be some revising to do. Especially after your first draft. By listening to others, you can improve your paper when revising. Also, if you listen to the other person's feedback, you can come up with some ideas of your own. One thing I might do differently next time in the workshop is to ask questions, instead of just listening to what they've got to say.

In addition to emphasizing responsibility for workshop participation, the workshop logs have another function: the last prompt asks students to articulate a plan for revision. The following excerpts show two students making decisions based on workshop experiences and feedback:

> All our papers got off the track of talking about or actually presenting an idea and then supporting it. We are all on track now! I received exactly the feedback I was looking for. . . . I also got insight into the flow and the understandability. I learned that I have to persuade better to exactly what I am trying to say and bring out Darwinism more than I did. . . . I am going to go home and rework the introduction and the general form of presenting an idea and then supporting it with concrete evidence. I am happy with the essay and looking forward to the revision. I am focused and know exactly what I want to do.

> I learned that I was ambiguous with my thesis and that my paper was slow in taking hold of the reader. I also learned that my organization needs work (in terms of point-by-point). I was a little

surprised by that because I understood it when I read/wrote it, but I guess the writer is sometimes too close to get the proper perspective.... I guess I need to start with my introduction, making it more specific to my new thesis. I also want to show more of [volunteer] life and get more detailed in my descriptions.

Workshop logs encourage students to state immediately a starting point for revision—long before the "night before" the deadline—and incubation can occur between the workshop and the due date (usually one or two weeks later).

Process Logs

The final type of log is primarily self-evaluative, although the last question looks to the next writing experience in an attempt to create a flow of learning because, as Joan Barickman says, "Successful education is composing old ideas and new experiences into new patterns" (1992, 50). Asking students to be reflective about the writing experience as a whole underscores the need to identify what ingredients of the process seem to be helping or hindering them, a necessary step in the development and refinement of new habits of thought about writing.

Process Log Question	Metacognitive Activity
What were my triumphs/difficulties?	Evaluate
What was the biggest issue I encountered and how did I resolve it?	Evaluate
How well did I meet my goals?	Evaluate
What might I do differently next time?	Set goals

It is here that students most often discuss changing notions about revision. Evaluating their successes and problems in meeting their goals seems to prompt increasing awareness of writing habits as well as speculation on future approaches, as revealed by the following log excerpts.

One student identifies his current method of planning as contributing to later organizational problems and proposes a solution:

> My biggest difficulty was not so much coming up with ideas but how to organize them. Help from workshops really showed me things I wasn't thinking. I had organization problems within each paragraph, too. My ideas were clear but they easily got muddled in the words. I feel my writing is improving in both solidity and creativity. I do *not* feel I plan well enough in advance when writing; my paper starts at one point and ends at another point altogether—good for freewrite but bad for a finished product. My papers have *focus* but not direction. As a result, my papers appear unorganized and hard to follow, even though effort did go into them. Next time I need to have a very detailed outline....

The second student assesses a new strategy which altered her perception of herself as a writer:

> This paper is my first triumph in the writing process. Once I started working with my paper in a kind of private workshop, momentum took over, ideas began to flow, and before I knew it I was well on my way to a final. . . . It does so much good to separate creative and critical forces in me. I actually let myself write badly as a means to an end and if I hadn't allowed myself to take the pressure off and just go with it, I never would have been able to find myself here: happy with a final draft. I didn't think it was possible! And to think I actually like "substantial revising." This whole process reaffirmed my faith in myself as a skillful writer. I knew I had it in there all along but it was locked behind some *horrible* habits.

Both students are making important observations about their experiences. Examining their writing processes has led them to discoveries that can inform future writing challenges.

A Conclusion

Students seem to realize that reflection is crucial to meaningful work, that they are qualified to make valuable observations, and that they can recognize and address writing problems on their own. At the end of each semester, when I offer students an open-ended opportunity to share their ideas about log writing, they discuss themselves as writers and, significantly, as thinkers.[3]

Students indicate that the use of writing logs allows them to evaluate the status of their texts-in-progress; generates a path for action by highlighting issues and questions for consideration; creates opportunities for new ideas to emerge; reminds students of steps otherwise overlooked; helps prioritize ideas; makes students acknowledge triumphs; encourages students to push themselves; and keeps students focused. In addition, many of the students praised the logs as necessary thinking opportunities. The following student's comments, representative of general response, illustrate the value of using writing logs during the process:

> In retrospect, the logs really helped me get a handle on what I was trying to write. This was *the only time* I really sat down and asked myself if I was going in the right direction or if I needed to change my focus [emphasis added]. I will be able to set higher goals for myself when writing now. . . . I will strive for higher goals because I have learned that I am capable of so much.

The response also reveals that the self-directed experiences have been instrumental in cultivating the student's sense of confidence about writing.

Making students responsible for planning, monitoring, and evaluating their writing processes puts them into the position of practicing reflective approaches to writing and thinking. Immersed in the multidimensional issues of writing, students must be able to define problems, consider alternatives, and find their own paths of meaning making. If students can recognize habits that aren't working and discard them, if they can explore alternatives and make thoughtful choices, if they can feel confident directing their own actions, then they have a foundation for dealing with complex issues in the future.

Notes

The author wishes to thank Dr. Liz Hamp-Lyons, Dr. Louann Reid, Dana Hagmeyer, and Hannah Kelminson for feedback at various stages of the project. She is especially grateful to Dr. Richard VanDeWeghe for guidance and encouragement throughout the process—and for his thoughtful, inspirational approach to teaching.

1. The data in this report were obtained from a study conducted over a one-year period involving three introductory college composition classes and examining approximately 1,400 writing samples. Log excerpts included in this report are unedited except for length and clarity (clarifying words appear in brackets).

2. For each essay assignment, students receive a detailed handout explaining the assignment and another handout listing criteria for evaluation/grading of completed essays. The "criteria sheet" offers standards for students to consider when responding to group members' essays, and the contracts written by the workshop groups specify student expectations for the presentation of feedback.

3. End-of-semester comments about reading logs reveal that students believe the format allows them to penetrate surface reactions; articulate new ideas and genuine "wonderings"; express and address feelings; organize thoughts; recognize personal assumptions or convictions emerging; explore how they've interpreted and analyzed the material; and build confidence in the ability to write about a variety of topics. Many students report that reading logs contribute to their perceptions of themselves as more critical readers and writers.

References

Barell, John. 1995. *Teaching for Thoughtfulness: Classroom Strategies to Enhance Intellectual Development.* 2d ed. White Plains, NY: Longman.

Barickman, Joan Estes. 1992. *Schoolwise: Teaching Academic Patterns of Mind.* Portsmouth, NH: Boynton/Cook.

Bizzell, Patricia. 1992. *Academic Discourse and Critical Consciousness.* Pittsburgh: University of Pittsburgh Press.

Britton, James, et al. 1975. *The Development of Writing Abilities (11–18).* Houndmills: Macmillan.

Brown, Rexford. 1987. "Who Is Accountable for 'Thoughtfulness'?" *Phi Delta Kappan* 69 (1): 49–52.

McPeck, John E. 1981. *Critical Thinking and Education.* New York: St. Martin's.

Moffett, James. 1983. *Teaching the Universe of Discourse.* 1968. Reprint, Portsmouth, NH: Boynton/Cook.

Myers, Chet. 1988. *Teaching Students to Think Critically.* San Francisco: Jossey-Bass.

Paul, Richard. 1990. *Critical Thinking: What Every Person Needs to Survive in a Rapidly Changing World.* Edited by A. J. A. Binker. Rohnert Park, CA: Sonoma State University Press.

Petrosky, Anthony. 1986. "Critical Thinking: Qu'est-Ce Que C'est?" *The English Record* 37 (3): 2–5.

Rosenblatt, Louise M. 1978. *The Reader, the Text, the Poem: The Transactional Theory of the Literary Work.* Carbondale: Southern Illinois University Press.

Sommers, Nancy. 1988. "Revision Strategies of Student Writers and Experienced Adult Writers." In *The Writing Teacher's Sourcebook.* 2d ed. Edited by Gary Tate and Edward P. J. Corbett. New York: Oxford University Press. First published in 1980 in *College Composition and Communication* 31 (4), 378–88.

12 "You learn from within yourself"

Helen Collins Sitler
Indiana University of Pennsylvania, Indiana, Pennsylvania

Kelly A. Carameli
Westmoreland County Community College, Youngwood, Pennsylvania

Brandi J. Abbott
Westmoreland County Community College

ENG 255 (Introduction to Literature) was a collaborative venture. The students were teachers as much as the instructor was. In keeping with the spirit of the class, we felt it only appropriate to collaborate on this manuscript, which is co-written by two students (Kelly Carameli and Brandi Abbott) and by the instructor (Helen Sitler). Together, we describe our experience in Introduction to Literature at Westmoreland County Community College.

Helen Sitler

A visitor peering through the window at the beginning of any of our class meetings would have seen an unusual sight. The desks of twelve college students and a teacher formed a circle around a stack of journals on the floor. We spent the first twenty to twenty-five minutes of each seventy-five-minute class reading one another's entries about the short stories or poetry for the day and writing responses to as many of our classmates' dialogue journals as we could. My teacher journal lay there, too. I was as eager as the students for other readers' responses to my thoughts about the reading. In the few minutes after journals were returned to their owners, silence ensued. We busily read our responders' comments; after that we were ready to proceed. Discussion, replete with references to one another's journal texts and written comments, began. Our discussions were rich and wide-ranging but always grounded in our personal transactions with the literature. As one student wrote in a course evaluation, "you learn[ed] from within yourself."

Because I was concerned with establishing a low-risk, noncompetitive learning environment, I had designed the course using a response-based approach which relied heavily on dialogue journals and class discussion. The students' own voices along with mine offer commentary on how our class functioned. We begin with brief explanations of dialogue journals and of reader-response theory.

The use of dialogue journals, or "written conversation," unites talk and writing in a functional, interactive way (Staton 1988). Journal writing provides students with an arena in which they can capture their first response to a piece of literature, an important step toward reflective analysis (Rosenblatt 1938, 1978). Such writing also extends students' opportunities for using language into productive channels usually denied them in classrooms. In journals, students can question, hypothesize, argue with other interpreters, and explore unfinished thoughts (Fulwiler 1989). Further, because the students share their dialogue journals with peers who respond as if in conversation, the process becomes interactive. By jointly creating a shared social world, journal readers and responders gain the "necessary mutual foundation on which to base a search for new knowledge" (Staton 1988, 314). In many ways, dialogue journals are a natural adjunct to a curriculum guided by reader-response theory.

Reader-response theory recognizes the centrality of the reader in any reading experience. Meaning lies not in the text itself but in the transaction of the reader with the text; thus the meaning any reader evokes from a short story or a poem has its basis in the life experiences and knowledge that the reader brings to the literature (Rosenblatt 1978). Furthermore, reader-response is a literary theory which unites emotion with intellect (Clifford 1991). In fact, the reader's emotional response provides a stepping stone to interpretation and analysis (Rosenblatt 1938, 1978).

In the classroom this means that students must first have the opportunity to connect personally with their reading. Following that personal connection, students must be invited back into the reading to interpret their evoked response. To accomplish this in ENG 255, we used dialogue journals, written responses to the journals from numerous class members, and class discussion.

Kelly Carameli

In flipping through my journal, I could not help but notice how it had changed over the course of the semester. In the beginning I was simply summarizing the story itself instead of responding to it. I think that after reading the comments from other classmates in my own journal, and from reading other journals, I finally started to get a better idea of what other readers needed to better understand my interpretations and impressions from different stories. It was interesting and intriguing to read how other people viewed a particular story and to consider the meaning they arrived at through keeping a record of their train of thought as they themselves read the story. I was fascinated by the wide variety of interpretations from a handful of people. In reading other people's journals, I was given a chance to see how a point or detail in a story might be seen differently.

Toward the middle of my journal, I noticed that there was more interjection of personal experiences and feelings, as well as my immediate thought on the story or poem. I believe this happened because I had a better understanding of what was expected in my entries and because I felt more comfortable and open with the others in my class. I think we all gave small pieces of ourselves to each other with every entry we wrote in our journals.

Helen Sitler

Students' increased awareness of audience and their realization that multiple perspectives were possible for any reading were cognitive benefits I had anticipated would arise from sharing journals. What I hadn't anticipated was the powerful social force the dialogue journals exerted.

These journals, shared widely among class members, were important in allowing us to connect with one another. Kelly notes her feeling that trust and acceptance developed along with the journal writing. In addition, the physical arrangement of desks in a circle (we all made eye contact) and open discussion prompted camaraderie. Students commented in course evaluations that "interaction with the students was the best" and "the class itself almost feels like an extension of home."

Another student, in her course evaluation, pointed out one further social effect of the dialogue journals. "I ended up doing more work than what was required because I loved the class and the stories!" On their own, the students had exceeded the number of reading assignments on the syllabus.

To accommodate students' interests and varying stages of development, I had left open spaces on the syllabus. Students were to choose their own reading from the text for those days, write journal entries, then come to class and read about the other students' selections. After the first round of exchanging these journals, the students were excited. I was amazed. In my teaching log I wrote, "Great news—they've read more than the assigned. . . . Comments from other journals got two times the amount of reading done!"

The students had acted as sales agents for their self-selected reading. Journal entries were so compelling that students went beyond the assignment of reading one more self-selected piece and instead read two, three, or more. This social aspect of the dialogue journals generated not only twice the amount of reading I would have dared to put on the syllabus but also stimulating discussions of the works that the students had chosen for themselves.

While sharing journals and class discussion guided our learning, a larger issue undergirded the classroom dynamics as a whole—establishing an enabling classroom environment. "To use the imagination freely, college students need a classroom atmosphere of trust, freedom, and fun" (Holladay 1988, 191). My students and I found that the response-based approach to literature encouraged such an environment.

Brandi Abbott

As a student in the reader-response literature class, I feel as though it is my duty to express myself through written words how I've learned, grown, and matured as a result of our class. Why do I feel so obligated? That's simple. So many people that I have come into contact with have approached literature as "dry" or "boring." Quite honestly, I began the same way. It wasn't until I began to connect my own personal life to the literature that I was reading that I realized all of those misconceptions about literature being boring were far from the truth.

Since our class was a reader-response class, I felt free to express my own thoughts and draw my own conclusions from each story. I realized that one story or one poem could have many different meanings, and not just one. The reason for this is just the fact that every person is different. For example, our literature class read a story about a family who loses their grandmother because of cancer. When I read the story, I was able to make a very strong emotional connection with the characters, whereas another member of our class never knew her grandmother and read that story from a totally different perspective. I discovered that even though we were reading the same story, in reality there were thirteen different stories being read.

Nobody reads a story in the same way, because each person brings her own different life and experiences to the story; therefore, the story yields thirteen different meanings as opposed to one. So many times (especially in grade school), we have been told that every story has one meaning, and the questions in the book regarding the story should be answered the same way. It is for this reason, I believe, that people approach literature as "boring," because they do not have the freedom to disagree with what the book or teacher says that story is "supposed" to mean.

If I could sum up our class in one word I would choose the word *free*. We were free to place our lives into the stories. We were free to draw our own different conclusions. We were free to write whatever we wanted in our journals. We were free to make our opinions known in class without being told that we were wrong and, most importantly, we learned and had a desire to do and learn beyond what our professor ever expected.

I am now (because of our reader-response literature class) a better reader and a better listener. I am amazed at the knowledge that I have acquired through our class. Placing and connecting our own personal lives to the reading was definitely key to understanding the literature and ultimately viewing literature as a whole in a different way, how literature should be regarded, as an exciting adventurous world.

Helen Sitler

One student's course evaluation expressed best my own hopes for this class.

> I've never had an English teacher that lets us analyze things in a large group. This helps so much because with other students' insights, everything about literature becomes meaningful and clear. My teachers in the past expected written homework and quizzes on what our interpretation of short stories and poems were. If it was wrong, it was too bad and this made me feel stupid. Helen's methods of teaching made me realize that everybody reads things differently. This class changed my attitudes towards many things, in a positive way.

I am saddened that the experience described above was a repeated theme among the students in this class. But I am not surprised, as it mirrors my own experiences in undergraduate English classes and, unfortunately, the way I taught literature for many years. When the opportunity arose to teach Introduction to Literature, I deliberately set out this time to create a more enabling learning environment, one which encouraged open discussion, numerous possible "right" answers, student-to-student connections, and learning "from within yourself."

My task was to teach an introductory literature course to students who were not English majors. To that end we discussed theme, plot, character, symbol, and technique in short stories through a response-based curriculum. However, as Tompkins (1990) and Zemelman and

Daniels (1988) note, the material that instructors cover is not truly what we teach. What we *do* is what we teach.

I would be pleased to discover in several years that Brandi, Kelly, and our other classroom colleagues can still discuss literature using appropriate terminology and remembering some things about certain authors. Nevertheless, the real success of this course is not that students' interest in literature was piqued or that they can speak about theme or symbol. The real success is that they found you can "learn from within yourself." These students discovered their own authority to challenge established opinions, to offer fresh perspectives, and to respect and learn from the insights of their peers. These lessons have the potential to extend far beyond Introduction to Literature.

Note

The authors wish to acknowledge all members of ENG 255 for contributing to the experience we describe here. We extend special thanks to Gina Kirkland and Donna Lake, students from ENG 255 who brainstormed with us and steered our writing in productive directions.

References

Clifford, John. 1991. "Introduction: Reading Rosenblatt." In *The Experience of Reading: Louise Rosenblatt and Reader-Response Theory*, edited by John Clifford. Portsmouth, NH: Boynton/Cook.

Fulwiler, Toby. 1989. "Responding to Student Journals." In *Writing and Response: Theory, Practice, and Research*, edited by Chris Anson. Urbana, IL: NCTE.

Holladay, Sylvia. 1988. "Integrating Reading and Writing." *Teaching English in the Two-Year College* 15: 187–194.

Rosenblatt, Louise. 1938. *Literature as Exploration*. New York: Appleton-Century.

———. 1978. *The Reader, the Text, the Poem*. Carbondale, IL: Southern Illinois University Press.

Staton, Jana. 1988. "An Introduction to Dialogue Journal Communication." In *Dialogue Journal Communication: Classroom, Linguistic, Social and Cognitive Views*, edited by Jana Staton, Roger W. Shuy, Joy Kreeft Peyton, and Leslee Reed. Norwood, NJ: Ablex.

Tompkins, Jane. 1990. "Pedagogy of the Distressed." *College English* 52: 653–660.

Zemelman, Steve, and Harvey Daniels. 1988. *A Community of Writers*. Portsmouth, NH: Heinemann.

13 Connecting Letter Writing and "Real Life" in the College Writing Class

Erika Scheurer
University of St. Thomas, St. Paul, Minnesota

Teaching college writing at all levels, from basic to advanced, I am always searching for modes and contexts for writing that fit the following criteria: (1) it is done frequently; (2) it is informal; (3) it leads to discovery; (4) it is meaningful to students, connecting to their reading and to their lives; and (5) it does not have to be evaluated by me. Until recently, the modes of writing that best fulfilled these criteria for me were journals and daily in-class freewriting.

Useful as these forms of writing are, they do have their drawbacks. Students (particularly beginning or unskilled writers) often do not see the point of personal generative writing—no matter how much we explain the theory behind it—and can have difficulty connecting it to in-class discussions of readings and to more formal essay writing. Through my conversations with these students over the years, I have learned that, to them, private writing (or generative writing read only by me) does not seem "real." The lack of motivation caused by this perception often results in students falling behind in their journals and putting minimal energy into the freewriting. A journal hastily written on the night before it is due certainly fits none of *my* criteria for "reality" either!

To ease my students' introduction to writing-to-learn, I needed a form of writing that combined the open, generative qualities of freewriting and journaling with the light, motivating pressure of an enabling audience.[1] The practice of letter writing fulfills these criteria and has become one of my most universally successful classroom practices.[2]

This past semester, in addition to the usual sorts of letters I have always had students write in my classes—cover letters on their essays and feedback letters to members of their writing groups—I had them write what I call "discussion letters." These letters, addressed "Dear Class" and signed, were written in response to assigned readings we would discuss in class the day the letters were due. I asked students to use the letters to make connections between the reading and their experience, to explore their thinking on an issue invoked by the reading, and to raise questions (much as they would in journal entries). They brought copies of their letters to class—one for me and three or four copies for discussion group members. About half of class time was spent reading their letters aloud in small groups, then having discussions based on their responses. Meanwhile, I quickly read through their letters to get a sense of where they were. A whole-class discussion then followed, based on what came from the small groups.

What I hoped was that students would use the letters as an informal means of using writing to think out their responses to the readings. The audience—a small group of classmates and I—would enable (not inhibit) students' thinking, particularly since I would not evaluate the letters but would only check that they had been written. Also, I hoped that this informal but audience-oriented writing would dramatize for students that, as Bakhtin has taught me, thinking always happens in dialogue with others (other writers, other readers, other voices within oneself). Finally, by asking my students to sign their letters and to read them aloud, I hoped to impress upon them the importance of writing words behind which, at least *for the moment*, they were willing to stand.

Letter writing fulfilled my teaching goals admirably. My students produced a good deal of writing (the first-year writing class produced about fifteen letters each, with the length limited to one page, single-spaced) and the writing by and large was informal, exploratory, and question-posing. My students, as you will soon see from their comments, found the process meaningful to their work as writers and readers. And—a quality not to be underestimated for its importance to writing teachers everywhere—I did not have to grade or evaluate the letters. Just requiring them to be written and read aloud in class was incentive enough. The process reinforced for my students the inherent connections between reading and writing, speaking and listening; they wrote in response to readings, then read their letters aloud, listening and responding to the letters of others. Finally, the genre of the letter helped to reinforce students' sense of the class as a community of readers and writers.

What follows is what I learned from the letters that students wrote and from a survey I distributed at the end of the semester focusing on their attitudes about and experiences with the letter writing. Two of the classes surveyed were 300-level advanced writing courses which focused on both theory and practice. The readings in this course were theoretical and challenging to them (from such journals as *College Composition and Communication* and *College English*). The third course was a first-year English class—Critical Reading and Writing—for which the readings were fiction and nonfiction prose. As for the advanced students, the texts these students read were difficult (e.g., Mary Louise Pratt's "Arts of the Contact Zone" and Toni Morrison's *Beloved*). Whereas my advanced students, by the end of the semester, certainly had more of a vocabulary for responding to the practice of letter writing than my first-year students (and their comments were more lengthy and developed), I was surprised to learn how strongly *all* my students felt about letter writing, even the most inexperienced and writing-phobic.

According to my students, one of the primary benefits of our approach to letter writing was the ease and comfort they felt in expressing their thoughts about the readings. Compared to writing a more traditional "discussion paper" of equal length, the practice of writing a letter helped students—especially those (in both courses) who were timid about writing—to feel comfortable with the writing process and with one another. In the excerpts below, I use "(f)" to indicate comments by my first-year writing students and "(a)" to indicate those of my advanced writing students.

> Letter Writing showed me that not all writing I do for class has to be a scary treacherous event. . . . (f)

> Writing letters to my classmates made me feel more comfortable with my classmates. Writing letters seemed more like a casual communication between two people, rather than an assignment that is written for a professor to be graded. (f)

> It is easy to talk to people through a letter. (f)

> The discussion letter was nice . . . and psychologically, it didn't freak me out as writing short essays, papers, sometimes do. (f)

> It made me focus on my audience, which was other students, rather than just on the professor. I found it easier to write. . . . I was less concerned about grammar and more focused on ideas, like if I was writing a letter to a friend rather than a "paper" for a teacher for a grade. (a)

> I felt more comfortable writing a letter than a paper. I know essentially they are the same thing, however the term "letter" does not conjure up as much fear in my mind as the word "paper." It also made it more personable and I felt as if we bonded as a class easier because of the "letter" writing. (a)

For some, this comfort transferred to their writing of more formal essays in the class. A few first-year students even began to merge the genres, addressing their essays "Dear Class" and signing them. One beginning writer commented directly about how letter writing made her more comfortable with essay-writing:

> Writing letters helped me be more open to my own feelings, opinions and helped me become more relaxed at writing essays. I got over the fear of writing essays because of the practice I had with the letters. (f)

As the student comments I have already quoted suggest, a pleasant side effect of the letter writing was a heightened sense of community in my classes. While I kept their writing groups constant, students' discussion groups varied (usually, I just had them count off), which gave them exposure to the writing of more people in class. One student described this community-building effect of the letters as follows:

> The addressing made me aware of my audience. "Dear readers" or "Dear class" made me relax; like I was reminded that we were all in the same "boat" and were trying to accomplish the same goals. (a)

The effect of this high comfort level with letter writing increased the motivation of a number of my students. They felt it was less a chore assigned by a teacher and more a means of self-expression and communication. One student explained this effect especially well:

> It has been a great benefit sharing them [the letters], and discussing them, without time pressure or grades, in a variety of group settings, led to the construction of a thriving network of trust that made future letters and discussions more honest, mature, and "real." The common idea of a letter is that you write it because you want to. Schoolwork is done because you have to. These assignments revise "have to" and "want to" in such a way as to make us anxious to write them. (a)

Along with the comfort and openness students felt in writing letters, they also felt some degree of responsibility for what they wrote. Some indicated that they did not want to "look stupid" in front of their peers and others emphasized the importance of being honest in both content and voice.

> I knew that if I read them aloud, then I owned those words. So if I wrote something that I didn't believe in then I was deceiving myself. (f)
>
> I felt more responsibility in writing those letters. (f)
>
> I made sure I understood the readings and I was honest in my letters. I think most students do put more effort into assignments that are read aloud—more so than just handing off a paper to the teacher b/c they don't have to *face* the response. I found it really helpful. (a)
>
> They were more personal, and signing my name made me want to be sure I was saying what I wanted to. (a)
>
> [Addressing and signing the letters] made it more my own. I felt like I was made more accountable for my opinions. (a)
>
> It was no longer "teacher writing." (a)

As every writer learns, being honest in your writing and looking foolish can coincide. We take this risk whenever we put pen to page, whenever we take a stand. In my first-year writing class, where we read and wrote about issues such as racism and homophobia, students learned this fact of the writing life early on. As one first-year student writes, one result of writing letters and reading them aloud was that "I became more cautious about how I addressed my views." This student, however, wrote some of the most controversial discussion letters in class; he was aware that his views would provoke response, but he felt comfortable enough to express them nonetheless.

Risk does not come only through addressing controversial topics, however. For some students, simply offering their thoughts and writing "I" (which is just about impossible not to do in a letter) involves risk. One student notes that taking responsibility in this way requires adjustment:

> The difference seemed to have been that my writing became more personal rather than just writing for writing's sake. Because I had never written this way in class before, I believe it took me a while to make the adjustments. (a)

Letter writing also brought other aspects of writing to life for my students, including the value of focus, the importance of response (as opposed to summary), and the consideration of audience. One effect I did not anticipate—limited almost exclusively to the more inexperienced first-year students—was a heightened sense of the importance of proofreading. Because I stress focusing on *ideas*, not style, in these letters (as

I do with journals and freewriting), I was dismayed to read about this "benefit" in some of the surveys. This response reminds me, though, that while letter writing serves as an excellent medium for generative writing, it is also still a *public* form of writing, even when this public is a friendly audience. Given this reality, I have moved beyond my initial disappointment to accept this benefit of letter writing; for students to learn the importance of proofreading on their own through writing for a friendly audience is far more meaningful than a teacher circling their errors. I am also reminded, however, that letter writing can supplement, but not substitute for, more private forms of writing such as freewriting and journaling.

In the end, I believe it is the "reality" of letter writing that makes it so successful with students—its simultaneous connection of their thought processes with those of others. As one first-year student expressed it,

> Sometimes when I read them aloud, something new would strike me. The way I said, or hearing someone else's input and ideas would cause me to develop new ones. . . . I did learn a lot about the issues we covered and it made me come face to face with them. It gave me a chance to form an opinion and be a crucial part of class discussions.

Grappling with ideas and experiences on the page leads to face-to-face conversation, which eventually leads to more formal writing and more conversation. Whereas writing cover letters and feedback letters for essays sends the message that *writing* is a form of ongoing conversation, the discussion letters teach my students a related, equally important lesson: that *thinking* is a form of ongoing conversation. For such conversations to work, the participants must feel comfortable enough to explore and question freely, yet invested enough to accept responsibility for their words.

For most of my students, both beginning and advanced, this approach to writing and thinking was new. As one advanced student noted, "I had to invent my own form of discourse with which to discuss the reading, whereas paper assignments are more often than not 'fill in the blanks and proofread' type projects." A first-year student registered an even more dramatic change in attitude because of letter writing: "I had the old opinion that writing is something that you are suppose to do, because it is an assignment. I now believe that writing can be very beneficial in everyday life."

The connections that letter writing effects between reading, writing, speaking, and listening, then, link to a more crucial, fundamental discovery for students: that the exchange of ideas, the life of the mind, is intimately connected to "real life."

Notes

1. I use the term "enabling audience" in the sense that Peter Elbow uses it: "When we think about them as we write, we think of more and better things to say" (1987, 51).

2. I am indebted to Toby Fulwiler, whose presentation at the 1995 CCCC Winter Workshop in Clearwater Beach, Florida, motivated me to try letter writing. His use differs considerably from mine, however.

Reference

Elbow, Peter. 1987. "Closing My Eyes as I Speak: An Argument for Ignoring Audience." *College English* 49: 50–69.

14 Living What You Read and Write

Darrell g.h. Schramm
University of San Francisco, California

Over the years I've been refining my methods for involving my first-year composition students with what they read and write, both intellectually and emotionally (that is, earnestly). While the reading and writing I assign may seem demanding, my students are clearly engaged; indeed, class discussions often go on so long that I am forced to curtail them in order to make time to write or to work in peer critique groups.

In brief, to encourage *engaged* learning, I assign weekly readings to which students must write a one-page typed response, handed in at the beginning of the period. Not only does this assure me that they have read the assigned material, but also that they now have something to say, something they've already written out and can offer in class discussion.

How do they know what to write about? What kinds of responses do they make, first on paper, and then orally in class? At the beginning of each semester, I present my students with two lists of questions grouped under two types of responses: on one hand, immediate and informational responses which may discuss function or structure but are not widely discursive, and, on the other hand, reflectively discursive responses which see far-reaching connections and reveal cultural, universal, and/or mythic meanings or reveal insights into the human condition. Though I am not happy with the titles of my two categories of questions and would welcome suggestions for change, I call them respectively "The Immediate and Speculative" and "The Reflectively Discursive."

The Immediate and Speculative

1. Discuss your emotional reaction to the reading. Why did you respond as you did?
2. What questions do you have about this reading? Speculate about these questions; try guessing at possible answers.

3. What experience or observation does this reading make you think of? Why?
4. Who seems to be the audience for this text? Are you a part of that audience? Why or why not?
5. Why do you think the author wrote this piece? How do you think the author's goals influenced the form and content?
6. What assumptions does the author make about the reader's knowledge or reception of this work? How do you feel about that?
7. Analyze the structure, organization, focus, written expression, tone, etc. What parts stand out for you?
8. How would you evaluate this piece of writing? Why?

The Reflectively Discursive

1. What did you learn from this reading about ideas? About others? About yourself?
2. How can you apply this text to your own life? To that of others? What is or would be the consequences or logical extension of this application?
3. Discuss your values or beliefs as applied to the author's subject or ideas. How might your values and beliefs have affected your reaction to this reading?
4. Compare the content of this text to another piece of writing (literature, history, philosophy, science, etc.) or to a work of visual or performance art (painting, film, music, etc.). In what ways is this assigned reading meaningfully different?
5. Choose a sentence or longer passage and write a far-reaching reflection on it.

Sometimes I assign a specific question or two for students' written response; sometimes I ask them to choose whatever question or questions appeal to them after they have read the text.

I have used this approach for all reading assignments—not just for essays, articles, and stories, but also for chapters from grammar and writing textbooks. Here is a paragraph from a longer response by Denise to two textbook chapters on research:

> I really do understand how it feels to write for a grade, though. I used to do it all the time. I'd write and not understand what I had written but I'd get an "A" because it was what the teacher wanted to read. I got tired of that. It's easier and much more enjoyable to write now because I can write about what I want without thinking about being tempted to plagiarize. That's grammar school stuff.

Denise is definitely engaged in her reading. She is making connections. Similarly, though his understanding may be somewhat simplistic, Matt, too, connects himself to his reading, even when it is a textbook chapter on writing an argument.

> What I picked up from Chapter 15 was mainly to write from my own personal experiences. Make sure the topic you pick can be agreed and disagreed on is the other main thing I learned. . . . Basically an argument is just a personal essay. Just about anything can be argued about but a topic I really believe in will be easier to argue than one I kind of believe in. . . . I think I'm going to like [writing] this essay because all it is is stating something I believe and telling why and telling the readers why they should too.

Janna, responding to the same chapter as Matt, connects the reading with her own experiences.

> Rawlins said that most people freak out when they hear the word argument as a way of writing a paper. That does not apply to me. I am not saying that I always find ways to argue with people, but if I disagree with someone or I feel strongly about an issue then I sure will let people know how I feel! Arguing is risky, though, because sometimes I say things before I think and end up not really saying what I mean; or when I am arguing with someone who always feels he or she has to be right then it is no fun either. As long as the people involved in the argument can argue fair without replying, "oh—that's stupid," then arguing can be a healthy way to release your feelings.

Another student, Irene, looking at the form, tone, and content of the chapter's sample essays, argues against the textbook's author, taking exception to his injunction to write an essay like those in the textbook. She goes on to give three reasons for her protest: she does not wish to write like anyone else but strives to be original; she does not wish to write arguments that seem too short and understated; and she wishes to write something less bland than those in the text, something more "passionate." Irene has felt free to contradict an assumption by a professional.

Maria finds it liberating not to be confined to a formula. "Why," she asks, "did I have to learn how to be so rigid and structured while writing my papers in high school, while here I am encouraged to be creative and not so 'anally retentive' by throwing out the five-paragraph essay format and outlines?" Maria has been able to engage herself in the reading by comparing it to a previous experience.

And so we discuss these issues of writing in class. Even the students who do not raise a hand in participation have something to say when called upon because they have thought and written about their reading.

However, my students do not engage themselves only with the technical textbook. Quite often the professional essays and stories they are asked to read and respond to by using these same questions engender the deepest thinking, the most exciting class discussions. I quote two such written responses in their entirety, the first by Denise in response to Stephen Jay Gould's essay, "The Great Dinosaur Rip-off" (1991).

> I always hated History classes in grade school. I hated everything about it. I hated having to memorize dates and people. I hated having to carry around that thick book.
>
> It was always a different textbook every year. It went by a different title and was written by a different author. But I almost convinced myself in seventh grade that I had been reading and carrying the same book for four years. The text always said the same thing. I always found myself memorizing facts about people who died before I was born. And I wrote reports about people I really didn't care about. I never found reasons to care about them, anyway. That's why I hated History. But as I moved into high school, I learned something new. During grade school, I never really did well in my History classes. I wanted to do better and do things differently in high school. I always thought that I wasn't trying hard enough. Things really started changing when I found out why. I hated history because it wasn't alive for me. I needed more than just words or people or dates. To really understand, I learned that I had to feel. I had to imagine and place myself in the past. Words mean nothing until you understand them. History is nothing until you try to become it. I worry about the kids of the future and almost feel sorry for them. Ten years down the road, their history books are bound to weigh tons. "Everything comes to us in fifteen-second sound bites" and "the most precious trait of adequate analysis—is erased." Things move so quickly. It's a shame that we blink. We miss so much.

It's a truism well worth stating that engaged writing is an act of discovery. We are carefully prepared yet almost unprepared for the revelation in Denise's statement "To really understand, I learned that I had to feel." It almost takes the breath away. But then she goes on to state something quite obvious, yet, because of the detailed background she has given us, we now sense strata of meaning beneath her declaration: "Words mean nothing until you understand them." Not so simple after all. She could base an essay on that statement. But she gives us more; making connections and using a parallel structure, she asserts, "History is nothing until you try to become it." Yes, yes. Grist for discussion, food for an essay. A possible thesis. And the way form fits content in the last three sentences of her response also deserves sharing and comment in class.

Jane, more than any other student in several semesters, was able to and chose to link her assigned reading with other pieces of writing, and invariably she wrote long, thoughtful responses that flowed beyond the one-page requirement. Here is her response to "The Death of the Moth" by Virginia Woolf (Woolf's essay can be found in Smart 1995):

> Like Orwell and [E. B.] White, Woolf uses animals to explain comparisons in human life and death experiences. The moth, although confined to mere existence, "what he could do, he did . . . enormous energy of the world had been thrust into his frail and diminutive body," seemed to be telling us to make the best out of what we have.
>
> Woolf also humanizes the moth to give the reader more of an emotional connection to its struggle with death and dying. "O yes, he seemed to say, death is stronger than I." Woolf's essay tells us that no matter what valiant effort is given, "nothing . . . has any chance against death." The moth symbolizes the "true nature of life."
>
> This essay also caused me to wonder if the moth was not just a reflection of ourselves. Through some unexplained higher power, either religious or scientific, are we also being observed by a higher deity from a distance? Are observations being made of us like those of the moth? Are we thought of only with feelings of pity because of our "hard fate" "flying vigorously to one corner, waiting, and then flying to another"? Are we only described as "tiny beads of life" "dancing and zigzagging" "against an oncoming doom"? Are we "little or nothing but life"?
>
> A line in Woolf's last paragraph especially touched and saddened me: ". . . when there was nobody to care or to know this gigantic effort on the part of an insignificant little moth, against a power of such magnitude, to retain what no one else valued or desired to keep. . . ." It reminded me of a passage in *Great Expectations* by Charles Dickens. The character, Pip, on a cold winter night looks out over the frozen marshes and wonders what it would be like for a man who has struggled all his life and still finds himself hungry, homeless and poor to "turn his face up to the stars and under the glittering multitude freeze to death and no one would ever know." In this instance, Dickens' character is much like Woolf's moth, little or nothing but life. For us all, death seems to be the common denominator.

Clearly, Jane has been reflectively discursive. Not only has she made associations with other readings in content and style, but she has engaged in ideas both intellectually and emotionally, applying the text to her own values and beliefs, asking questions, comparing ideas, analyzing the tone of the essay, as engaged with the writing as she has been with Woolf's text.

Since I have created this double list of questions, my classrooms have been invigorating and delicious in discussion, in feedback, in small group work. Students are engaged. Through these questions for response, they have fashioned the links between the reading life and the writing life, between the written word and the lives they lead. Reading and writing have become for them a way of making meaning, as Ann Berthoff says (1981), a way of growing, a way of clarifying who they are. And we, students and instructor, are all the richer for it.

References

Berthoff, Ann. 1981. *The Making of Meaning: Metaphors, Models, and Maxims for Writing Teachers.* Portsmouth, NH: Boynton/Cook.

Gould, Stephen Jay. 1991. "The Great Dinosaur Rip-off." *Bully for Brontosaurus.* New York: Norton.

Woof, Virginia. 1995. "The Death of the Moth." In *Eight Modern Essayists,* edited by William Smart. New York: St. Martin's.

15 Searching for Words to Cross Cultures

Susan Tchudi, Stephen Adkison, Jacob Blumner,
Francis Fritz, and Maria Madruga
University of Nevada at Reno

The teenaged girl leaned against the rough stone wall of the tunnel. A mass of visitors, each carrying a white carnation, pressed past her into the darkness. By the light of a single bulb, she wrote carefully in her journal. Another student listened intently to an old soldier as he told of his time in this labor camp, of his lost youth and lost brother. The student made brief notes in his journal to follow up that afternoon. The site of this activity was the former labor and POW camp in Mittelbau-Dora, Germany, on the fiftieth anniversary of its liberation in April 1945. We were conducting an international writing workshop, and our hosts had arranged for us to visit Dora on this historic occasion. When our bus left the POW camp, fifty-plus students were subdued, thinking, and a good many of them were writing in their journals.

Sometimes writing teachers get caught up in how to motivate students to write. We have become increasingly convinced, however, that good writing, meaningful writing, springs from the writer's own desires and interests. People who use writing as a way of deepening their understanding and powers of observation become committed to writing as a way of life, a way of being. Our experiences in the writing workshop in Mühlhausen, Germany, reinforced our commitment to use writing that springs from inner motivation, a desire to know, to understand, to express.

The Mühlhausen Writing Workshop, sponsored by the Huron Shores (Michigan) Writing Institute, involved sixty students aged twelve to sixty-plus from seven countries—Germany, the United States, Lithuania, the Czech Republic, Russia, Italy, and Finland. For two weeks we met at the Mühlhausen Volkshochschule, the "people's" high school, a venerable old school hall now given over to community education in Mühlhausen. Working in groups small and large, we talked, drafted, edited, and revised our ideas on topics ranging from our own childhood experiences to the future of the world. The students varied in their control of languages; most were bilingual, either English/German, or English or German and one of the other languages—Lithuanian, Czech, Finnish, Italian, Russian. Several students were tri- or even quadralingual. What was common to all of us was our determination to share our experiences and perceptions with one another. Everything we did—both work and play—was set within the frame of the writing workshop. We composition instructors met with small groups of students who wrote about the experiences they were having, the acquaintances they were making, their own histories which helped others get to know them, their thinking on problems in the world, and their visions of the future. The multicultural and cross-generational makeup of the workshop provided us with many new ways of seeing, with new knowledge about the world, and with a desire to communicate our various views and visions.

As we've noted, one of the most powerful experiences for the workshop students was our visit to Mittelbau-Dora, a World War II labor and POW camp near Nordhausen, Germany. Of the 60,000 victims who ended up at Mittelbau-Dora, 20,000 died. Our trip was planned to coincide with the observances of the fiftieth anniversary of the camp's liberation; the students had the opportunity to join many of the camp's survivors and the veterans who had liberated it as they remembered their own experiences at Mittelbau-Dora. Workshop members entered deep into the tunnel that had been dug into the mountainside to house manufacturing facilities for V-2 rockets. Deep within the mountain we saw where the prisoners had worked and slept and died. We carried white carnations into the darkness to lay at the memorial inside the tunnel. We saw survivors with their names and numbers on badges lighting candles and laying wreaths and flowers in memoriam. In other parts of the camp, we saw where prisoners of war had been kept, where the SS guards had lived, and, finally, the crematorium which toward the end had burned twenty-four hours a day to dispose of the bodies of dead prisoners. Later that afternoon, everyone gathered to hear the survivors, both former prisoners and liberators, speak. In small knots throughout the large tent set up at the site, young people listened intently as these survivors remembered and told their stories, stories of atrocities, of inhumanity, of evil, and, sometimes, of love.

Workshop participants—representing different ages, cultures, backgrounds—reacted. Some projected themselves into the experience. Ruta, a Lithuanian woman, wrote a poem—"It Seems to Me That I Was There in Dora"—in which she explored the tension between wanting to forget and wanting to remember the destruction: "I won't hurt, won't torture/Myself for a long time./ I had to come back./ However I cannot in another way. It hurts./ A lot./ Perhaps it will pass./ I'll stay for some more." Kati, a fourteen-year-old American girl, used the metaphor of footprints to show how memories endure:

> Memories are like footsteps.
> Almost forgotten, covered over: never gone.
>
> Millions of footprints: of ones lost, and ones that
> Are alive, but cannot live.
> Soldiers march, hold their guns; make more prints.

A young man from Germany, Frank, wrote a short story about a German who, having created a radio to listen to BBC broadcasts, is arrested and interned at Dora. He relates his protagonist's experience in the mountain:

> Darkness. Dust. Noise. Shouting people.
> I'm inside a tunnel. Blowing stones out of the mountain. I haven't seen the light of day for six months now. The darkness is destroying my eyes. Working 12 hours a day, I'm only able to fall asleep after I'm done with my work. No hunger, maybe because of the hard work I have to do, maybe because of the desperation that seems to be the only thing of substance you can lean on here.

Other students observed and made judgments. Axel, a young man from Finland, sensed evil at Dora. "Down in the mine, you catch a glimpse of the evil that once reigned there. The darkness and the looming granite walls are infected by it. . . . A bad air hangs over the mountain, one that won't blow away. As I left, I thought 'Do the trees and the flowers growing on the hill know their ground, are they also infected?'"

Martina, a German teenager, saw a survivor's number and wondered:

> a man
> a Jew
> already very old
> is wearing it on his jacket.
>
> pride?
> heroism?
> having survived?
> shame?

Another German teenager, Susanne, reflected on shared cultural responsibility for Dora:

> Guilt and doubt come to my mind.
> Sadness and rage at the same time.

> German people persecuted minorities
> for different beliefs.
> German people forced innocent persons
> into concentration camps.
> German people made their prisoners work
> extremely hard under cruel conditions.
> German people eliminated religious minorities.
> I am a German girl,
> I feel, think, and speak
> like a German human being.
> And therefore I'm to blame for all that happened.

A few days after Dora, we loaded up the buses for Berlin, a place that also elicited powerful memories, intense cultural exchanges, reflection, and recognition. We had the opportunity to see through one another's eyes, to hear stories of others' feelings about the once-divided city of Berlin and the wall. Claudia, a former Berliner, wondered where the Berlin of her youth was. "I turn away and go searching for something I hardly find here. Every step beats my questions in the stones of the sidewalk: Mother Berlin, are you here? Do you still recognize me? Will you take me again in your great arms? . . . I want to kneel down, press my ear on the asphalt and listen to the vibrations of the city." Alessandra, an Italian student, imagined the creation of the wall. "I think the image that struck me most was the black cross with the names of the wall victims. During the time of a night, men destroyed families, relationships, and divided a city in two different parts, creating distance and even hate. We imagine all this, but people really lived it." But like many students Alessandra celebrated the present: "The breaking of the wall is a symbol of how things can change." This idea of the wall coming down was a recurrent theme in many students' writings. Christopher, the youngest participant at age twelve, wrote a narrative in which he explored the destruction of the wall:

> As he walked down the dim lamp-lit street, his boots echoed, seeming to shatter the silence. He stopped at the fluorescent spray-painted cement wall, he felt the grainy surface with one hand, feeling the problems it had created, its evil.
>
> He took his hand away and placed it on his hammer, raised it high over his head, and with both hands, swung down. "Clink." He continued, "Clink, Clink, Clink."
>
> Two minutes later a man wearing a bathrobe and slippers came. He had a hammer and screwdriver and began to hammer in the screwdriver and chip out pieces.
>
> A minute later two boys no older than twelve began to chip away at the wall with rocks.

> After that they came by the tens. Men, women, children.
> Jeans and T-shirts, pajamas, sweats.
> Stones, pickaxes, sledgehammers.

In reflecting on their experiences, students moved from the particulars of Dora and Berlin to more generalized insights about cultural differences, looking for ways to connect. Katja, a German teenager, expressed a feeling many of us shared:

> hopeful days
> was there no hope any more
> the end of humanity sealed.
> no hope?
> will the sky darken?
> yet one hope exists
> and the sky lights up
> the hope to meet the other ones
> to overcross the sea of prejudice
> a new country to be seen
> new aspects to be heard
> new aspects to be spoken
> mean hope.

Although Berlin and Dora were dramatic, our daily workshops at the Volkshochschule and at the youth hostel where we lived were no less intense. Participants created cross-cultural dialogues; participated in photography workshops; visited a potassium mine; taught one another childhood games; created three-dimensional utopian and dystopian models of the future; visited local businesses and artisan shops; and attended a German version of *A Midsummer Night's Dream*. All of these became subjects for reflection and writing.

In our final workshop meeting, everyone—workshop leaders and participants—read his or her chosen piece for publication in *Breakwall* (Tolly 1996). In addition to some of these we have included here, students read about their homes and families, utopian and dystopian futures, love, and politics. But the cultural reflecting and connecting was a consistent theme. An American teenager, Christie, put many of the hopes Katja expressed into concrete terms in a reflective piece entitled "Ich suche nach einem wort: I search for a word":

> *Ich bin Auslander*. I am a foreigner for the first time in my life. *Ich bin Auslander*. I search for a word to describe everything I am experiencing. I search for a word to explain how similar life is in America, but it is extremely different. I search. *Guten Morgen, vie gehts?* Good Morning, how are you? Germany and America—miles and miles apart. We speak different languages and we still come to understand. I search for a word to explain the unique

qualities in each country and in the wonderful people. To accept others as they are, to open one's mind and to fill it with knowledge. *Ich suche nach einem wort.* I search for a word. *Ich spreche nicht so gut Deutsch.* I don't speak German very well, but I can help people with their English. Many different cultures gather together for a writing workshop in Mühlhausen, Germany, conducted in English—Germans, Americans, Russians, Lithuanians, Italians, a Finn, and a Czech. I have searched for many words to describe many different things. I will continue to search. I will continue to learn. I will continue to have a love for diversity and experience. I search for a word. *Bitte, sprich langsamer.* Please speak a little slower. The power of understanding. *Die kraft haben.* To have the power. I search.

Of course, it would be a lie to say that all of our exchanges were flawless and filled with human understanding. There were times when we couldn't make our precise meanings clear. Some participants spoke so little German or English that they often remained on the fringes or had to have everything translated. Occasionally, we had differences of opinion. For example, we spent the evening of our visit to Dora teaching one another games from our childhoods. One participant felt that such a playful activity following the Dora visit reflected typical American insensitivity and superficiality. Some of the older workshop leaders and participants felt the younger ones stayed up too late and made too much noise. In addition, language barriers were not insignificant. Especially in translating pieces from one language to another, bilingual participants felt frustrated in trying to find the right words. And we Americans were again embarrassed by our lack of facility with other languages. But, as Katja and Christie have said, we overcame very different histories and made contact with one another, and the writing that the students did in the workshop reflected this.

Based on our experience, we are strongly convinced that students would greatly benefit from more educational opportunities emphasizing cross-cultural and cross-generational experiences. Of course, a visit to a labor/POW camp in former East Germany is not an experience that we can realistically offer to most of our students. However, educators can search out many powerful experiences in their own back yards. In our collective experience, we have taken students to tutor children on an American Indian reservation; taught courses with eight different native languages represented; and taken students to plays, concerts, and museums, as well as to speak with community elders. One of our summer institutes emphasizes interdisciplinary approaches to understanding the many points of view represented in regional issues. Our composition and literature courses have actively sought to bring in the voices of many cultural groups. Virtually every small town and all large cities have historical and cultural societies representing the cultural roots of their populations; museums, musical events, and theater provide more opportunities. The possibilities are literally limitless. Having seen the power of important experience in creating motivation to write, we plan to continue searching for ways to offer more cross-cultural and cross-generational opportunities to our students.

Note

We would like to acknowledge the contributions of other workshop leaders, Stephen Tchudi and John Eliason; the Huron Shores Writing Director, Marilou Ikens; and the staff of the Mühlhausen Initiative.

Reference

Tolly, Anne, ed. 1996. *Breakwall* (Volume VII). Rogers City, MI: Huron Shores Summer Writing Institute.

16 Media "Target Assignments" Invite Students to Tune In, Turn On, and Write

Meta G. Carstarphen
University of North Texas, Denton

Much to the chagrin of every classroom teacher, students today seem more intrigued by popular entertainment than by academic assignments. Statistics about the pervasive influences of the media on contemporary youth and adults are not reassuring. As Art Silverblatt reports in his book, *Media Literacy: Keys to Interpreting Media Messages* (1995), "in the average American household, the television set is on for over seven hours per day. . . . And remember, television represents only one media system."

Concern about media influences on our society is not likely to abate, as new technologies force rapid convergence of established communication tools with innovative ones. Industry insiders speak confidently of the not-too-distant future when the majority of American households will boast access to hundreds of new television channels, scores of newspapers via computer, and magazines on demand thanks to our long-distance communication services.

Conceptually, media literacy encompasses strategies to "decode" messages in a meaningful way. A basic definition of such competency, offered by the 1992 National Leadership Conference on Media Literacy, sets forth these parameters: "It [media literacy] is the ability of a citizen to access, analyze, and produce information for specific outcomes" (cited in Vivian 1991, 300). Though intentionally broad, this statement invites a proactive approach from educators who want to challenge their students to attain mastery over media messages instead of accepting the defeat of their minds by the trivia of mass entertainment. However, it is just as important to recognize that thoughtful interaction with the media can offer pathways to strengthen students' basic capabilities in reading, writing, and reflective observation.

This certainly has been my experience in teaching media survey courses. Typically, such a course is a beginning college student's introduction to the history and operations of each major component of mass communication: newspapers, magazines, radio, film, television, motion pictures, sound recordings, and books. Heavily imbued with historical facts, dates, and profiles, the texts for these courses naturally emphasize (in terms of teaching) presentational styles which are long on lecture and (in terms of learning) individual performance on standardized tests. Add this aspect to the fact that such courses are institutionally arranged to encompass large enrollments, and the opportunities for innovative student participation are usually very limited indeed.

Underlying all of these logistical aspects is a question that, to me, points up a very important philosophical dilemma: how can such a course prepare potential communication professionals for their chosen fields if their thoughts are restricted to marks on a machine-scored test page? How can we groom professional writers and critical thinkers if we don't nurture as much respect for the content of their thoughts as we do for the accuracy of their form?

My solution has been to institute a semester-long research project called Target Assignments. At the beginning of the term, students receive a list of at least fifteen topics related to various aspects of the media. I invite students to reflect upon their reaction to a particular topic. Students get to select ten topics from the list as a minimum but are invited to do more for extra credit if they so choose. Their goal is to have their Target Assignments completed by the announced date, typed according to specifications, and submitted as a total report. Collectively, the Target Assignments are worth one hundred points, or the weight of a unit exam.

What kinds of topics are included? Varied, in both complexity and perspective. Some invite the students to monitor familiar media in an unfamiliar way, such as recording their experiences in listening to five AM and five FM radio stations they have never paid attention to before. Another type of assignment asks them to gauge media effectiveness by analyzing a newspaper article's use of graphics, photos, and charts in order to determine how much these added to their understanding of the story.

Still other kinds of assignments invite students to be social media critics by evaluating the interrelatedness between media and society as they see it. These slightly more rigorous topics challenge students to cite examples of television shows which they feel perpetuate a kind of stereotyping, or evaluate strategies that talk show hosts may be using to influence their audiences, whether through logical or emotional appeals.

None of the media experiences that the students are asked to write about are inherently new. Our students are professional media consumers. But what is new for them is the occasion to isolate that singular media moment as if it were significant (which, of course, it is) and render an opinion. Their responses show that they can relish such self-reflective moments.

One student, Allison, is pretty insightful about an episode on the Geraldo Rivera show where radio talk-show host Howard Stern was, for a change, the visitor: "As a guest . . . Howard taunts Geraldo. Stern made jokes of the Geraldo 'broken nose' incident and sex life on the host's show. Breaking every rule of courtesy, Stern is changing the behavior on TV. . . . Why people worship Stern is not the issue. The issue is that Stern is changing the unspoken respect that governed media behavior."

David, in another assignment, looks at newspapers' use of graphics and makes some judgments which go beyond what the textbook had to say about the differences among media:

> In the world of slick magazines and slick television, the daily news media is at a disadvantage. Newsprint lacks the immediacy of television and the sexiness of magazines. However, by effective use of visuals, newspapers are making up some of that ground. The tangibility of a map or a chart in front of you is not something that television can duplicate, and the timeliness of the photos is something that monthly magazines can't do as quickly. By adapting to the graphics needs of a society raised on TV, [the] newspaper is far from being left in the dust.

I am refreshingly surprised by the amount of passion students bring to this assignment as well as the unique insights. One student, Robert, reviewed a documentary called *Ethnic Notions* about the history of African Americans in film and television, making some insightful comments in light of that tradition about current television fare starring African Americans. A female student, responding to the question about identifying stereotypes on television, picked the popular show about teenagers, *Beverly Hills, 90210*. From her perspective, she quite eloquently showed how this program "unfairly" portrayed high school students as privileged, overly concerned about sex, and good-looking.

I grade these assignments to reinforce the basic goals of writing fluency and critical thinking. Therefore, students receive full points for successfully writing coherent narratives to the minimum required length of one-and-one-half pages for each assignment. No opinion is wrong as long as the student cites examples and shows some reflective thought about the topic. At the same time, in classes where enrollment is seventy-five students or more, grades on content and format take precedence over penalties for errors in mechanics and style.

More often than not, however, students willingly exceed my expectations and their own. If I simply announced to the class that each student would be responsible for a fifteen-page research assignment, many would faint in disbelief. Yet they end up writing at least this much, often more, in their cumulative reports. I also ask them to bind their reports attractively, yet I give no specific parameters. Many use their own savvy to create eye-catching covers, attractive margins, graphics, and other elements to influence the appearance of their own media products.

Not every student will produce a television show, write for a newspaper or magazine, or take to the airwaves as a disc jockey. But every student is immersed in media and should be media-literate. Through Target Assignments, students can also use their media savvy to push up their competencies in reading, writing, and critical thinking.

Note

The author gratefully acknowledges the contributions of students Robert Green, David Holt, and Alison Jay, who were enrolled in JOUR 1210.

References

Silverblatt, Art. 1995. *Media Literacy: Keys To Interpreting Media Messages*. Westport: Praeger.

Vivian, John. 1991. *The Media of Mass Communication*. Boston: Allyn and Bacon.

17 Activating the Viewing Process

Richard H. Fehlman
The University of Northern Iowa, Cedar Falls

Shirley Brice Heath noted that "the central business of English" should involve "turning back and self-consciously reflecting on how one has been using language—examining these processes of talking, listening, writing, and reading" (as paraphrased in Elbow 1990, 17–18). But what often appears missing from such declarations is any emphasis or direction given to the importance of reflecting about "viewing" as a language process. Maybe this is the result of a cultural prejudice which suggests that viewing is a passively mindless practice, or maybe it is merely a lack of experience on the part of educators in the area of teaching critical viewing. In either case, what follows is a short activity called a "view aloud": an exercise which retards the normal process of viewing (a newspaper comic in this case) so that students might sense how complicated a comprehending and interpreting process it might be. It is a simple exercise which draws on the wealth of viewing experiences outside of class and allows students to question these experiences during class in the name of active, critical viewing.

I begin the exercise by asking for volunteers: individuals in class who are willing to respond to questions about the meanings they make as they respond to the visual language of a typical comic. I begin by putting the following image on the overhead (Watterson 1993).

I ask students: What do you see? What is this a picture of? Often they say "a teacher," although recently one student said it was a "grandmother." I then ask them to read the language cues in more detail: tell me, How is it that you *know* this is a teacher? Many begin to read not only the print language ("a teacher would be concerned about dates if she were teaching history") but also the visual imagery ("the teacher has a pointer . . . there is a map attached to a blackboard . . . she is reading from a book").

I continue my questioning, asking students to be even more conscious of their perceptions: Have you had teachers like this? Are most teachers women? Are most of them unattractive, elderly women? How do you feel about her as a teacher? Is she a good teacher? Is she teaching in a normal manner? Students often describe her as "somewhat boring" because she is not making eye contact with her students and because she is reading off mere facts. Here I might ask: Who are her students? Are they elementary students or high school students? Where are the students? Are we, the viewers, seeing the teacher from their point of view?

It is here that some students identify the comic teacher as Miss Wormwood, Calvin's teacher in the "Calvin and Hobbes" comic strip. At this point, I might add the title to the image on the overhead (Watterson 1993).

Calvin and Hobbes

I might suggest to students that the more they know about the text, the more they are able to apply that knowledge quickly—almost automatically—to the meanings they are making, to help verify or modify those meanings. Here I might ask those students who are familiar with "Calvin and Hobbes" to share the cosmology of the comic series with their peers: what they know about Calvin, Miss Wormwood, and their relationship that helps them understand this one picture better than those who are reading it for the first time. If they know Miss Wormwood, for example, then they know that they are probably seeing her from Calvin's point of view—that of a precocious grade schooler who sees her, and sees learning from her, as a frustrating experience, one which tends to cramp his ideas and imagination.

I might also suggest to my students that whether or not they were familiar with this particular comic strip, a similar processing of textual information had gone on from the minute they realized or classified the first frame as a comic: from the first picture—if they had ever read a comic before—they knew that the information would be a narrative, often beginning in medias res like a short story, that there would be more of the story ahead (maybe four or five visual moments, or frames) often utilizing dialogue in captions above the characters and almost always having a humorous conclusion.

And with that in mind, I ask them to predict—as they do in reading a text—what is going to happen. What will the next frame contain? Many suggest the classroom or a picture of a student. But, I ask, what will the student be doing? How will the student be portrayed? To which some respond "bored" or "disinterested," although a few suggest that the student may be interested, busily copying down notes. I continue: what will *not* be pictured in the next frame? Of course, the responses here are quite interesting and varied, and, the more the suggestion is out of the realm of the narrative established in the first frame (like a beer commercial, as one student suggested), the more students giggle at the ridiculousness of the prediction.

In critically deconstructing one frame, it is clear that because students are experienced readers/viewers they anticipate a great deal about the text to follow. So the next step is to reveal the second frame (Watterson 1993).

Calvin and Hobbes

Many students are surprised by this picture, especially those who thought that the next image would contain a student, and they work hard—mentally—to make sense out of an image which tests the predictions they have made. What is this image? What are the horizontal lines—and the strange lettering? But more important, what is the source of this image? Is it from the teacher? In the classroom? From a student? Almost always, a student or two suggest(s) that it looks like a pattern of interference across a television set. Is the teacher showing a video (Watterson 1993)?

Calvin and Hobbes

Often my students are abuzz when they see these three narrative images together and then transact with them and try to make sense enough to guess what will happen in the rest of the story. Some see the planetary imagery coming from the second frame and interpret it as a picture of a student's thoughts as he or she "tunes out" the teacher shown in the first frame. Students often point to the print language to justify this meaning: "mysterious planet" as juxtaposed with the language in the first frame ("and so, in 1654")—one being futuristic, fictional, and exciting, and the other being historical, factual, and perhaps dull.

So what will the next frame contain? More guesses, as the narrative begins to complicate itself. Many students suggest that the next frame will repeat the image of the teacher or present a picture of a bored student. That is why the next frame (Watterson 1993) is interesting as students again are asked to modify their predictions.

Calvin and Hobbes

They know now that the fourth frame is merely a repetition of the second frame, so when they see it they are not too surprised. What does surprise them, however, is the change in the imagery from the first to the fifth frame (Watterson 1993).

Calvin and Hobbes

So I ask, how is the language different? They note that the teacher's image is larger and closer to the front of the frame, that her disinterested facial features and gestures have changed (she is angry at someone as she points accusingly into the frame), and that the dialogue now is printed boldly for emphasis as if she were yelling these words.

Students now deduce that someone—a student—is not paying attention; thus they predict—knowing now that the middle frames are the thoughts of that student—that they will see him or her. And, of course, they do (Watterson 1993).

Calvin and Hobbes   by Bill Watterson

CALVIN AND HOBBES © Watterson. Dist. by UNIVERSAL PRESS SYNDICATE. Reprinted with permission. All rights reserved.

Like narratives in other media—print as well as audio and/or visual—there is both conventionality and predictability in the narratives of the daily comic. And the representation of that student in the final frame, contrasted to the previous frame of the teacher imposing her will forcefully on him, seems to fit, and grow from, the rest of the tale. But if there is predictability, there is also surprise. The image of the student—

pictured from above, cornered at his desk, gesturing with head propped against his arm, staring vaguely—might suggest a hopeless acceptance which is far from humorous when one reflects on it. This is the point where students and I talk about how, and whether, these final images are funny. It is often interesting to them that the punch line is both intertextual and self-reflexive: a joke about learning in terms of television viewing which draws on their experiences with both. Schooling is addressed as "programming," and control in the classroom is discussed in terms of who is in charge of changing "the channel." Interestingly enough, the comic itself says as much about viewing in our culture as it does about learning and teaching, and I often use it as a jumping-off point for discussion about both of these issues, especially in terms of what power or control learners/viewers should have in either process.

There are other ways to use the view-aloud strategy; it is a technique that works just as well with film and television texts as it does with a comic. In all cases, the view aloud gives students the opportunity to understand that normal viewing is neither passive nor mindless, that the ease they bring to the viewing process is deceptively thoughtful and complex. It also suggests, especially through this comic, that viewing, like learning itself, is often a process of gaining control of meaning-making experiences—and the more students can learn strategies for taking control, the more critical and valuable their learning experiences will be.

References

Heath, Shirley Brice. Presentation at the 1987 English Coalition Conference. Paraphrased in Peter Elbow, *What Is English?* (New York and Urbana, IL: MLA and NCTE, 1990), 17–18.

Watterson, Bill. 1993. "Calvin and Hobbes." Cartoon printed in the *Waterloo (Iowa) Courier*. November 12, 1993.

III Reflecting and Connecting through Presentations, Projects, and Portfolios

If carefully designed, a product can drive learning. In planning a presentation, preparing a project, or reflecting on the pieces in a portfolio, students learn by doing. The power of reflecting and connecting to effect greater understanding through students' use of language to learn can be seen in the activities described in this section. Many of these activities are interdisciplinary in nature, encouraging students to make connections and to reflect on their learning in several areas. Other activities encourage students to make connections between new knowledge and old, and to reflect on their progress in gaining knowledge and skills.

Larry Johannessen offers several activities for an interdisciplinary study of the Vietnam War. Dana Nevil's multicultural poetry project encourages students to read and reflect, while working both collaboratively and independently. Offering a model for similar presentations, Daniel Kain describes a research project to bring together students in fourth grade and ninth grade to celebrate the one hundredth birthday of Montana statehood.

Students also use language actively in the classes described by the next two essays. Ann Wheeler's students complete a senior project in which they consider the relevance of their education as they examine what they have learned and make connections among the various areas taught in English. David Miall describes his project method of teaching literature, offering several specific strategies for students to use in responding to literature individually and then employing those responses as the basis for a larger collaborative project.

Teachers at all levels have become increasingly interested in the value of portfolios to help both students and teachers make connections over time and reflect on their progress. Barbara King-Shaver describes a districtwide interdisciplinary pilot project using writing portfolios across the curriculum at various grade levels. Thomas Philion explains how he used two portfolio projects to help preservice teachers connect with the world of teaching that they will enter and reflect on their approach to teaching. Finally, Patrick Monahan demonstrates the power of portfolio reflection through specific assignments for high school students.

18 Vietnam War Literature and the Arts

Larry R. Johannessen
Benedictine University, Lisle, Illinois

With the lights out and shades drawn, I turn on the slide projector and show the first in a series of slides of the Vietnam Veterans Memorial in Washington, D.C.. My students scan the thousands of names chiseled into the V-shaped memorial's black granite walls. A hush comes over my students. "React!" I call out. "What do you think?"

"How many names are on those walls?" one student wonders.

"A lot," someone answers, as I go on to the next slide.

"What are those names for?" another student asks.

"They are the names of the soldiers who died in Vietnam," a student sitting near me calls out.

"No! That's crazy," comments still another. I click to the next slide.

"It's true," a student in the front of the room says. "They all died in Vietnam."

"So many names," someone says. "So many."

My students are moved in much the same way as the more than seventy-five thousand people who come each week to the nation's capital to visit the memorial, or what has become America's wailing wall.

This is the way I began a unit on the literature of the Vietnam War a few years ago when I was teaching eleventh-grade American literature. This activity illustrates the impact that the art which has come out of the war can have on students. In fact, Freedman (1985) argues that the Vietnam War was the first war fought on television and to a rock-and-roll soundtrack. As a result, Freedman maintains, it is through art, particularly visual and aural, that we may come to understand the war and its aftermath. In addition, because the war was fought on television and to a rock-and-roll beat, the literature of the war reflects these influences. In fact, a number of scholars (Anisfield 1988; Christie 1989; Gilman 1988; and Johannessen 1992) point to rock music as a major in-

Portions of this chapter appeared in revised form as "Fostering Response to Vietnam War Literature through the Arts" in *English Journal* 86 (September 1997): 57–62.

fluence on this literature, an influence that gives it a remarkable intensity, makes it very appealing to students, and distinguishes it from the literature of previous wars.

For these reasons, starting my unit on Vietnam War literature by having my students view slides of the most visible and powerful visual work of art to come out of the war is just the first step in how I use the arts to enhance student learning about the Vietnam War and the literature of the war. After discussing student reactions to the slides, I inform the class that they will be doing oral reports on the music, dance, art, theater, and photography of the war and that we will be studying some of the literature written about the war. I explain that just as the Vietnam Veterans Memorial had a powerful impact on them, they will be studying various kinds of art to see how it affects them and how this art is reflected in the literature. Then I pass out the assignment sheet shown below (adapted from Johannessen 1992, 153–154).

The Vietnam War and the Arts

Directions: Select one of the following topics and then, using the information you gather, prepare and give an oral presentation that answers the questions posed in your topic. In your presentation, you must show the art, photography, or other visual works—or play the music—that is the focus of your report.

1. The protest songs of the 1960s reflect events that were taking place. How do these songs reflect the political controversies over the Vietnam War? How is this music reflected in the literature of the Vietnam War? Which songs and/or artists seem to be most important? Why?

2. Many rock-and-roll songs were popular with GIs who fought in Vietnam. Which rock-and-roll songs and/or artists were most popular with those who served in Vietnam? Why? How is this music reflected in Vietnam War literature? How does this music reflect the political controversies of the time?

3. In the 1960s and early 1970s, artists began depicting the war in Vietnam. How do artists such as Peter Saul and others portray the Vietnam War? How do these works reflect the political controversies of the time? Which artists and/or works of art seem to be most important? Why? How are these portrayals of the war reflected in Vietnam War literature?

4. Magazines, newspapers, and television brought images of the war into American homes on a daily basis. Some of these images became touchstones for the growing unrest at home over the war. How did photographers and television news camera crews portray the war in Vietnam? Which images were most important in terms of the political controversies of the

time? How are these images reflected in the literature of the Vietnam War?

5. Classical music was also influenced by the war in Vietnam. The music of Leonard Bernstein and Richard Wernick are two notable examples. How does this music reflect the political controversies of the time? Which music and/or artists seem to be most important and why? How are this music and the themes it contains reflected in the literature of the Vietnam War?

6. Dance was not exempt from the Vietnam War. Yvonne Rainer and others were influenced by the war. How did dance reflect the issues surrounding the Vietnam War? Which artists seem to be most important and why? How are the themes of dance reflected in the literature of the war?

7. As early as 1972, some pop music began to deal with a new issue—the Vietnam veteran. How is this issue reflected in the music of artists such as Marvin Gay and Curtis Mayfield, and how is this subject treated in pop music of the 1980s? How is this music reflected in the literature of the Vietnam War? How does it reflect changing attitudes toward the war and Vietnam veterans? Which artists and/or musical compositions seem most important in terms of this issue? Why?

8. The visual art produced by combat artists during the war, as well as that produced by Vietnam veterans and other American and Vietnamese artists, depicts the war and its aftermath in striking ways. How does this art depict the war and its aftermath? Which works and/or artists seem most important? Why? How are these views of the war reflected in the literature? How do they reflect the controversies or issues of the time or changing attitudes toward the war?

9. Popular music from the 1980s illustrates new attitudes toward and views of the Vietnam War and those who served in the war. How does this music see the war in Vietnam and the Vietnam veteran? Which songs and/or artists seem most important in this regard? Why? How does this music reflect the change in attitudes and views in society? How is this music reflected in the literature of the Vietnam War?

10. The Vietnam Veterans Memorial in Washington, D.C. has been called everything from the "black ditch" to a powerful work of art. How does this memorial reflect the lingering wounds of the Vietnam War? What is your assessment of this memorial? Is it a "black gash of shame" or a work of art that has the potential to help heal the wounds of the war? How is the controversy over the memorial and/or the meaning of the memorial reflected in the literature of the Vietnam War?

11. Since the early days of the war, documentary films and television programs have dealt with a number of issues and controversies of the war. Some of these films and programs have won critical acclaim, influenced public opinion, and brought about public awareness of issues related to the war. Which of these films and/or television programs are most important? Why? How are the issues, themes, and/or controversies dealt with in these films and programs reflected in the literature of the Vietnam War?

12. Directly or indirectly, popular films and television shows have dealt with the war since the mid-1960s. In fact, as with rock music, these films and television shows reflect not only the political controversies but also the changing attitudes toward the war and toward Vietnam veterans. Select a time period, such as 1964–72, 1973–1982, or 1983–present, and answer the following questions about the feature films and/or weekly television shows of that time period. How do the feature films and/or weekly television shows portray the Vietnam War? How do these works reflect the political controversies of the time? Which films and/or television programs seem to be most important? Why? How are the issues, themes, controversies, and views of the war reflected in Vietnam War literature?

13. From the early days of the war, with plays such as *MacBird!* and *Viet Rock,* to recent popular productions such as Cameron Mackintosh's *Miss Saigon* and Shirley Lauro's *Piece of My Heart,* the theater has dealt with the Vietnam War. How do the plays during the Vietnam War reflect the political controversies of the time? How have Vietnam veterans and others portrayed the war and its aftermath? Which playwrights and/or plays seem to be most important and why? How are the political controversies or themes and issues in these dramas reflected in the fiction of the Vietnam War?

After going over the assignment and the topics, I give students some time to think before choosing a topic. While students might do this assignment on their own, I have them do it in pairs or small groups because the school and/or local libraries probably will not have enough materials for every student in a class. I usually assign students to pairs or small groups based on their interest in particular topics. The final reports are due while the class is reading literature dealing with the war.

This activity works in a number of ways. First, many of the thirteen topics have tremendous appeal to students. For example, students who are interested in rock and roll are fascinated to discover how this music reflects the sentiments of the anti-war movement during the 1960s and early 70s. In their reports they note that draft resistance became a favorite theme in songs such as Arlo Guthrie's "Alice's Restaurant" and Phil Ochs's "I Ain't Marchin' Anymore." They are equally fascinated to discover how the music of Bruce Springsteen and others reflects the changing attitudes of Americans toward those who served in Vietnam. In addition, as they examine the music in light of the literature they are studying, they discover a number of important connections. For example, in reading Tim O'Brien's memoir, *If I Die in a Combat Zone*, they note that O'Brien was opposed to the war and yet rejected the call by the antiwar movement to resist the draft or desert the military. It is much easier for students to understand O'Brien's opposition to the war as a result of the connections they make between the popular music of the day and the attitudes of many young people concerning the war in Vietnam. They also note that while his memoir is not necessarily an antiwar book, it nevertheless asks readers to consider whether the war was worth the cost. Some students point out that his change in attitude toward those who fought in the war is reminiscent of the point of view reflected in songs such as Billy Joel's "Goodnight Saigon" and Huey Lewis's "Walking on a Thin Line." Students are able to connect the literature with art and see how these in turn reflect the ideological civil war that raged across the land and led to a questioning of the national character. In addition, they see how the art and literature speak to the aftermath of the war and how the war continues to have an impact on their lives.

Studying the art of the Vietnam War has other rewards as well. For example, one pair of students who began looking at films produced in the late 1970s was very upset to discover that early post-Vietnam films such as *Taxi Driver* portrayed Vietnam veterans as psychopaths. This led them to examine later films such as *Uncommon Valor* and Sylvester Stallone's Rambo films in an attempt to understand the change in attitude toward Vietnam veterans. They were able to see how films reflect public attitudes and sentiments and how they play an important role in cultural myth making. Ultimately, they were able to apply their knowledge to Bobbie Ann Mason's novel *In Country*, in that they were better able to understand the characters, particularly the Vietnam veterans.

Another important benefit of having students study this art is that it gives them an opportunity to respond in English class in ways other than through linguistic expression. As Smagorinsky (1991) argues, bringing the arts into the English classroom is one way to provide students whose linguistic intelligence might be the weakest in their repertoire other vehicles through which to communicate understanding. Furthermore, studying the arts enables students to transport knowledge gained in one domain to another. They begin to see how the different subject areas are related.

In a follow-up class discussion of the Vietnam War and the arts, I ask students to draw conclusions. Many are often quick to point out how the war politicized American fine artists and how the art in recent years, like the literature that deals with the war, seems to be an attempt at healing some of the wounds of the war. However, some students note that controversies still exist. For example, students who reported on the visual art note that while popular films such as Chuck Norris's Missing in Action series portray the Vietnam veteran as a warrior-hero, many of the paintings, photographs, and sculptures created by Vietnam veterans show a different view. They point to the exhibit *Vietnam: Reflexes and Reflections*, which toured the country in the 1980s, as an example of the art produced by veterans that shows the agony of the veterans and the Vietnamese people. "This art," one student said, "reveals that the veterans don't feel like heroes, and it doesn't show any victory like some of the popular films." In addition, students who reported on the Vietnam Veterans Memorial discuss some of the controversies over the memorial. They point to the fact that the nation could not agree on a single memorial to the Vietnam War in Washington. It needed both the somber wall, engraved with the names of the fallen, and a statue of three soldiers, innocents who look one year out of high school. This discussion reveals the importance of having students study the art of the Vietnam War. Students have gained a sophisticated understanding of the role of art in society.

As a follow-up writing activity, I often ask students to relate the art they have researched and reported on orally to the literature we have studied in class. One of my first-year college students who studied how the war has been portrayed by American and Vietnamese artists (see, for example, *As Seen By Both Sides: American and Vietnamese Artists Look at the War*, by C. David Thomas) relates how veteran artists saw the war to Philip Caputo's memoir, *A Rumor of War*. "The pain and the sadness expressed in many of the paintings by Vietnam veterans," she writes, "remind me of Caputo's hollow comment when he leaves Vietnam: 'We had done nothing more than endure. We had survived, and that was our only victory.' There are no victory parades for Caputo or for these artists. There is only survival and pain and sadness."

This excerpt illustrates the impact that the art of the war can have on students and how studying the art can help them make meaning out of the literature. After students have completed their study of the art and literature of the Vietnam War, they have a much more sophisticated understanding of the war and of the literature and art dealing with the war. War, too, is no longer a vague abstraction, something they read about in history books, or see in a Rambo adventure film, but rather a very real possibility, with consequences that they had never before imagined.

References

Anisfield, Nancy. 1988. "Words and Fragments: Narrative Style in Vietnam War Novels." In *Search and Clear: Critical Responses to Selected Literature and Films of the Vietnam War*, edited by William J. Searle. Bowling Green, OH: Bowling Green State University Popular Press.

Christie, N. Bradley. 1989. "Teaching Our Longest War: Constructive Lessons from Vietnam." *English Journal* 78 (April): 35–38.

Freedman, Samuel G. 1985. "The War and the Arts." *New York Times Magazine* March 31: 50.

Gilman, Owen. 1988. "Vietnam and the Paradoxical Paradigm of Nomenclature." In *Search and Clear: Critical Responses to Selected Literature and Films of the Vietnam War*, edited by William J. Searle. Bowling Green, Ohio: Bowling Green State University Popular Press.

Johannessen, Larry R. 1992. *Illumination Rounds: Teaching the Literature of the Vietnam War*. Urbana, IL: NCTE.

Smagorinsky, Peter. 1991. *Expressions: Multiple Intelligences in the English Class*. Urbana, IL: NCTE.

Thomas, C. David, ed. 1991. *As Seen By Both Sides: American and Vietnamese Artists Look at the War*. Amherst: University of Massachusetts Press.

19 Crossing Borders with a Multicultural Poetry Project

Dana Nevil
Georgia State University, Atlanta

Over six decades ago in *Literature as Exploration*, Louise Rosenblatt asserted that "when there is active participation in literature—the reader living through, reflecting on, and criticizing his own responses to the text—there will be many kinds of benefits" (290). The following multicultural project promotes the active participation in literature and produces the benefits of which Rosenblatt writes. While studying in a doctoral program and teaching high school full-time, I have explored multiculturalism in theory and practice. I worked to develop this student-centered project so that my students could independently explore culturally diverse literature. The project's emphasis on student choice generates enthusiasm and encourages students to reflect on and connect to poetry, other cultures, and the ideas of their peers. Instead of assigning poetry of a certain culture for study, I allow the students to choose any culture and select their poems. The resulting reflections and insights found in the students' written responses and discussions are most compelling and illustrate the project's significance.

I designed this project in an attempt to change two aspects of my classroom. First, I wanted to increase the student's active role in the class. I concur with John Mayher's assertion: "my students learn only when *they* uncover it, not when I cover it!" (1993, 11). Second, my students needed exposure to more diverse literature. Reading Arthur Applebee's findings in NCTE's research report *Literature in the Secondary Schools* (1993) prompted my action in this area. Applebee's extensive national surveys reveal that minority authors are poorly represented in all literary periods. He found that of high schools' required book-length works, 98.7 percent of the authors were white and 85.9 percent of these authors were white males (61). Furthermore, in all genres, no more than 14 percent of the literature was written by minorities (73). The National Council of Teachers of English has recognized this deficiency, and, in its "1993

Report on Trends and Issues," the Commission on Literature places multiculturalism as the first of six key issues concerning literature instruction. The members of the commission state their primary goal as "creat[ing] lifetime readers and writers of multicultural texts." The commission members also assert that "literature teachers must learn to empower students to teach themselves" (*English Record* 31).

With these issues in mind, I created the following project. This exploration in multicultural poetry encourages students to read and reflect upon multicultural literature, while allowing them to work both collaboratively and independently. The project also focuses on whole language skills, with the students reading poems, writing responses, discussing with and listening to their peers, and presenting to the class. The project has been completed by tenth graders, but it can be a meaningful experience for students at many levels, including middle school, high school, and college. It could also be tailored easily for elementary students.

Instructions for a Multicultural Poetry Project

For teachers, this project requires no outside reading and no extensive preparation. They must simply ensure that an adequate number of poetry anthologies containing culturally diverse poems are made available for the students to read and share (see the Suggested Readings list at the end of this chapter for sources with which to begin).

Part One of the project requests that the students divide into groups consisting of four to five members. Each student must choose a different culture and find five poems from this culture that he or she finds interesting and understandable. In the past, my students have chosen cultures or groups including African, African American, Appalachian, Asian, Caribbean, German, Indian, Latino, Native American, Russian, and Southern.

Part Two of the project requires that the students complete written responses not only to their poems but to the other group members' poems as well. I often take the students to our computer lab to compose. Focusing on reader response, I furnish questions to initiate the students' writing. They are not required to answer all of the questions but are instructed to consider the following:

> What thoughts, concerns, or questions do you have as you read each poem?
>
> Do you identify with the feelings or ideas presented in the poems? If not, what about the ideas presented is unique or different from your ideas or perspective?

Do the poems contain any common themes?

Do the poems remind you of anything you've experienced?

What insights into the particular culture or group do these poems give you?

Part Three of the project brings the groups back together for several activities, which include comparing their responses to the poems, sharing their insights on the cultures, and reflecting on their learning experiences. The activities consist of the following steps.

First, the students are instructed to read or discuss their responses to a culture. One person in the group takes notes and writes the group's ideas, reflections, and conclusions. The students repeat this process for each of the cultures explored by their group.

Next, the students look for common themes among the cultures such as love, struggle, change, death, and tradition. They submit their findings and conclusions in writing.

Third, the students discuss the project itself and submit their opinions and ideas for future projects. They are encouraged to reflect on the experience and what they have learned from it.

Fourth, each group member chooses one poem to submit for the class's multicultural anthology to be compiled by the students. (The students enjoy sharing the poems most meaningful to them and reading their peers' choices.)

Finally, the group chooses one poem to read and present to the class.

Student Responses

I determine the project's success from my students' written responses. Repeatedly, these responses justify the project's worth and my students' growth. The students may make grammatical errors, misspell words, or write awkward sentences, but the significant results are manifested throughout their responses.

The following responses from tenth graders affirm that introducing students to multicultural literature can establish students' connections to diverse cultures. Divided into categories, these individual and group responses (presented without correction) show the students' wide range of reflection, connection, and understanding.

Addressing Stereotypes

The students' addressing and overcoming stereotypes is one of the most successful elements of this project. They realize the inaccuracies of their preconceived notions and subsequently change their impressions of a culture.

> Due to propoganda and accusations made by movies I saw Russians only as serious like super spys and double agents. If not in those ways they've been identified as poor inarticulate people who are really huge in stature. These poems change my outlook toward Russians totally. (Anrikae)

> The [Asian American] poems were a lot different from what I had anticipated. I actually didn't know what to think of, besides karate, however I was impressed to find out that there is much more to Asian American culture. The poems told about how life begins and how beautiful it is. (Pam)

> In these poems [Mexican], it seems that the culture would be happy. Because when you see anything about Mexicans they seem to always have fiestas and fun. But every culture has a little hardship. (Rykita)

> When I think of Native American Indians, I don't usually think about them as being romantic, but as very stern and full of pride. So to read "Love Song" was an insight for me on the culture. (Maia)

> Phillip thought that these poems [from India] would be about needing food, but they weren't. (Traci)

> Mostly when people talk about Africa, they talk about the poverty. But these poems portray the beauty of Africa. (Rykita)

> We learned that cultures are diverse in many ways and often what we think about them is distorted or wrong. . . . (Maia)

Connecting to Their Culture

Another important result of this project is the students' feeling of pride in themselves or their culture. Most of my students are African Americans and they love reading African American poems and connecting to their culture.

> These poems give my a positive insight on the poems because it is showing that African Americans can do more than just rap, sing, run, and jump. It has interested me in read poems by black authors. . . . I am also glad too because now we can show the world what real black women and men can do. Not just run and jump but read and write poetry. (Antwan)

> The most interesting poem out of all the poems was "My People No Longer Sing" [African poem]. The poem says that you should never forget about your culture. . . . When you get sick

and tired of being tired, sick, and hurt, that you can always look back and remember your people, and feel happy and proud. (Kenya)

I do identify with the feelings of these poems [African American]. The poems touch your soul and get deep within, because they are so true. (Tannesha)

Being a southern american myself I can relate to the poems. It makes it easier for me to understand, especially since I have thought about living for the present for what it is and not thinking about the past. I think, after reading these poems, that I have a better understanding of my own culture: Southern American. (Traci)

When you read these poems they seem to make you think about all the struggles your ancestors went through, it really makes you proud to be who you are. (Kearston)

Connecting to Other Cultures

The next two responses reveal that the students sometimes relate and connect to another culture, and they often reflect on the reasons for those connections.

We all liked these poems [Native American], because they are so much like the African American poems. Khalid liked them because he could relate with the struggles of their people. (Keverne)

I would like to say I didn't like how the Europeans came over and alienated the Indians from their own land telling them where to live. . . . It's the same way the Europeans did us Africans. We share the same pain when it comes to education and freedom. (Steward)

Connecting to the Poems

The students frequently connect the poems they read to their lives, reflecting on past or present experiences. This is the first step for the students in having a significant and memorable literary experience—the kind that encourages them to read independently, to make reading a lifelong practice.

I like these poems about Asian American culture because the poems remind me of everyday life. Because in the "Lives" it remind me of when we had to travel into a thunderstorm to go to Florida and my heart was beating like a drum too. These poems are real to me and it reminds me of everyday life. (Nikia)

One of the poems I feel I relate to and it is called "Round Women" be E.K. Caldwell who is Native American. The poem itself talks about women who are in full figure and how they have be taught to dislike their bodies because skinny women are the more ideal ladies people prefer. I myself understand this poem because I am a round woman. (Shundra)

The poem I like best is called Women Work (Maya Angelou). And the reason why I like this is because it tells all about what a woman does while she's at home. The things she says in the poem is what I do at home.... Some days when I work really hard just like the woman in this poem I wouldn't mine for a little sunshine on me or raindrops on me to call my own. (Rachel)

New Insights and Appreciation

Finally, many students reflect on their new insights about the cultures and the significant knowledge they have gained because of the project. They often express admiration and appreciation for individuality and cultural differences, while realizing that we humans are intimately connected in spite of our differences.

What I really like about this project was that it was easy and it actually teaches as well as develop your knowledge to different cultures. We need to do projects like this more often. (Ramon)

These poems all talk about the chinese reaching america and there everyday struggle. They are describing how they were treated and how they felt when they were being kept back in the detention center. My favorite line was "Here even a proud man bows his head low" I think that that line tells us how unbearable it was to be there and to be treated like that. (James)

I did not relate to the Appalachian poems because I'm a city boy and I've never been related to the country. In fact, this could be one of the poems that I learn the most from. (Keverne)

Poems from Russia were mostly about struggling for what you want to achieve, they were also about Russian life (a struggle in itself). These poems gave me a little insight on what it might be like if I were living there. I enjoyed these poems because they were different from any kind of literature that I ever have read. (Ngozi)

I have always wanted to know how Native Americans felt when their land and their homes were taken away. This was so long ago, however, I feel more informed after reading these poems. They seemed to have given me something that helps me understand their feelings from long ago.... I think that I learned a great deal about Native American culture through reading these poems. (Traci)

I can truely say that I learned a very good thing from these [German] poems. I learned that just because this culture is sometimes looked down upon, doesn't mean that the culture is bad. This also goes for any other culture that has written poems. (Phillip)

We learned that cultures are diverse in many ways and often what we think about them is distorted or wrong and that people do have individual thoughts even if they are from the same culture. (Maia)

These poems gave me a new way of looking at Mexicans, and how the heritage of everyone is different. (Jamille)

Pam liked the message that everyone doesn't have to be the same or look the same to be accepted in society. (Shundra)

We were surprised about how similar some of the cultures were to each other. We thought that they would be complete opposites. Usually the culture's differences are talked about. With this project we were able to look for the similarities between cultures. (Traci)

Conclusion

The selected responses reveal the students reflecting, connecting, and gaining new insights about themselves and other cultures. From reading multicultural poetry, the students recognize that both differences and similarities exist among cultures. Most commonly, they connect to the poems from their culture; yet, they also admit their enjoyment of reading about other cultures and their unique connections to certain poems. The students proudly voice the new knowledge they've acquired. Finally, when the project is completed, they not only possess a set of culturally diverse poems of their own choosing, they also possess greater knowledge of themselves and the world. In "Five Kinds of Literary Knowing" (1992), Robert Probst maintains, "Literature should socialize, humanize. It should offer us the chance to sharpen our insights into the human condition" (66). In my classroom, literature has produced this effect. My students' reflections on and connections to multicultural literature have made them more understanding of themselves and of all humanity.

Works Cited

Applebee, Arthur N. 1993. *Literature in the Secondary School: Studies of Curriculum and Instruction in the United States.* Urbana, IL: NCTE.

"1993 Report on Trends and Issues." *English Record* 44: 1, 31.

Mayher, John S. 1990. *Uncommon Sense: Theoretical Practice in Language Education.* Portsmouth, NH: Boynton Cook.

Probst, Robert E. 1992. "Five Kinds of Literary Knowing." In *Literature Instruction: A Focus on Student Response*, edited by Judith A. Langer. Urbana, IL: NCTE.

Rosenblatt, Louise M. 1983. *Literature as Exploration.* 4th ed. 1938. Reprint, New York: MLA.

Suggested Readings

Bruchac, Joseph, ed. 1983. *Breaking the Silence, An Anthology of Contemporary Asian American Poets.* Greenfield Center: Greenfield Review..

Bruchac, Joseph, ed. 1994. *Returning the Gift: Poetry and Prose from the First North American Native Writers' Festival.* Tucson: University of Arizona Press.

Carson, Jo. 1989. *Stories I Ain't Told Nobody Yet.* New York: Orchard. Appalachian poetry.

Feelings, Tom. 1993. *Soul Looks Back in Wonder.* New York: Dial. African American poetry.

Gonzalez, Ray, ed. 1992. *After Aztlan: Latino Poets of the Nineties.* Boston: Godine.

Harper, Michael, and Anthony Walton, eds. 1994. *Every Shut Eye Ain't Sleep: An Anthology of Poetry by African Americans Since 1945.* New York: Little, Brown.

Linthwaite, Illona, comp. 1987. *Ain't I A Woman!: A Book of Women's Poetry from around the World.* New York: Peter Bedrick.

Nye, Naomi Shihab, ed. 1992. *This Same Sky: A Collection of Poems from Around the World.* New York: Four Winds.

Soto, Gary. 1990. *A Fire in My Hands: A Book of Poems.* New York: Scholastic. Mexican American poems.

Yep, Laurence, ed. 1993. *American Dragons: Twenty-Five Asian American Voices.* New York: HarperCollins.

20 Investigation Waltz

Daniel L. Kain
Northern Arizona University, Flagstaff

Imagine a room full of fourth graders cheering on a ninth-grade pioneer doctor who is urging her student patient to swallow a spider as a pain reliever. Or another noisy rabble calling for the execution of the wicked Sheriff Plummer by the infamous Vigilantes. In both cases, the engagement of performers and audience alike is assured.

Engaging students involves more than a catchy topic. True engagement calls for learning experiences that connect to student interests (Beane 1990), that access multiple intelligences (Armstrong 1994), and that provide opportunities to use knowledge in meaningful ways (Marzano, Pickering, and McTighe 1993). As a teacher of junior high students, I realized I needed engaging activities to encourage student achievement. The project described here offers a simple approach to achieving engagement of that quality.

The project develops like a waltz: a series of moves in a three-step pattern, flowing, smooth, and involving. Each 1-2-3 of the dance refines the learning and responsibilities of the students. I will describe the project in terms of the context my students used—the celebration of one hundred years of statehood for Montana. However, this approach could work for a great variety of situations: local or regional events (a city's anniversary, the birthday of an important person), seasonal events (Earth Day), current events (natural disasters), and so on.

Before I break down the dance into its moves, let me paint the larger picture. I was teaching a speech course at a junior high school, and my ninth-grade speech students connected with younger students in our district (fourth graders) to celebrate the one hundredth birthday of our state by creating and performing special presentations based on Montana history. My speech students learned not only about their state's history, but also how to research topics of interest to them and how to work together in groups to design and perform audience-appropriate presentations. The younger students learned about history, and, more important, they saw role models of older students who knew something and who could present their knowledge in interesting and exciting ways.

The project, which is a combination of elements of the cooperative learning strategies known as Group Investigation (Sharan et al.

Investigation Waltz **141**

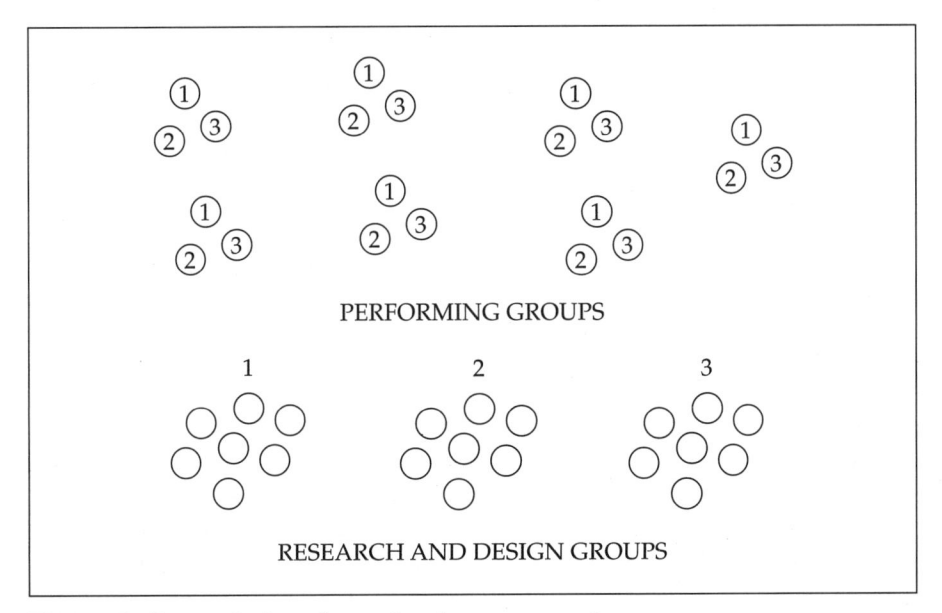

Figure 1. Group designs for waltz of engagement.

1984) and Jigsaw (Aronson et al. 1978), can be visualized as a three-step process that encourages students to take increasing amounts of responsibility. The three moves of this waltz of engagement are the research move, the design move, and the teaching/performance move. Each will be addressed in turn. First, however, the structure of the dance needs to be clarified.

The Structure of the Waltz of Engagement

Like most traditional dances, this waltz of engagement requires the proper structure and design. In order for the students to do the research and design necessary for the performance, I planned backward from the performing groups to create working groups of students. Given a class of twenty-one students, I knew I wanted the students to perform in seven groups of three students each. Thus, I organized seven groups of three students with a heterogeneous mix by race, gender, and ability. From these seven groups, I formed three groups of seven, so that each group of three would have one representative at each larger group (see Figure 1). This is easily done with the numbers indicated above. (That is, a "one" from each performing group forms the larger group of "ones.") However, though I designed the groups in this manner, I did not inform the students of their partners for the performing groups until after much of the research phase was completed.

Step One: Research

We began the waltz with a prolific thinking activity: brainstorming. As a whole class, we listed all the questions, issues, and concerns the students could think of that focused on the changes our state had undergone in the previous one hundred years. Given the context of a celebration of Montana's Centennial, we brainstormed a long list of topics that might be interesting to explore. In keeping with the spirit of brainstorming, we did no editing of ideas. The students understood that they were ultimately to develop their ideas into a presentation for younger students in the city's schools, so there was an immediate purpose to their thinking. The key element of this step is to get maximum participation in the social context of a whole class. If the students don't come up with ideas, they will be at a loss later on.

We organized our thinking around the connections between what fourth graders might be interested in knowing and what would be interesting for the ninth graders to investigate more in-depth. For example, one student suggested that they could compare a typical day for fourth graders in 1889 with one in 1989. The students developed a long list of possible topics to investigate, and then we broke into the three larger groups (the seven-member groups) for students to discuss the topics they found most interesting and to discuss research strategies that would go with potential topics.

For the research element of this step, I required the students to use both secondary and primary resources. We arranged visits to the school library to examine secondary sources. It's a little trickier finding primary sources when dealing with an event a century ago, so we interpreted *primary* rather loosely. Still, students can get fairly creative with their information-gathering skills. For example, one group ultimately decided to research the Vigilantes, those citizens of early Montana who fought against crime and corruption. While it would be impossible to find a living Vigilante, the students discovered a knowledgeable police officer through an interview with a history teacher, and the interview with the police officer revealed that the world's leading authority on Vigilantes was a retired professor living in our city. They arranged to visit this professor at his retirement home and interview him on the subject. Other groups arranged similar interviews: a group researching the typical day of a fourth grader in 1889 and another group that investigated medical practices in 1889 both secured interviews through a local museum. In both cases, they examined pictures and artifacts to help them understand the time they were exploring. They made connections among the things they were reading, what they were learning in interviews, and the museum artifacts.

I gave the students adequate time to conduct their research, and they learned the importance of delegating duties and sharing the workload. Some students, for example, found they would have to conduct interviews after school hours. These students then made arrangements for other members of their groups to visit public libraries or make phone calls after school hours. Each group's research involved different kinds of activities, so each group had to devise its own research plan and individual responsibilities. I consulted with each group, offering suggestions about resources and strategies. But the students organized and conducted their research.

Step Two: Design

The second step of this waltz of engagement was for the three groups of seven to design performances that would allow the smaller groups to present the results of their research to fourth graders in an engaging and appropriate manner. The larger groups knew they would have to design performances that met a few parameters: an audience of fourth graders, three-member performance groups, a classroom environment as the stage for their performance, and portable props to be carried by performers on a school bus.

Each large group spent several days trying out possible performances and learning these well enough to be able to return to their groups of three and teach not only the information they had learned, but also the basic plans for the performances. In two cases, the presentation involved narrative skits with limited audience participation. The students in the medical-practices group, however, built their presentation around extensive audience participation. They anticipated, correctly, that fourth graders would love seeing remedies such as the spreading of honey on their classmates or swallowing a pretend-spider to ease pain. The larger groups recognized that the smaller groups would be free to adapt their plans to fit the resources and talents of each small group. However, they needed to return to their performing groups with the basis for the presentations well established. This way, each small group would have three performances on topics of interest to fourth graders ready to take into an elementary school classroom on the day we selected for the celebration of the Centennial.

Step Three: Perform

After the groups of seven had designed a presentation, each student was assigned to a prearranged group of three, where he or she became a teacher/learner. The student, for example, who had helped prepare a presentation on the Vigilantes now had to teach that presentation to the other two members of the small group. This teaching also meant adapting the proposed presentation to fit the characteristics of the smaller group. The fresh input of new thinkers meant that the original presentation might be broadened in scope. Or perhaps a particular portion of the original presentation that seemed embarrassing or uncomfortable to the small group was omitted. Whatever the reason, as group members taught each other what to do in their performances, each group developed its own version of the show. In an extreme example, one small group more than tripled the time (with good effect) of the medical practices skit, adding numerous props and comic lines to what the group of seven had designed.

The smaller groups took several class periods to adapt, learn, and practice their performances. Then, the students assumed their final role—that of performer. Loaded down with props and costumes for three minishows, the students piled on a bus and were distributed to various elementary schools. My students experienced not only the practical benefits of public speaking but also the significant and rare experience of interacting with an authentic and different audience. All too often, our students perform in contrived circumstances for their peers and teachers and no one else. In this instance, the students found it an eye opener to speak to students five years younger than themselves. Both the responsiveness of the younger students and their knowledge amazed my ninth-grade students. Questions asked by the fourth graders and answers offered by these same students convinced the ninth graders that "kids are a lot smarter now" than when they were in grade school. On another level, the speech students learned quite quickly how to tell they were losing an audience, because the fourth graders were not as "polite" as students in speech class are forced to be.

Conclusion: Benefits of the Waltz

Through a relatively simple structural arrangement, each of my students functioned as thinker/researcher, teacher/learner, and performer. In the same way the rhythm of a waltz draws in the dancer, this project pulled each student along toward a meaningful, focused goal. Students were given choices all along the way: the topic to investigate, the strategy for research, and the way to present their findings to a real audience. They were able to tap various ways of knowing and their own strengths and intelligences as learners and performers. Because each student was indispensable to his or her small group, both as a teacher and as a performer, no student could allow others to do all the work, which is a complaint commonly voiced about group work (De Jong and Hawley 1995). The format of this "waltz" offers a way to approach learning so that traditional boundaries between disciplines fade away in light of student engagement. It is not that students merely do history or speech or drama, but that they are engaged in learning that goes beyond all such boundaries. The students perform many of the lifelong learning activities advocated by Marzano et al. (1993): complex thinking (investigation of a question), information processing (various information-gathering techniques), effective communication (both in teaching their partners and performing for younger children), collaboration (the entire project), and creative thinking as a habit of mind. The benefits of such engagement are indeed powerful.

References

Armstrong, Thomas. 1994. *Multiple Intelligences in the Classroom*. Alexandria, VA: ASCD.

Aronson, Elliot, Nancy Blaney, Cookie Stephan, Jev Sikes, and Matthew Snapp. 1978. *The Jigsaw Classroom*. Beverly Hills, CA: Sage.

Beane, James A. 1990. *A Middle School Curriculum: From Rhetoric to Reality*. Columbus, OH: National Middle School Association.

De Jong, Cherie, and James Hawley. 1995. "Making Cooperative Learning Groups Work." *Middle School Journal* 26: 4, 45–48.

Marzano, Robert J., Debra Pickering, and Jay McTighe. 1993. *Assessing Student Outcomes: Performance Assessment Using the Dimensions of Learning Model*. Alexandria, VA: ASCD.

Sharan, Shlomo, Peter Kussell, Rachel Hertz-Lazarowitz, Yael Bejarano, Shulamit Raviv, and Yael Sharan, with the collaboration of Tamar Brosh and Rachel Peleg. 1984. *Cooperative Learning in the Classroom: Research in Desegregated Schools*. Hillsdale, NJ: Erlbaum.

21 Distinguishing between the Myth and Reality of Self

Ann Wheeler
Arthur High School, Sullivan, Illinois

"Mrs. Wheeler, why haven't we done more activities like this? Why did you wait until two weeks before graduation to do such a neat unit?"

Music to an English teacher's ears, especially when coming from seniors in the last weeks of school! Four years ago, after the voices had faded, I, too, wondered why I hadn't done more "neat units" that require students to reflect on what they've learned and to make connections among the various disciplines taught in the English classroom. Because it requires both of these, my "Mythology of Self" unit continues to be a favorite for me and my students as it evolves and improves with each graduating class.

Actually, the unit grew out of desperation—my own. That particular year I had a group of seniors who were the misfits of our small rural high school. Even the few academic standouts had succumbed to the cynical, "What's the point?" mind-set of the majority of their peers. Though my class was designed for the college-bound senior, only a handful planned to attend a four-year college; most would go to the local junior college or to work in nearby factories. The students knew their scores were among the lowest, their behavior the worst, and their futures the bleakest—and they let everyone else know they knew.

Where do such classes come from? How does such a collection of individuals end up in the same class? (One teacher believed it had something to do with the number of sunspots that occurred the year they were born. . . .) What had they been told about themselves by their parents, their teachers, their peers? How much was true and how much was myth? I wanted to understand and, more important, I wanted them to understand themselves better before they graduated. So, with this combination of desperation and curiosity, I developed a unit I called "The Mythology of Self," a unit which required reading, thinking, reflecting, discussing, creating, and connecting.

In developing this unit I considered works and activities that would help students examine what they believed, why they believed it, who had influenced their beliefs and how, and what, if anything, they could do to change these beliefs. After much thought and digging through folders, books, and videos, I discovered a variety of quality material that would help me meet my goals. For example, I had taught Conrad's *The Secret Sharer* for years. Now, with the use of a reading log, I emphasized even more the struggle of the individual to recognize and accept both his good and bad "sides." Discussion centered on why we hide and try to deny a very real part of who we are. From an old speech text I found a "Personal Inventory" that the students and I used to help them focus on how they saw themselves. This instrument's open-ended statements, such as "People who don't know me very well think I am . . ." and "I value more than anything . . . ," both intrigued and frustrated students. When I asked them to reflect on why they answered the way they did, the sorting out of thoughts and feelings continued.

A real find was the Bill Moyers PBS program in which he interviews Sam Keen, a modern-day philosopher and author. Keen talks about how his life changed dramatically once he was forced to ask himself who he was. Telling stories about one's life, analyzing the contents of one's pockets, drawing the floor plan to one's childhood home, and then discussing various events associated with these rooms were activities that we then used in class. The students had to think about themselves and then share their thoughts orally in small groups or in writings to me. For example, while they "walked through" their floor plans with their classmates, they remembered the corner where the Christmas tree was always put, or the closet where they hid when they knew they were in big trouble, or the porch where they played with dolls until their parents divorced and the family had to move. What an eye opener for me. I saw a completely different side to these young adults who at times had convinced me they could never have known the innocence of childhood.

Besides their original poetry and artwork, we read and discussed excerpts from Eudora Welty's *One Writer's Beginnings*, Sue Hubbell's *A Country Year: Living the Questions*, Annie Dillard's *Pilgrim at Tinker Creek*, and David Douglas's *Wilderness Sojourn: Notes in the Desert Silence*. These are excellent examples of reflective writings that illustrate personal dilemma, doubt, humor, and spirituality. References to works we had studied previously, including *The Red Badge of Courage*, *To Kill a Mockingbird*, and *Macbeth*, surfaced during group sessions, but now in a different context. What had caused Henry, Scout, and Macbeth to believe as they did? Most of these connections were made by students with little prompting by me.

Through reading, writing, speaking (both formally and informally), drawing, listening, and observing, every student both asked and answered questions about self, peers, and me. (It wouldn't be fair for me to ask them to bare their souls and not do the same.) From a collage, in which the student was to include pictures of what was important to him or her, to a memoir that recounted an event that made a difference in his or her life, each activity peeled back one more layer of that protective skin he or she had grown in order to survive the uncertainties of life. By the end of the unit, virtually days before they were to graduate, these students had gained a better understanding of themselves, their peers, and me. They could more easily distinguish between the myth and reality of who they were.

When the students and I evaluate this unit every year, I am reminded of the less obvious strengths it has. It works for different learning styles, appealing at different times to the kinesthetic, auditory, and visual learner. Another plus is that students work at their own pace on individual projects and then adjust that pace when part of a group. Classmates often mentor or peer-edit to help someone in the group. Obviously, the mix of dependent and independent learning, the variety of activities, and the fact that students help one another all combine for a successful educational experience.

Students truly reflect and connect in this unit. While completing the activities, these students are thinking in-depth and finding relationships while integrating all of the disciplines associated with English, even though they might not be able to articulate that this is what they are doing. With modifications to keep materials current and ideas fresh, this unit remains one of my most popular and challenging.

Reference

Moyers, Bill. 1991. *Your Mythic Journey with Sam Keen.* Produced and directed by Betsy McCarthy. St. Paul/Minneapolis: KTCA.

22 The Project Method in the Literature Classroom

David S. Miall
University of Alberta, Edmonton

Experiencing Literature

If the central experience of reading literary texts is, as Frye (1970, 75) has suggested, incommunicable, then we should not be attempting to tell the literature students in our classrooms what a text means. We can teach about literature (about genre, rhetoric, history), but we cannot instruct students how to respond, what to feel and think as they read a text. If we attempt to do this, we are likely to derail students' own responses and implicitly deprecate their feelings and thoughts, as well as disenchant students with the whole enterprise of becoming literary readers (Miall 1996). How, then, can we nurture the responses of students to texts, empower and strengthen those responses, and make them more authoritative? In this essay I discuss one method that I have used with success in my own literature classrooms, working with both university and high school students. It is called the project method. Now being used with increasing success in elementary classrooms (Katz and Chard 1989), it has considerable potential for application with literary studies at a senior level.

First, we have to persuade students to take their own responses seriously. It may seem evident to them from their other classes (including previous literature classes) that learning must be teacher-directed—what are teachers paid for, after all? Teacher direction also usually appears to be more efficient. The teacher can offer coverage of the ground required and lead a large group of students through the same topics. But while it is possible to learn under these circumstances, such learning (in contrast to essay preparation or homework done alone) tends to be erratic and fortuitous. Students may learn when a point being made by the teacher relates to something they already know or are interested in, but much will bypass them because they have no way of assimilating it to their own experience of the text.

Learning with such a teacher is rather like taking a guided coach tour through a city. You will see most of the main sights, assuming you look in the right direction, and you will gather a few facts about the history of each monument you pass, but your impression at the end of the day is likely to be a somewhat disconnected jumble of impressions. You learn about a city far better by walking the streets for yourself with a map and guide in hand. You may not get to see so much, and you will take longer over the tour, but you will feel and hear the city on your own terms and at your own pace, and you will see many scenes that the coach tour ignores. So it is with learning in a literature class. The learning that students do at their own initiative unquestionably takes longer and demands more effort, and it may become tiring or distressing at times (like the city explorer who wanders into a side street and becomes lost), but it ends by giving far more real understanding.

One of the project method's features, clearly, is a redefinition of the role of the teacher. But its most important feature is that it involves a change of expectations on the part of the participating students. They must give up the security (and the irritations) of the guided tour in return for a less comfortable, and sometimes unsettling, journey on their own feet. But they will be in control of the itinerary.

Working in Groups

Group work is at the center of the project method that I will describe. It is the most creative part of the learning process, because it is here that the dialogue that takes place in response to literary texts is realized amidst a group of learners. To read a text requires that you supply your own knowledge of the world and the judgments you have made about it, but the text in turn may call into question the adequacy of your knowledge and impel you to shift your perspective. You may learn to judge differently, or to feel differently about some significant aspect of your life. This is the defamiliarizing work that literary texts achieve through a variety of structural and stylistic devices: through defamiliarization the text involves you in the conflicts of ideas and feelings that come from unsettling the existing structures of your thought (Miall 1993).

But what world knowledge does a text require? What feelings seem to be called into question? And what new processes of thought do the defamiliarizing devices of the text call into being? Individual readers will, of course, have their own answers to these questions, and it is important to allow time (whether in class or out) for these responses to develop. Well-structured discussion in a group then enables students to compare ideas about the existing structures of thought that are drawn upon by the text, and to consider what new feelings and ideas it creates. Group discussion not only enlarges the range of ideas available but may also enable students to enact, unprompted and extempore, some of the conflicts and arguments that the text initiates. A group discussion realizes in this way somewhat more of the potential dialogue in a text than the individual student will manage to do alone within the same time.

But working in a group of four or five students requires aims and a method. Unless students are agreed on a particular strategy, discussion within a group is likely to stray from one aspect of a text to another without arriving at any useful conclusions; discussion may wander off the text altogether. For this reason it is important, first, that a group defines the aims of its work at the beginning via a discussion to which all members of the group contribute, according to their interests in the text. Second, the group will agree on a particular method that will achieve one or more of the aims.

When meeting a new class of students at the beginning of the year, I usually spend the first few sessions giving them experience in a range of methods for use with literary texts. Some of these are general, others are specifically aimed at working with a particular genre (a poem, a drama, or a short story). Each is designed to draw upon what is distinctive about the student's own direct response to the text. Three such methods are webbing (sometimes known as mind mapping), ideas and contrasts, and the structure diagram.

In webbing, students are provided with a pack of self-stick notes (the small size). Each student working alone puts down in a word or two (with line or page references where appropriate) the most striking or interesting features of the text, with each idea on a separate note. (More advanced sessions of this activity can employ different colors for the different classes of ideas.) The students in a group then examine each other's notes, discuss and query them, and sort them into a pattern that makes sense to all of them on a tabletop. They can classify some of the main groups of ideas by adding a label. This, in itself, or transcribed to a poster or overhead slide, can be made the basis for a report to the whole class.

For the ideas and contrasts method, a short passage is chosen from a text, either literary or critical: for example, a short poem, a page from a novel, or the first two or three paragraphs of a critical article or review. The method requires first that students underline words or phrases that seem to carry the main ideas. Then an opposite or contrasting term is generated for each underlined word or phrase, where possible, and written in the margin. Some of the contrasts may already be expressed or implicit in the text; in other cases, the contrast may be absent. In either case, the method begins to reveal much about the underlying structure of the argument employed by the writer, whether poet or critic, and serves to bring to the fore its dialogical texture.

The structure method can be used on any kind of text, whether a sonnet or a novel. The students ask the question, If you were dividing this text into several sections (say, from three to seven), where would the divisions come? Having decided on, say, six episodes, students draw these on a sheet of paper in a pattern like a simple flow chart. Six boxes are shown, where each box is accompanied by the page or line numbers of the episode it contains. In a short phrase written in each box, they then describe the episodes and add such other annotations as seem required. This method serves to raise questions about why the writer chose to focus on these episodes, and why they are put in this order. Students might annotate the boxes, for example, to raise issues created by the writer's handling of each episode or the question of how each relates to the next.

The Project

The project builds on such methods, and develops them into a more comprehensive and elaborate treatment of a given text or group of texts. It also usually requires that students work in their groups outside of class time and over an extended period, perhaps two to four weeks. The group will usually consist of four students and should be formed from students who share a similar set of interests.

A project generally will have three phases (Katz and Chard 1989). In the first phase, represented by the kind of work described in the three methods above, students explore their existing responses to a text, and share them through a specific method that allows them to represent and organize their responses. While doing this work, they will discover issues, raise questions, or notice problems that require further work. During phase two, students agree on the main questions to be pursued and assign tasks to each individual in the group. Students will then use the library, local museums, or other sources (including the teacher) to undertake research on their specific questions. For example, while one student might examine the life of the author and the influences on that particular text, another might seek information about a historical event referred to, while a third tries to locate visual resources to illustrate the text (cartoons, paintings, or the like). In phase three, students bring together their information and find an effective way to present it to the whole class. I usually encourage students new to this method of working to use a poster display for this purpose (other methods might include oral or dramatic presentations, but these generally require greater skill and experience in order to be effective). Organizing a poster is itself an intellectually demanding task, and often leads to further stimulating discussion.

I usually arrange for students to present their projects during the same class session. Thus, on the agreed-upon day, a number of posters will be displayed on the walls of the classroom, and we give some time for students to circulate, to examine the work, and to note any points they wish to raise. Finally, each group is invited to introduce its poster briefly and participate in discussion about the work done. After the session, the posters are displayed for several weeks in the department library, where students can examine them at their leisure.

The project report sessions at the end of phase three are among the most invigorating and remarkable occasions I have experienced in a classroom. For students who have understood how to make the methods work, who have collaborated effectively on a project, and who have embarked as a result on a study that matters personally to them, the project can also be a high point of their educational experience, as many students have told me (informally or in course evaluations). At the same time, working with projects takes careful preparation if students are to benefit from them. In particular, such work requires that students learn to trust one another, to trust the teacher, and to commit themselves to the rather different kind of learning process it involves. For the teacher also it can be a challenging experience: not only do we give up a large measure of control, which may be unsettling, but the process itself is often defamiliarizing, when students raise questions or surprise us with perspectives on a text that we have never considered.

An Example Project

I conclude by reprinting a report on a project that was produced recently in one of my classes. For Amanda and her collaborators (pseudonyms have been used), this was the second project undertaken in a full-year course on British Romantic writing. Among the resources for this course is a hypertext on the Romantic period that I have been developing, available to students in a computer lab on campus. Amanda used this resource primarily for the advice it contains about methods of presentation. She also referred to several other methods that I introduced earlier in the course.

Project Report on Shelley's "Julian and Maddalo"

When we first read Perkins's excerpt from "Julian and Maddalo" [in David Perkins, ed., *English Romantic Writers*], I was intrigued and wanted to pursue it further. Because I was interested in studying this poem for my final essay, I thought the project report would be beneficial to my essay preparation. Due to the length and nature of the poem, I think that "Julian and Maddalo" was an excellent choice for our project report.

I first consulted the hypertext for further information on Shelley and the poem but found the most guidance in the section dedicated specifically to project reports. It was here that I uncovered the suggestion for a structure diagram—an excellent way to present a poem that was too long to include on the poster but was, at the same time, unknown to the class [Perkins's anthology omits the second half of the poem]. Because such a detailed analysis would be helpful to my overall understanding of the poem, I offered to contribute a plot diagram and summary to the poster display.

To begin my analysis, I color-coded significant aspects of imagery, character, and tone. While doing this, I paid attention to shifts between the ideal, reality, and the imagination as we had practiced at the beginning of the year. I then recorded the line numbers of these small sections and included a brief summary or significant quotations. I was then able to take these short sections and combine them under broader headings. This helped me to establish shifts in the plot, as well as changes in voice, tone, and theme throughout the poem.

The results of this analysis were six distinct sections which I labelled "introduction," "rising action," "conflict," "climactic movement," "resolution," and "epilogue." The Maniac's section was the most difficult to label since it was a huge shift in tone—almost a digression—yet still integral to the plot. It was climactic but too long to be considered the climax of the poem, so I settled on "climactic movement" as a label for this section.

This basic plot structure provided us with the necessary basis from which to build our poster. Andrew studied Julian and Maddalo and their conflict, while Alan considered the role of the madman, each of which corresponded to a section of my plot diagram. We also selected key passages from the other sections to portray a theme, tone, or concern of the poem.

To add visual appeal to the poster and to show the poem's setting, I collected photographs of Venice from travel brochures. Rather than cluttering the poster with arrows, we color-coded sections which related to one another. In so doing, we created a poster that presented plot, introduced the characters, established the setting, and hopefully inspired others to read the poem.

The hypertext was also very helpful in providing suggestions for the oral report. Since the poem was new to everyone, we decided to highlight the plot and, in so doing, offer some of our own speculations. Because the Maniac's section was so intense and emotional, we chose it as a sample to present to the class. We hoped that this too would create interest and make other students want to read the entire poem.

References

Frye, Northrop. 1970. *The Stubborn Structure: Essays on Criticism and Society*. London: Methuen.

Katz, Lilian, and Sylvia C. Chard. 1989. *Engaging Children's Minds: The Project Approach*. Norwood, NJ: Ablex.

Miall, David S. 1993. "Constructing Understanding: Emotion and Literary Response." In *Constructive Reading: Teaching Beyond Communication*, edited by Deanne Bogdan and Stanley B. Straw. Portsmouth, NH: Boynton/Cook.

Miall, David S. 1996. "Empowering the Reader: Literary Response and Classroom Learning." In *Empirical Approaches to Literature and Aesthetics*, edited by Mary S. MacNealy and Roger J. Kreuz. Norwood, NJ: Ablex.

23 Reflection and Portfolios Across the Curriculum

Barbara King-Shaver
South Brunswick Schools, Monmouth Junction, New Jersey

It seems impossible to attend an educational conference or pick up a professional journal without encountering the issue of assessment. An attack on traditional methods and a call for authentic methods of assessment are in the forefront of educational reform. Since World War II, norm-referenced, multiple-choice tests have dominated assessment in the schools. Recent work in this area, however, offers alternatives to standardized tests. As Glazer and Brown (1993) have noted, "Assessment and instruction have become integrated, ongoing procedures. . . . Students need to learn how to monitor their own growth and needs." For these reasons, many educators are turning to portfolios as one alternative method for assessing student work.

Teachers in South Brunswick Schools in Monmouth Junction, New Jersey, have been using various forms of portfolios for over five years. The portfolio models used in the district range from K–2 Literacy Portfolios to Tenth-Grade Best Works Writing Portfolios Across the Curriculum (see Figure 1). Teachers are committed to the development of portfolios and portfolio assessment because they believe that the main goal of assessment is to find out what students can do. Portfolios enable teachers to see how students are problem-solving, communicating, and self-assessing. The reflective component of the portfolio, the part in which students think and write about their own learning, is valuable in helping teachers assess where their students are and in helping students monitor their own learning.

An essential component of all portfolios in South Brunswick is the metacognitive element of reflection. As Roger Farr states in his article on language arts assessment, "There must be one central focus of language arts assessment—assessment must serve students" (1991). This is true in all disciplines, not just the language arts. Self-reflection focuses on the students. It gives students the opportunity to look carefully at

1. Grades K–2 Literacy Portfolio
2. Grades 3–12 Best Works Writing Portfolios
3. Elementary and High School Math Portfolios
4. Tenth-Grade Best Works Writing Portfolios Across the Curriculum
5. Working Portfolios used by individual teachers and students as a regular part of their classwork

Literacy portfolios have been used in grades K–2 as a method of assessment in South Brunswick Schools since the fall of 1989. Literacy portfolios for grades K–2 include components of all the language modes: reading, writing, speaking, and listening. Using these portfolios, student growth in language arts is assessed over a period of three years. Working with personnel from Educational Testing Service (ETS) in Lawrenceville, N.J., the teachers and administrators using the K–2 Literacy Portfolios developed a scoring guide rubric for assessing the contents of the portfolios based on descriptors developed by the classroom teachers. The rubrics were then used for two years by readers who, working with ETS personnel, validated their reliability. Trained readers—teachers from within the district—were able to obtain similar scores or scores within at least one point of each other when reading and rating the same literacy folders.

Best Works Writing Portfolios have been used in the district since 1991. Math portfolios were begun in 1992 and have become part of the tenth-grade writing-across-the-curriculum portfolio. A growing number of teachers have begun using portfolios as a regular feature of their classes in different disciplines. Joyce Lott has written about one teacher's use of writing portfolios in her book, *A Teacher's Stories*. In addition, several science teachers are now using portfolios as part of their courses, and the Advanced Placement English students are keeping poetry portfolios.

Figure 1. Portfolio models in South Brunswick schools 1992–94.

their own learning processes, and it encourages students to take ownership of their own learning. Research in cognition indicates that meaningful learning is reflective, constructive, and self-regulated (Wittrock and Baker 1991). The reflective component of portfolios meets the definition of meaningful learning. Reflecting on a learning experience asks students to consider what they have done, what they have done best, how they plan to get help in areas they need to work on, and what they plan to work on next.

Writing a Reflective Piece

The two key steps in preparing a portfolio are selecting the pieces of work to include and reflecting on these selections. The purpose of both of these steps is to help students take ownership of their learning. In doing this, the reflective writing piece is key. As a form of self-assessment, the reflective writing piece distinguishes portfolios from writing or work folders. It provides students with a place to reflect on their own work and to establish goals for their own learning. Written reflections can explain why the samples were selected, point out their strengths and weaknesses, note what the student learned from completing the samples, and discuss plans for future learning. In addition to a written reflection accompanying each selection in the portfolio, a final reflection on the portfolio as a whole is usually included.

Students need practice in order to become good evaluators of their own work. Younger students and students just beginning the process often make comments such as, "I like this piece because it is my favorite" or "This writing shows how good my handwriting can be." Comments become more substantial as students practice both talking and writing about their work reflectively. More experienced students write comments such as, "This piece is special to me because it is about the last time I saw my grandmother" or "The piece was focused and did not meander from the topic" (Tierney 1991). Conferencing with peers or a teacher helps students practice talking about their work, and this practice helps students write better reflective pieces for their portfolios. Question prompts also help students as they plan their reflective writing pieces. In addition, teachers may use sample reflective writing pieces completed by other students.

Reflective pieces of writing that accompany a portfolio may vary in format, depending on the purpose of the portfolio. In general, reflective pieces are written in either a narrative essay form or in a letter form. If a letter format is used, the letter may be addressed to the teacher or to an assessor, e.g., "Dear Assessor" or "Dear Reader."

The reflective process, beginning with selection of works and ending in a reflective writing piece, helps the teacher as well as the students. As the students come to understand their own strengths and weaknesses, teachers discover clues about their students' learning. These clues can lead to new ways of teaching and, therefore, to better learning. But the best reason for asking students to reflect on their learning is to make them independent learners responsible for their own learning processes.

The South Brunswick Tenth-Grade Writing Portfolio Model

In the summer of 1992, teachers from science, social studies, English, and mathematics met to discuss ways to support writing across the curriculum. Out of these discussions came the idea for a two-year pilot program for developing writing portfolios across the curriculum in tenth grade. This group of teachers identified three main goals for their project:

1. To promote writing and language use across the curriculum
2. To look at authentic methods of assessment (portfolios)
3. To help students become reflective learners who take more responsibility for their own learning

The teachers involved in the writing portfolio project included writing assignments as part of their ongoing classroom lessons. In addition, they had students keep cumulative folders of their work. Students were asked to select examples of their best work from the cumulative folders and to write reflections on their selections.

The summer meetings were followed by training on reflective writing at a fall inservice day. At the fall meeting, the teachers decided to use prompt questions when helping their students write reflections. The prompt questions they constructed were based on a model provided by Donald Graves at the NCTE Annual Convention in St. Louis, Missouri, in 1989:

1. What can I do now that I couldn't do before?
2. What am I good at?
3. What do I need to learn next?
4. How will I learn it?

Participating teachers developed their own variations on these prompts (see Figure 2).

In the spring of 1993, the participating teachers met again to share their students' writings and reflections and to construct a rubric for assessing writing. In order to construct a rubric, the teachers first listed descriptors of good writing. The main charge put to these teachers as they developed descriptors was: What do we want and expect students to be able to do in math, science, social studies, and English by the end of tenth grade? There were many areas of agreement, and, from the descriptors of good writing that were identified, a rubric for assessing writing was developed (see Figure 3). After looking closely at the reflective components of the portfolios, the group decided that reflective pieces of writing should not be scored using the writing rubric because they were highly personal and varied widely in form. Teachers decided that it was not useful to employ a rubric designed for expository writing when reading reflective pieces. The participating teachers did use the rubric to score sample portfolio pieces from all disciplines involved. They were able to come to agreement on the sample papers, with most scores being the same or adjacent.

Math Reflective Prompts

1. What was Chapter 2 about?
2. What did you understand best in the chapter?
3. What was most difficult for you? Why do you think it was difficult?
4. If you could do it all over, would you change anything in terms of studying or note taking?

Another Teacher's Math Reflective Prompts

1. What can I do in math now that I couldn't do before?
2. Which math skill(s) am I good at?
3. What other things do I need to learn in math this year?
4. What could I do to help me improve my math grade?

Social Studies Reflective Prompts

1. Why did I select this piece of writing as my best work?
2. What do I like best about this piece of writing?
3. What do I see as the strengths of this piece of writing?
4. What do I see as the weaknesses of this piece of writing?
5. What have I learned about writing from this assignment?
6. What have I learned about social studies from completing this assignment?

English Reflective Prompt
Think about a commitment statement you made at midyear. Discuss whether or not you have completed the commitment you set for yourself. Why or why not?

Another English Reflective Prompt
List skills or writing techniques that were new to you this year. Choose one item that helped you improve as a writer and explain it. Choose one item that has given you trouble or confused you and explain it.

Science Reflective Prompt
Select your best piece of writing in biology thus far. Write about why you selected this piece.

Figure 2. Prompt questions for reflective writing.

During the 1993–94 school year, additional samples of student work were collected in WAC portfolios. The teachers involved fine-tuned their own scoring skills by practicing with the rubric. They also experimented with different reflective models. By the end of the school year, the participants were ready to share their work with their colleagues and introduce the model across the tenth grade.

	4	3	2	1
Purpose	Establishes and maintains a single, distinct focus and clearly addresses the topic or task	Establishes a single focus and attempts to address the topic or task	May drift or shift focus and minimally addresses the topic or task	Focus is uncertain or missing and does not address the topic or task
Support	Has explicit details that effectively support points	Has appropriate details but they are not totally effective; details have little elaboration	Details are subjective, some repetition, no elaboration	Details are random, inappropriate or nonexistent
Organization	Has a distinct interesting introduction, a logical progression of ideas with transitions and a distinct conclusion	Attempt at an introduction, an uneven development of ideas, some transitions, and a weak conclusion	No discernible introduction, loosely connected ideas with weak transitions, and no discernible conclusion	No discernible introduction, random ideas, no transitions, and no conclusion
Sentence Structure	Great variety in structure and length, sentences are appropriate to purpose and there are few if any errors	Some variety in structure and length, some errors	Little variety in structure and length, many errors	Sentences are simple, monotonous, incomplete, and incorrect
Wording	Effective, varied, rich vocabulary	Some variety, less effective and rich vocabulary	Little variety, some inappropriate or limited vocabulary	Limited, inappropriate vocabulary
Mechanics	No obtrusive errors, technically correct in spelling, punctuation, capitalization and usage	Few obtrusive errors, no patterns of errors	Errors are frequent and obtrusive, patterns of errors are evident	Frequent errors impede comprehension

Figure 3. South Brunswick scale for Writing Across the Curriculum.

What Student Reflections Have Shown

Student reflections have shown that students can self-assess their progress across disciplines. In one regular Algebra II class, students used prompts to reflect on what they could do well, what they needed to learn, and what they could do to improve. This last prompt—asking students to reflect on what they could do to improve—forced many students to think about this for the first time. Before, they had relied on the teacher to tell them what to do next. A student who really thought about what he, not the teacher, should do, stated, "In order to help me improve my math grade, I think that I should read the section that is being covered before we discuss it, so when it's being talked about in class, I won't be lost. In addition, I think that if I truly don't understand a section, I should go for extra help." In English class, another student commented on her own strengths and weaknesses: "One of my biggest strengths is my ability to be concise. . . . One area that I can improve is the use of the passive voice. Although I try very hard, I'm not always successful at excluding it from my papers."

Reflections also show that students are able to select favorite "best works" writing pieces and explain why they chose them even if the pieces selected were not their best grades. As one English student noted, "I like my 'Deep Sea Diver' poem. I got a C+, but when I look at it I see it is hard to read for someone else, maybe it's just my way of thinking. I guess I could have got a B+ if I did write it so someone else could understand it." A biology student explained why knowing the subject makes for better writing:

> I have selected my piece of writing on the poor, maligned bacteria as my best work because I felt that I knew and understood that topic a little more than my other topics. I felt I could actually relate to what I was writing. Unfortunately, the lack of time was a weak point in my writing because I didn't have time to do enough planning ahead. All in all, I learned that if you write with feeling, the text becomes stronger and more powerful. From a scientific point of view, I learned how humans can neglect and stereotype important organisms in the ecosystem.

This young man not only learned science from doing his writing assignment but also learned more about the writing process itself, as did a student in social studies: "I didn't know I had to include all the things I did in writing in my English class in my history paper."

Several of the teachers keeping portfolios that contain reflective pieces have noted that, in addition to helping them find out more about their students' learning processes, the reflections have brought student and teacher closer together. As Gene Maeroff observes, "thumbing through a portfolio with a student or watching a student perform a task—whatever the psychometric worth of such assessment—adds a degree of intimacy that can be refreshing in an age of depersonalized appraisal" (1991, 281). Commenting on what she could do to improve in algebra, one student noted, "I think I should find better ways to study. I should do all the problems over from homework. Also, I should not get nervous before I take tests or quizzes because I lose points for not concentrating and making careless mistakes." This response showed her teacher that the student's problems rested not just in an inability to solve the equations but also in her attitude, her feelings toward the test. This information gave the teacher the opportunity to talk with the student in a different way to help this young woman overcome her anxiety. In her text on student portfolios, Joyce Lott, an English teacher in the same school, presents several anecdotal stories of becoming more involved with students personally as she began reading their portfolios and reflections. In reading the papers and reflections of an Indian American student, for example, Lott notes that the student taught her that writing—the way we express ourselves—cannot be separated from our cultural identity (Lott 1994). Reading students' reflections often takes the teacher to unexpected places.

This pilot program has shown that teachers across the curriculum value writing and the keeping of student writing portfolios across the curriculum. It also shows that teachers learn to recognize the importance of the reflective component of portfolios. In fact, several teachers have begun building reflections into every major assignment in their classes, as have some of their colleagues who heard about the pilot teachers' work. In addition, this project has shown that teachers from a variety of disciplines can come to agreement on what constitutes good writing and how to help our students learn better.

References

Brandt, Ronald S. 1992. "On Performance Assessment: A Conversation with Grant Wiggins." *Educational Leadership* 49 (May): 35–37.

Brandt, Ronald S., ed. 1992. *Performance Assessment: Readings from Educational Leadership*. Alexandria, VA: ASCD.

Farr, Roger. 1991. "The Assessment Puzzle." *Educational Leadership* 49 (November): 95.

Gifford, Bernard. 1990. "Issue: Authentic Assessment." *ASCD Update* 32 (September): 7.

Glazer, Susan Mandel, and Carol Smullen Brown. 1993. *Portfolios and Beyond: Collaborative Assessment in Reading and Writing.* Norwood, MA: Christopher-Gordon.

Lott, Joyce. 1994. *A Teacher's Stories: Reflections on High School Writers.* Portsmouth, NH: Heinemann.

Maeroff, Gene I. 1991. "Assessing Alternative Assessment." *Phi Delta Kappan* 73 (December): 272–81.

Meyer, Carol A. 1992. "What's the Difference between *Authentic* and *Performance* Assessment?" *Educational Leadership* 49 (May): 39–40.

Mitchell, Ruth. 1992. *Testing for Learning: How New Approaches to Evaluation Can Improve American Schools.* New York: Free.

O'Neil, John. 1992. "Putting Performance Assessment to the Test." *Educational Leadership* 49 (May): 14–19.

Perrone, Vito, ed. 1991. *Expanding Student Assessment.* Alexandria, VA: ASCD.

Shepard, Lorrie A. 1989. "Why We Need Better Assessments." *Educational Leadership* 46 (April): 4–9.

Sizer, Theodore. 1992. *Horace's School: Redesigning the American High School.* Boston: Houghton Mifflin.

Tierney, Robert, et al. 1991. *Portfolio Assessment in the Reading-Writing Classroom.* Norwood, MA: Christopher-Gordon.

Willis, Scott. 1991. "Transforming the Test." *ASCD Update* 32 (September): 3–6.

Wittrock, M. C., and Eva L. Baker. 1991. *Testing and Cognition.* Englewood Cliffs, NJ: Prentice-Hall.

24 The Resource and Professional Development Portfolio Projects

Thomas Philion
The University of Illinois at Chicago

Over the past year or so, I have developed two portfolio projects which help me to foster reflection and connection in my secondary English methods classroom at the University of Illinois at Chicago. One project is something that I call the Resource Portfolio Project. The other is something that I call the Professional Development Portfolio Project. In this essay, I present an overview of these two activities and reflect upon the educational principles that inform them.

The Resource Portfolio Project

Like most teachers, I have to work hard to make my teaching relevant to my students. A criticism that I often hear from my students is that the teacher education coursework at the University of Illinois at Chicago is too removed from the realities of secondary English education. My students—many of whom already have worked extensively in schools or other cultural institutions—do not want to spend the majority of their time in my classroom speculating as to the nature of their teaching philosophy or reflecting upon their experiences in learning to read and write. What they want from me are concrete and practical ideas for teaching high school English.

The Resource Portfolio Project is my way of addressing my students' receptiveness to the obviously practical, without sacrificing the habits of reflection that my own experience tells me are crucial to the creation of a sophisticated teacherly identity. On the first day of my methods class, I ask my students to brainstorm, in small and large groups, different topics and/or issues that they feel they need to know more about before they enter the Practicum in Teaching (student teaching). I write their ideas on the blackboard, and I explore with my students the rationale behind their choices. Then, I share with my students a large collection of articles and artifacts that I have gathered over the years in response to my own needs and interests and to inquiries from beginning English teachers. When I finish my presentation, I tell my students that high school English teachers rarely have someone hovering over them in order to see if they have been acquiring all of the various information that they need in order to accomplish their work in an exemplary fashion. Professional English educators, I suggest, take it upon themselves to acquire information when they find themselves deficient in some area. I tell my students that over the rest of the semester I expect them to construct a Resource Portfolio of articles and artifacts focused on issues of concern to them as they enter the profession of secondary English education. Engaging in this endeavor, I suggest, will provide them with the lifelong learning skills that they will need in order to develop and grow as teachers of high school English.

Over the duration of the semester, I take a number of steps to facilitate my students' completion of this assignment. I maintain the small groups established on the first day of class so that students can coordinate their research goals; thereafter, students share resources and discuss problems in these small groups. Early in the semester, I take my students to one of my English Department's computer labs so that I can show them how to join relevant electronic discussion lists sponsored by NCTE. Later, I show my students how to send e-mail, how to access the World Wide Web, and how to access the resources of our library, especially ERIC. If a special interest develops, I invite guest speakers to our classroom or organize a field trip. As the need arises, I copy and distribute information of interest to my students.

At midterm and finals, I hold conferences with my students in order to get a better sense of their approach to this project: What problems have they encountered? What information have they acquired from other courses at the University of Illinois at Chicago? What connections have they made to professional communities beyond our campus? How have they made decisions about materials to include in their collection? I give my students both oral and written feedback on their portfolios and direct them to new sources of information.

At both midterm and finals, I give students grades on their portfolios. The criteria sheet that I currently use focuses on the quality of presentation, organization, content, and reflection. All portfolios must be well-bound, attractive, well-organized, and varied in content. Additionally, all portfolios must have a reflective conclusion in which the students write a rationale for and an evaluation of their work.

The Professional Development Portfolio Project

The Professional Development Portfolio Project works like the Resource Portfolio Project, but the focus is different. In this case, I direct my students' attention to the one activity that they most wish to avoid: critical reflection upon their approach to teaching.

Because I know that my students respond best to projects that are job-focused and practical in nature, I write scrupulously about this project in my course description.

> The creation of a Professional Development Portfolio is probably the most difficult challenge that you will face in this class this semester; conversely, it is probably the most important activity in which you will engage. Beginning English teachers need to be able to present to mentor teachers, students, and prospective employers the nature of their thinking about the teaching of English. The Professional Development Portfolio is my way of asking you to reflect upon and develop your assumptions about the teaching of English, and to develop a coherent plan for sharing those assumptions with others. More practically speaking, your Professional Development Portfolio will be your introduction to your university supervisor and mentor teacher(s) during the Practicum in Teaching. The idea here is commonsensical—the more insight your mentors acquire into your perspective with regard to the teaching of English, the better able they will be to respond to your needs and interests and to advise you as to courses of action.

As with the Resource Portfolio, I present the Professional Development Portfolio as a tool for entering the profession of secondary English education. However, I emphasize that the portfolio is more than simply a "tool" for acquiring a job or a good recommendation; it is also a springboard for a critical conversation about English pedagogy.

The required contents of the Professional Development Portfolio are as follows: an introduction, a statement of teaching philosophy, an eight-week unit plan, a prospectus for a teacher research project to be completed during the Practicum in Teaching, and a reflective conclusion. Additionally, I suggest that students include other texts that may help them to indicate to others the nature of their preparation to teach: a piece of creative writing, an annotated bibliography of professional reading, a written recommendation, a videotape of a classroom lesson, and/or a written account of an actual teaching experience. My aim here is not only to encourage my students to take ownership of their portfolio, but also to engage them in what I see as the hard work of teaching—planning extended units and making tough decisions about what to teach, how, and why.

Over the duration of our semester together, I try to construct a classroom environment that supports this complex endeavor. Students share drafts and revisions of their required portfolio pieces in small groups at several points throughout the semester. At each of these points, I provide my own feedback. Students can consult several writing models that I place on library reserve, as well as the detailed list of writing suggestions and expectations that I include in the class coursepack. Occasionally, guest speakers visit our class to discuss their teaching and unit plans, and students usually refer to one or more of the methods texts that I order for our course. Our large-group conversations and individual journaling also provide us with opportunities to reflect upon pedagogical goals and methods. Especially useful are the discussions that follow my reading of journal entries written by current student teachers out in the field. I find that these journal entries usually invite a provocative discussion about conflicts and problems confronted by student teachers.

Probably the most significant interactions that I have with my students with regard to this project are the two face-to-face conferences that I conduct over the duration of our semester. At this time, I can advise students about the development of their required writing. Usually, students do not struggle with the teacher research prospectus; the form here is familiar and straightforward (identify an issue, explain what you know about the issue, and construct a plan for future research). However, students grapple endlessly with the statement of teaching philosophy and often have a very difficult time figuring out, in their unit plan, how to speak to an audience of adolescents about pedagogical goals, evaluation procedures, and classroom activities. I find that my conferences with students enable me to understand these difficulties and to ask questions that complicate in a useful way the emerging ideas of my students.

At the end of the semester, I evaluate my students' Professional Development Portfolios using a criteria sheet similar to that for the Resource Portfolio. Professional Development Portfolios are assessed in terms of their quality of presentation and revision, clarity of expression, rhetorical cohesion, and quality of reflection. As in the Resource Portfolio, all students evaluate their work in a reflective conclusion.

Reflective Conclusion

In his essay "Collaborative Learning and the 'Conversation of Mankind'" (1984), Kenneth Bruffee writes that the first steps in learning to think better "are learning to converse better and learning to establish and maintain the sorts of social context, the sorts of community life, that foster the sorts of conversation members of the community value" (640). I can think of no better quote to sum up the educational principle that informs these two different portfolio projects. By asking students to acquire resources for their future teaching, to engage in the difficult task of creating long-term plans for teaching, and to engage in conversation about those activities, I am attempting to create the sort of community life that typifies exemplary secondary English education communities. I believe that if my students can create in our classroom a community of learners focused on reflection and connection, then they will be better positioned to make the transition to full-time teaching. They'll know what to do if they find themselves in teaching situations that are not supportive and nurturing, and they'll know how to respond in situations that are exemplary in nature.

While this notion seems to me to be the overriding educational principle at work in these projects, I think that there are additional explanations for why these projects work, both for me and for the majority of my students. Both of these projects satisfy my students' desire for practical information that connects in some way with the real circumstances of their future teaching. Additionally, I think that my students welcome the opportunity to develop their own goals and objectives, to make connections to other coursework in their teacher education program, and to conceive themselves as professionals. Although they might not always admit it, the challenge of fulfilling the demanding expectations of these two projects is just as crucial to their overall satisfaction with the projects as is the opportunity to construct their own goals and objectives.

As for myself, I like these projects because they enable me to stress the value of taking responsibility for one's preparation to teach, of working collaboratively with others, and of looking critically at one's pedagogical perspective. In both of these projects, students must ask themselves why they are interested in some ideas and not in others. Why acquire information related to Young Adult Literature? Why include this grammar worksheet? What does it mean to label oneself a "whole language teacher"? I derive great satisfaction from the intersection of the practical and the theoretical that occurs in these projects.

However, the main reason I like these projects is that they help me to reflect upon my English teacher-education pedagogy and to connect with professional resources and communities that I never would have explored without them. It is this unexpected outcome for which I am most grateful.

Reference

Bruffee, Kenneth. 1984. "Collaborative Learning and the 'Conversation of Mankind.'" *College English* 46: 635–53.

25 Keeping the Candle Lit through the Fierce Winds: Encouraging Personal Mastery through Portfolios

Patrick Monahan
Downers Grove South High School, Downers Grove, Illinois

L ife has a peculiar way of never quite letting one reflect. I think to write is to reflect is to understand. That is why I write. The words on paper are like fresh air sweeping through my jumbled thoughts and feelings."

With these words, Tera Welbourn, twelfth grader, opens the preface of her learning portfolio, and, in her imagery, beautifully captures the challenge of high school learning. Perhaps nowhere in education are students more jumbled in their learning, rushing quickly from class to class, from teacher to teacher, participating in an often unrelated, headlong series of classroom events. Not surprisingly, in such a mad dash, students sometimes miss or mistake their learning.

I was first attracted to portfolios by the opportunities they provided for reflection, initially on writing. Roberta Camp and Denise Levine (1991) write, "Reflection makes visible much in learning that is otherwise hidden, even from student writers themselves" (197). Early in my experience with portfolios, I recognized their benefits in revealing learning to students. I did not anticipate, however, their capacity to surprise students with their own successes. Rachel, a twelfth grader, describes such an epiphany in her reflection on an independent project:

> Because I had to search for just the right quote that demonstrated a major theme in the novel, I began noticing things . . . there were several. I was . . . one-fourth of the way through my next novel when a breakthrough happened. A passage just seemed to jump out at me. A class discussion had been in the back of my mind as I was reading and I made a connection. As I read on I noticed

more passages. All of a sudden I was reading critically, thinking while I read—and it was amazing that all sorts of things began popping out of me.

In her portfolio Rachel has the chance to think about her reading, and she is impressed by her capacity to extend beyond comprehension into interpretation. Indeed, she is genuinely amazed by her learning, which is magnified by her sense that she has achieved it independently. Rachel's moment is one which teachers want to repeat with all students, but what can we do in our classes to encourage such surprises?

The surprises of learning, I believe, emerge from two related and deeply personal qualities. The first is Personal Standard (Wiggins 1991). As children come to define their best performances, whether it is their best time in a track meet or the most complex story they have ever written, they establish a benchmark for their performance, a standard which they may strive to reach and pass in the future. Knowing one's best is one of the central components of mastery.

The second quality is Personal Signature (Costa and Kallick 1995), the capacity of children to see their work as a representation of themselves. Like an artist or an architect, a student should come to know that his or her name is a guarantee of quality and excellence. Even in work that is less than their best, students can find moments of excellence, and, as they make these discoveries, they begin to develop a sense of pride in their work.

The portfolio is not a new idea, nor have children in the past been denied them. My mother kept mine on the refrigerator. Periodically, and when I wasn't looking, she removed my "best" work from the door to make room for more. Today, teachers are encouraged to allow children to make such choices, determining what projects and materials to add to their collections and what to remove. Unlike a folder, the portfolio is selective, reflecting the choices of a child.

The literacy portfolios I ask students to make are messy. Each quarter, students collect samples of their work and, in a series of reflective commentaries, explain to an interested observer how each item specifically represents their learning. I provide students with a description of the types of evidence they may want to include. Four are closely linked to the idea of pride, an important component of personal standard. Three are linked to the idea of knowing one's best and becoming aware of the criteria which define good work, which is also a component of personal standard. Two are linked to Personal Signature. A description of these portfolio categories is presented in Figure 1.

Keeping the Candle Lit through the Fierce Winds

> A learning portfolio is a collection of items selected from students' work which provides evidence of their learning. This portfolio also includes a series of reflective commentaries through which students explain to an interested observer how each item of their work specifically represents their learning. Types of evidence include:
>
> **Highlights**: Samples of work (whole or partial texts) which students consider their best efforts. In commentaries, students identify the features of their work which illustrate their strengths.
>
> **Firsts**: Samples of students' attempts at a new skill or a new approach in their learning. In commentaries, students describe the success of their efforts and what they have learned.
>
> **Breakthroughs**: Samples of work in which students experience deep insights. In commentaries, students describe the nature of these insights and describe the effects of them upon their understandings of learning.
>
> **Skills**: Evidence of the acquisition of small but important grammatical or stylistic skills. In commentaries, students describe their new understandings of these concepts.
>
> **Pictures of Development**: Two samples drawn from similar types of work, one early in a term, one later. In commentaries, students comment on the differences between these samples, underscoring their learning.
>
> **Processes**: Samples of students' sketches, notes, and drafts. In commentaries, students describe the processes they employed in completing an assignment and evaluate the effectiveness of these processes.
>
> **Transformations**: Samples of work in which students did not meet their expectations or the expectations of the assignment. In commentaries, students demonstrate through analysis that the work has been instrumental in their learning.
>
> **Voice**: Samples which represent the unique qualities (personalities, habits, principles, style) of the student. In commentaries, students describe the features of the work which represent them.
>
> **Treasures**: Excerpts from reading or writing which affect students powerfully. In commentaries, students record these moments and reflect upon their personal meanings.

Figure 1. Types of evidence for learning portfolios.

Sometimes after each project, but usually at the end of each of the first three quarters, I ask students to make selections, and they accumulate eighteen to twenty-four items and commentaries during the year. In reflections, students may accomplish a number of important outcomes linked to personal mastery. First, they are able to place their learning in the context of their personal development. Reviewing their work over time, they are able to define and appreciate their achievements and shape their goals for the future. For example, in a Picture of Development reflection, Jen expresses her satisfaction with the growth she observes in two introductions, one from first year, another from senior year. As a first-year student, she explained why Laura is the main character in *The Glass Menagerie*. She wrote,

> She is also the main character because of the fact that, without her, the story would have less meaning. True, if Tom or Amanda were gone, the story would be less, but without Tom you have Amanda trying to get Laura a better life. Without Amanda, you still have Tom's problems and Laura's, but without Laura, you only have a conflict of mother pushing son. But this is my opinion.

Writing the word "FRESHMAN" above her paragraph and the word "MIRACLE" by her grade of C, Jen surely laughed when she pasted in her senior introduction from an essay on *Crime and Punishment*. Here she wrote,

> Within Dostoevsky's *Crime and Punishment* exists a complex character named Rodion Raskolnikov. Portrayed with dual personality, Raskolnikov sometimes acts in one manner and then suddenly in a manner contradictory. In order to emphasize this dual personality, Dostoevsky creates two other characters in the novel who represent the opposing sides of Raskolnikov's character—Sonia and Svidrigailov.

In her reflection on her senior work, Jen comments on wanting a "real topic." Rather than picking an easy one, she has decided "to reach and trust [her] instincts." She explains, "I used all the concepts I had learned, trusting myself and my ideas, . . . and not rushing. I took my time on this paper and gave the book a chance to settle in my head." In closing her reflection, she notes, "As I try and trust myself, I learn that I am capable of greater things." In comparing her first-year performance with her senior effort, Jen has developed confidence in her abilities. She knows that good ideas will come to her if she waits for them. Observing her work over time, she has found good reason to trust herself.

Through reflection, students may also accomplish a second important outcome: anchoring curricular experiences and ideas in their personal lives and beliefs. Here, reflections assist students in situating a distant curriculum within their own experiences. For example, in a Breakthrough reflection, Laura reveals the evolution of her essay on *King Lear* and her growing ownership of her ideas. She writes,

> When my paper was returned to me, it was covered with blue pen and basically said my ideas were wrong. I remember writing that Goneril and Regan should have taken care of their father because they owed him and it was the custom to do so. My teacher said that gratitude and custom didn't seem very good descrip-

> tions of love. . . . I remember how frustrated I was because I thought he was just trying to make me write about his ideas. After struggling for a long time, I had a breakthrough. I wrote it down in my notebook because it came so suddenly I was afraid if I hadn't written it down it would've disappeared. Children should take care of their parents because they love them and feel responsible for their well being.
>
> My grandma is in a nursing home right now. . . . When my mom is not working, she spends a lot of time with my grandma. Even though my grandma may not recognize her sometimes, my mom feels she should be there by her side. She never says she's too tired, or it doesn't matter any more. Now I realize she's not going because she owes her or is obligated to do so. She goes because she truly loves her.

Laura's understanding of *King Lear* is anchored in the story of her mother and grandmother. She has placed this drama in the larger context of her life. When Laura submitted her portfolio for the second quarter, she dedicated it to her grandmother. This self-sponsored addition signaled her growing commitment to her work and provided a clear indication that curriculum mattered for her.

By reflecting, students may also accomplish a third outcome: establishing or demonstrating control over their learning. A personal sense of mastery is very closely linked to this sense of control. As students reveal their habits of mind, talking about the strategies that have resulted in their successes, they are made more aware of their capabilities and personal resources. For example, in a First reflection, Eve describes her thinking that led to a successful interpretation of "Storm Warnings," a poem by Adrienne Rich:

> I read the poem ten times before beginning. . . . Then, I tried to imagine the scene and the feelings. . . . The line that made an impact on my thinking was "These are the things we have learned to do." The light bulb went on in my head, and the meaning of the poem came to me. . . . A few days before I was talking to a school counselor. She asked me how things were and I replied, "Normal." She then said that normal is very subjective and not always good because people who live in abusive situations have gotten so used to it that it becomes normal. This conversation immediately came to mind when reading that line. I then looked in the poem to see if there was enough support to write of an abusive environment.

In her performance, Eve demonstrates her capacity to transfer her learning. She realizes the importance of carrying her experiences with her in her efforts to make sense of the poem. More important, she displays her capacity to control her thinking consciously and deliberately.

Through such reflection, she most certainly developed a sense of mastery in her work.

During reflection, students may also accomplish a fourth outcome: placing value on their efforts. As they review their work, they come to question its worth. In a Transformation reflection, Hedda expresses her frustration with her performance at the same time that she reveals her high expectations for herself:

> It might be suitable to explain this weird form of "paper." This is 100% recycled paper, made by me. Though it takes . . . time and patience, I get real satisfaction in the fact that I decide what goes in to make it, and sometimes what comes out can be very beautiful. . . . It is the same sort of satisfaction I desire in doing an English paper. . . . I determined a bulk of . . . my problem is . . . my process for writing. . . . Ideally, I'd like to sit in front of the typewriter, or computer, and write like mad. But in a masochistic sort of way I procrastinate. Let me show you the extent of my avoidance. It is 4:41 a.m. Monday morning, and here I am typing away. . . . I'm determined to come out of this class with a healthier outlook.

Hedda's remarks on her handmade paper show her desire for excellence. She is proud of her paper and wants to be as proud of her writing on the paper. While she is disappointed in her work, she sees her problems and has made a commitment to improve.

In Transformation reflections, some students move beyond seeing their problems to finding solutions in their own work. At times, they even imagine or create new solutions. In his Transformation reflection, Eric comments on his habit of organizing on a simple five-paragraph level:

> In essay writing, I come up with a theme and usually three major points. . . . The problem arises when I don't expand on those major points. In effect, I beat around with the same point. . . . For example, in my third paragraph I discuss Dilsey's charity. I explain how she has charity through various examples, but I do not explain the different types of charity or how charity might change from time to time. . . . My second paragraph is perhaps the most developed because I describe the different ways Dilsey keeps in touch with reality. I don't do this with other sections. They are both accompanied by the note "You can do more here." In fact, I can.

Within his reflection, Eric is able to define his problem and, in his own work, to find a sample of better performance. He also suggests how he might handle some of the work differently. While poor performance and low grades usually diminish students' confidence, the portfolio provides a setting for recovery and personal redemption. Students often reflect hardest on work which has not met expectations.

As the portfolio project moves into its final stages, I ask students to write prefaces to their portfolios. The reflection which comprises the preface is more comprehensive than that which accompanies each entry. At its simplest, the preface encourages students to clarify a specific area of learning. One student, for example, had struggled throughout high school with her writing. She explains, "I've never considered myself a good writer.... I always knew that writing was one of my weak points.... I came into English this year with a feeling that this year would be no different. However ... gradually I was improving." The portfolio encouraged this student to look very closely at one area of weakness, and, as a result, she discovered ways to improve.

On a deeper level, in some prefaces students identify very individualized goals for learning. They provide a framework for their reader's observations. One student writes,

> I had three goals which I hoped to achieve over the course of the year. Style ... Up to this point, my essays have been rather bland .... Organization. Just one look at my room is enough to convey the disordered character of my personality. And Liveliness ... I need to exhibit some passion.... This book is [my] history of transition.

In part because students have defined their growth in portfolio entries, and in part because portfolios encourage students to celebrate their successes, many students include in their prefaces very confident statements about learning. One young woman playfully notes her own habits of criticism and warns her reader against such behavior: "In my analysis of my writing, you may notice a ... cynical tone at some points. This is only because I like to criticize my own work. It only makes me work harder. Do not let this make you believe that I am open to your criticism." Another student expresses his confidence in another way: "My class this year has been full of challenges to go beyond what was expected, and to achieve not simply for a grade, but for personal satisfaction at knowing that I learned something valuable. This process of self discovery is an important one."

Perhaps the most gratifying prefaces are those in which students reconceptualize learning itself. The portfolio, in its emphasis upon personal learning, sometimes results in these types of reflections. One student beautifully captures her new conception of learning:

> I am a bricklayer in this institution of learning. I entered this class with the desire ... to improve my ability to lay bricks. I thought

that [I needed to] discover the right size to cut the blocks, the precise way to spread the mortar, and the most decorative way to display my work. Before this year, writing meant laying the bricks correctly.... Earning my living as a bricklayer has been one of my primary endeavors.... I have learned to lay the bricks exactly as my employer wanted. This year, I can proudly say I have begun to build a cathedral. I have stepped back from the bricks and the work to see the "big idea."

The quality of portfolio reflection is, I have come to understand, a matter of emerging commitment. Early in the year, portfolio reflection remains generally perfunctory. Then, as a means to encourage students to expand their efforts, I ask them, prior to the second submission, to share their portfolio with a classmate and to trade letters describing qualities which make it effective. Suddenly, the project takes on new meaning, and in subsequent submissions, students work hard to restructure their work. Prior to the last submission, students learn that they must write a preface and also share their portfolios with a parent or trusted adult. These requirements again engender commitment.

As I read portfolios, I am struck by the seriousness with which they come to be regarded. They assume the qualities of their creators and illustrate the unique curricula of their makers. Portfolio advocates have noted this highly personal nature of portfolio reflection and have suggested that this type of thinking represents an important stage in adolescent development. Roberta Camp and Denise Levine write, "[Reflection] is particularly critical for young adolescents who are attempting to make sense of their world and their place in it, to understand themselves and the nature of their relationships with others, and to clarify their values and establish habits of mind" (203).

The title of this chapter is drawn from a poem by Tera Welbourn, which she composed for the cover of her portfolio. In her preface, she confidently explains her feelings about reflection: "I believe that what I've learned from life should never be forgotten. These are the lessons that bleed.... After all, what is the purpose of dissecting a novel, ... if you do not use the author's ideas and messages to enrich your life." In her poem entitled "These Words," Tera writes about reflection and its power:

> During our search
> we struggle
> to keep
> the candle lit through

> the fierce winds,
> determined not
> to forget.
> Only words,
> > asleep beneath
> > the shadows,
> > at rest in
> > images past...
> > console us.
> > We grasp blindly,
> > finding our hands
> > full of them.
> These words...
> These words...
> > Too heavy
> > to hold, escaping
> > through our
> > fingers, doves in
> > hurried flight.
> > Their song
> > echoes still.
> These words...
> > Oh ancient words!
> > immortal words...
> > Once they've
> > found a home...
> > will bleed
> > eternally.

Note

A related article on portfolios, drawing on some of the same student material, appears as "Attending to the Rhythms and Intonations of Learning: Listening for Changes in Students' Portfolios" in *Assessment in the Learning Organization: Shifting the Paradigm* (1995), edited by Arthur L. Costa and Bena Kallick (Alexandria, VA: ASCD).

References

Camp, Roberta, and Denise Levine. 1991. "Portfolios Evolving." In *Portfolios: Process and Product*, edited by Pat Belanoff and Marcia Dickson. Portsmouth, NH: Boynton/Cook.

Costa, Arthur L., and Bena Kallick. 1995. *Assessment in the Learning Organization: Shifting the Paradigm*. Alexandria, VA: ASCD.

Kaiser, Rachel, Jennifer Rehak, Laura Guenser, Eve Zyzik, Hedda Auza, Eric Vymyslicky, and Kimberly Zielinski. 1992–94. Selected excerpts from twelfth-grade portfolios.

Welbourn, Tera. 1994. "These Words." Unpublished poem. Used by permission of the author.

Wiggins, Grant. 1991. "Standards, Not Standardization: Evoking Quality Student Work." *Educational Leadership* 48 (5): 18–25.

IV Time for Reflection

The title of this section has at least three meanings that are pertinent to this volume. In the first sense, learners need to have time set aside specifically for reflection on their language performance. This is the message of the two authors in this section. JoAnne Miller helps her sixth-grade students become independent learners by setting aside time for them to engage in focused goal setting and self-assessment. Reflection, she says, gives students a chance to "see [their] own growth." Teachers, too, need to set aside time to reflect on their own classroom practices and what these practices reveal about their assumptions and goals. Linda Shadiow poses crucial questions that serve to guide this reflective process. Shadiow's own answers to the questions she poses have enabled her to "find the ground and the horizon upon and within which [her] professional practices are set."

A second meaning of "time for reflection" is that reflection not only takes time but also must be engaged in repeatedly over time. Reflection involves stepping back and objectively considering one's performance, whether it's classroom teaching practices or one's own writing efforts. And this is a process that might well occur at the beginning, middle, or end of a teaching unit, semester, or year. By allowing time between reflections, we can gauge our own growth and changes in attitudes and abilities.

Finally, there is a third meaning for our section title. Now that you have read some or almost all of the essays in the volume, it is indeed time for reflection. It is time to reflect on the practicality and the value of implementing one or more of the instructional strategies that you have read about, and it is time to reflect on your own answer to the question, "How do students learn?" On such reflections, much of the quality of students' learning—and our teaching—depends.

26 Nourishing Independence through Self-Assessment

JoAnne P. Miller
Davis Middle School, Hillsdale, Michigan

There are several vehicles for learning. One has a front seat that accommodates only the teacher. The students sit in the back, unable to see ahead, and are expected to trust the teacher to drive carefully as she takes them down the road of education. Another has a space off to the side for the teacher. She stands out of the way lest the creativity of the students be stifled by her directions. Each student drives himself, and sometimes the classroom resembles a bumper car arena.

A new concept vehicle was developed specially for writing workshop. It has a front seat big enough for the teacher and all the students too. The teacher still sits behind the wheel, but each student is encouraged to read her own road map, knowing the teacher will help her when she needs the guidance.

Writing workshop entered my sixth-grade classroom and transformed it. When I asked my students to join me in the "ownership" (Atwell 1987) of the direction of our journey toward literacy, I saw a dramatic increase in their engagement with learning. Students wrote with vigor and commitment because I recognized the value of their thoughts and demonstrated my enthusiasm for their choices. I realized that "[t]eaching is less about what the teacher does than about what the teacher gets the students to do" (Perkins 1993).

What if, I thought, a student's involvement didn't end with a finished piece of writing? What if the responsibility for personal direction extended to the assessment process? What would happen if I helped students focus on what they were learning and how they were using their new learning to become better writers? Might not the learning through engagement continue and become deepened if we never asked students to relinquish ownership of their work?

Learning to Self-Assess

It was easier for the students to adapt to writing workshop than it was for them to adapt to assessing their own work. In their world, teachers had always been in charge of giving grades, and grading/evaluation/assessment had always meant checking whether the completed assignment had right or wrong answers. In writing workshop, process is as important as product, with growth in ability being the measure of "correctness." I wanted to help students stand back from their writing so that they could assess themselves in an objective way. To do this, I needed to develop and teach specific activities that would help the students understand how they demonstrate excellence as writers. I saw three areas:

> **Goal Setting** for focus
>
> **Journal Writing** to develop the habits of an author
>
> **Best Piece Assessment** to identify how personal writing is effective

Goal Setting

We set goals so that the path of life has a direction. Students sense this wisdom and feel more comfortable if they know what is expected of them. The establishment of goals for writing workshop is a responsibility shared by the student and me. At the beginning of each of our six marking periods, I establish "external criteria," a minimum number of finished pieces which must be completed by everyone, as well as how many different genres will be required. Students are responsible for "internal criteria" and decide which pieces of free writing they wish to develop, taking them through conferences, revisions, and editing with support and assistance from their peers and me. Although I provide the structure, the final decision making for personal direction lies with the student (Rief 1990). Along with the two goals that belong to everyone—"I will finish three pieces" and "I will write in two genres"—each student decides two other areas where he needs to concentrate effort to become a better writer.

Throughout the marking period the students review their goals. This way they are reminded of the behaviors and skills on which they chose to concentrate.

During the last week of each six-week marking period, the students assess how well they have met their goals. The act of stepping outside themselves to look at their actions and products for the marking period focuses their attention on what they did during writing workshop.

Stephanie's third goal was to "Do a careful and thorough job of revision." In her assessment she was specific about what she did.

> I was dedicated when I was writing. I looked at specific revision strategies like alternative leads, adding better descriptive words, and trying to show, not tell. In "Journey in the Mind" I tried to describe what I saw and what I felt emotionally. I never came right out and said, "I like to be alone." But I used positive and bright words as I described my visit to the beach. That gave the feeling of happiness.

It's not unusual for students to be unrealistic when they first assess their own work. Zach said, "I work hard. Some of my stories are good . . . write more in my Journal next time."

When this happens, I speak privately with the student to discover what he really meant. We look together through the writing workshop portfolio of finished pieces to see what was accomplished and how that compares with the goals that were established at the beginning of the marking period. A clarification of the connection between goals, actions, and products is usually helpful in establishing the necessary objectivity.

Focused goal setting and a realistic self-assessment of how successfully goals were met are the first steps for developing independent learners. They are essential steps if each student is going to assume the responsibility for the direction of his or her own learning.

Journal Writing

Authors have two jobs: they develop an idea to write about and they write. Students need to establish an independence from their teachers as they become authors. Through journal writing, students can be taught the skills of generating topics and writing fluidly on their own.

Journal writing is freewriting, a continuous flow of thoughts and ideas. The key is to put your writing implement on the paper and to write, even if you have no direction at first. This is what many published authors do when they run out of ideas or get stuck. If students will just write, something will come up that interests them. Getting students to write, however, can be a Herculean task.

During journal writing, I ask the students to move their desks into a circle. Those students who have established the habit of nonparticipation are stymied by this furniture arrangement. No one can hide and do nothing. I am careful to assure a situation that feels tolerable to students by having us write no more than five minutes at the beginning of the year. Even with this cautious limitation of time, I still must periodically look up from my own writing and give an encouraging nod or smile to those who aren't writing. By November or December almost all of my sixth graders are capable of sustained writing for twenty-five minutes or more.

The opportunity to have others hear what's going on in your life is a seductive incentive to write, and we end each Journal Time with an opportunity for several students to share their written thoughts. It's common for students to come to school on Journal Day anxious to get started so they can share what has happened to them recently.

As the students become acclimated to the routine of journal writing, disruptive students find that their audience has dwindled; the other students become absorbed in their writing so that they can read to the class. With no response from their peers, the usual disrupters become writers too and develop the habits that authors need in order to be successful.

Deciding what to write about goes hand in hand with writing. Teaching students how to come up with an idea independently is necessary if we are to liberate them from the belief that learning can happen only if a teacher is present. Periodically we have a "topic search" (Atwell 1987 and Koch 1992), a guided brainstorming in which the students are helped to identify attitudes, beliefs, or incidents they might want to write about. The topic search begins with a general theme. The students put this topic heading on the top line of their writing journals. Then we proceed with a guided brainstorming which follows this form:

> We're going to think about Heroes. Jot down two or three people you have not met who are your heroes.... Now jot down two or three people you have met who are your heroes.... Finally, jot down two or three ways you might be a hero to someone else.... Check two to three of your responses that you would like to write about.... Now choose one to write about today.

The form for brainstorming is similar regardless of the topic. Even if the student chooses not to base her journal entry on the topic suggested, she becomes familiar with a way to generate topics. The topic search will be a method for students to use independently to discover ideas to write about in the future.

Organized and intentional journal writing helps students to become authors. The last week of the marking period is the time for students to become their own critics as they assess the effectiveness of their involvement with topic generation and freewriting. Looking back at what has been written one to five weeks earlier gives each student more objectivity in viewing himself.

Andrew explained how he looked for new topics when he said, "I looked around the room for things to write about. On page 3 you see I got the idea from a poster in the classroom and wrote about it."

Samantha spent each Journal Day intent on her writing. In her Journal Assessment she wrote,

> I have five entries in my Writing Journal. I really put a lot of thought into it. I journeyed through me to find what was on my mind. . . . I listened to my classmates' ideas to get ideas for myself. I opened myself up. Any idea that rolled into my head was at least considered. . . . During Journal time I kept writing. I know this because all of my entries are long (at least three pages).

The act of reflecting on their entries over time gives students insight not possible on a daily basis. If reflection detects a lack of indicators of excellence in their entries, I have the opportunity to explore with individual students specific behaviors and attitudes that they can practice during the next marking period.

Best Piece Assessment

As the teacher I must help each student make good choices in deciding when his piece needs further work and when it is finished. When a student submits a finished piece, he attaches all drafts and conference sheets to an "Application for Acceptance." This is a simple sheet with identifying information, a short statement from the student on where he got the idea, a list of revision strategies used, and signatures from those with whom he conferred and had an editing conference (Galley 1994). This is where I can exert quality control by not accepting a piece before it has been reasonably revised and edited. It also provides an opportunity for me to do some individual teaching to show a student specific things that she can do to become a more alert and self-regulating writer.

In the last week of each six-week marking period, each student decides which of the three finished pieces that she has done is the best. As a class we list the literary techniques we learned, the revision skills we used, and the editing we focused on during that marking period.

Each student then reflects on what made his best piece good. Using quotations from the piece and explanations of how certain literary devices were used to add interest, power, etc., each student becomes his own reader and critic. Appreciation of one's own skill (which the passage of time brings) can create a sense of satisfaction. Jeremy was delighted with the poem he chose for his journal writing, one he had finished three weeks earlier and hadn't read since. He called me over while he was writing his self-assessment. "I didn't know I meant to have this theme of loneliness when I was writing this piece," he sighed, with awe on his face. "It's a great poem."

With distance between the writing and the self-assessment, Jeremy could see his own growth. And seeing personal excellence can become a spur to further effort and an encouragement to try harder. Jeremy's assessment reflected his own pleasure, not only in his finished piece, but also in the process he followed. In the writing of his piece, he used the best methods of freewriting that he had developed during journal writing as well as the skills of prewriting and revision that he had learned from minilessons which had preceded daily writing time.

> I spent time on this! I thought about it a lot. I was sitting in the dining room eating my quarter pounder with cheese and an idea rolled into my head. I really didn't want to lose that idea, so I excluded myself from conversation, afraid I would forget. When I was done, I stormed up the stairs like a jack rabbit being chased by a rattlesnake. I sat up there at my desk for two hours writing.
>
> I put feeling into this. I felt like I had to write this, not want to, had to, not for a grade either. I've had this on my mind for awhile. Here are some quotes that show my feelings. "We will wonder until we destroy the things we wonder about..."

Conclusion

Independent learners set goals for themselves, establish the habits that will lead to success, and are objective, perceptive observers of themselves and their products. As writers they are both author and audience, both creator and critic.

Through the teaching of techniques for self-assessment, we can shift the attention of our students away from reliance on us for a nod of approval or a frown of dissatisfaction. We can help them become the learner and the teacher as writing and assessment become so interconnected that there is no separation between the two.

References

Atwell, Nancie. 1987. *In the Middle: Reading, Writing, and Learning with Adolescents.* Portsmouth, NH: Boynton/Cook.

Galley, Sharon. 1994. MELAF (Michigan English Language Arts Framework) materials. Michigan Department of Education.

Koch, Richard. 1992. *Writing Workshop I Seminar for Teachers.* Hillsdale, MI.

Perkins, David. 1993. "Teaching for Understanding." *American Educator* (Fall): 28–35.

Rief, Linda. 1990. "Finding the Value in Evaluation: Self-Assessment in a Middle School Classroom." *Educational Leadership* 47 (March): 24–29.

27 How-Two: Learning about the Horizons of Our Teaching Selves

Linda Shadiow
Northern Arizona University, Flagstaff

Things take on importance against a background of intelligibility. Let us call this a horizon. It follows that one of the things we can't do, if we are to define ourselves significantly, is suppress or deny the horizons against which things take on significance for us.

Charles Taylor, *The Ethics of Authenticity*

For quite a while the stories I told relatives and nonteacher friends about my work in high school classrooms constituted an unrelated parade of how-to's. Describing things I did in the classroom to introduce a Cervantes novel or the noun clause seemed to have entertainment value and make me feel like a teacher. Somewhere along the line, however, I did sense what for me was an emerging distinction between "teaching" and "being a teacher." Looking back, I see that I was so hypnotized by the singular moments of teaching success or failure resulting from my use of an expanding collection of how-to's, it took me a while to recognize that each choice was making a contribution to an accumulating sum. Periodically stepping back to see what patterns my instructional choices formed, and to see the landscape of significance within which those choices were being made, introduced me to the *how-also* element of my professional practice. On one level, it is as simple as going home from NCTE conferences with a bulging packet of handouts from Idea Exchanges (the how-to's), separating the sheets into "possibly" and "not likely," and then, before filing or discarding those piles, seeing what I could learn about my evolving teaching self from reviewing the how-to's within each (thus, the *how-too*). On another level, it is the same complex task I ask of students as their own work accumulates over a semester and which is something more than a perfunctory accounting of their reflections or responses to a series of assignments. It is, instead, a willingness to review, to re-vision, and to rethink—a reflexive process where the doing and the thinking about the doing are interdependent but not duplicative and, in the discovery of their influence upon each other, lead to thinking *beyond* the doing.

Choice Making and the *How-To*

At times over the years, the choice making that teaching involves threatened to swallow me whole—select a book, select a passage, select an approach, select a student, select a topic, select a digression . . . the rhythm of classroom interaction has stops and starts, each seemingly punctuated by choices. The quick pace and gathering speed of the curriculum left little time to inventory my choices, let alone consider what I might learn from the results of such an accounting. While I had read Dewey's *Democracy and Education* (1916) in my preservice days, the significance of his point that mere activity does not constitute experience was not something I purposefully contemplated (131). Since the how-to's of more experienced and successful teachers were readily available, I reasoned I could benefit from their success (I hoped to duplicate it), and could save both students and myself from the painful ramifications of my inexperience.

In retrospect, the how-to's collected from every source I could put my hands on served as a comfortable but dangerous hiding place. I believed other teachers had some kind of natural gift that I lacked but could compensate for with bulging file folders of their promising practices; these were classroom activities I had never thought of, and the student responses they described were not evident inside Room E-13 at BSHS. Confidence in my own work strangely decreased as the size of my file folders increased, and I had little if any awareness of the double-edged nature of these early choices. It did not occur to me that "What teachers do is neither natural nor necessary but based on choice," nor did I sense any accompanying imperative: "Since choice may harden into custom or dissipate into whim, one asks for justification" (Buchmann and Floden 1993, 145).

The how-to's were hypnotic in their promises and potential but lulling in the insatiable appetite they created for more. Maybe it was when I tried to develop a comprehensive categorization system (in the days before a computer program would have made such a step an easy one), that I realized I might be misusing the well-intentioned generosity of my colleagues. More likely this realization resulted from the painful criticism offered by a candid (heroic?) student trying to survive in a classroom too influenced by teachers who were *not* a part of the context and orchestrated by a teacher who was but who did not understand that fact. Some current professional literature labels this as a "methods fetish" (Bartolome 1994, 174) and even suggests that an antimethods pedagogy would better serve education (Macedo 1994, xviii). In order to look more critically at the how-to's I chose, I first needed to find a manageable starting point. I offer, for the remainder of this essay, a description of the process that has helped me in the critical *how-two* aspect of my work. Rather than presume that these sample questions apply to contexts other than mine, I use them to illustrate, not to prescribe. It is in the same spirit that colleagues through the years have shared their *how-to*'s, that I now add *how-too*.

A Brief Inventory: Question Set A

On a sheet of paper, put down the items that come immediately to mind as responses to the following questions. Doing this now, even in the margins of this essay, is likely to be more beneficial than waiting until the conclusion of the essay because subsequent suggestions are related to your responses here.

1. What are the names of three books (or the names of three authors) you would recommend as important reading for educators?
2. In your own history as a student, what are three different incidents that stick out in your mind as significant?
3. In your life as a teacher, what are three classroom lessons or practices that you view as having been successful?
4. In your life as an educator, who are three students through the years that you have found yourself telling other people about? And, briefly, what is an aspect of each story that makes the student and the story memorable?

Educator Vito Perrone (1991) observes that for reflective teachers, he has found that collections of observations, rather than singular descriptions, are "a means of getting [teachers] closer to their practice" (86). It is the collection which emerges from a seemingly straightforward inventory that is the basis for looking toward horizons against which the cases are set; the subsequent exploration provides the opportunity for thinking beyond the doing. The poet Pablo Neruda uses a metaphor of the cartographer setting out to discover one's internal landscape in his poem, "We are many." When I first read the poem I was struck by the explicit aim in the concluding lines: "that when I explain myself / I will be talking geography" (1958, 101). The challenge to strive toward this degree of professional consciousness, however, is accompanied by the possible pitfall of egocentric navel-gazing. While I am interested in my horizons—my professional geography—it is because of the potential that such an exploration carries for teaching me about what Ricoeur (1978) calls the "voluntary and involuntary moments of consciousness" (3) that guide my teaching and thus have consequences for the students with whom I work.

Patternings and the *How-Too*

A search that presumes steps toward achieving a cross-contextual consistency holds the same potential limitations as an uncritical use of a collection of how-to's. The fossilization of promising practices encompassed by the notion of *consistency* (a move "toward duplicative repetition or order") ignores the dynamic context of daily classroom life, whereas aiming for a professional wakefulness in exploring the *coherence* of those practices moves "toward patterns where irregularities can be recognized and encompassed, not exorcised" (for a discussion of this distinction, see Buchmann and Floden, Chapter 11). It is in a coherence which permits rather than eliminates conflict and doubt that we ultimately accept the intellectual responsibility I had previously found defensible ways to avoid. While there would be a security in formulating some bogus rules for a teaching practice *consistent* with my professional and political beliefs, the dynamic nature of students and their classroom contexts would again be excluded. I would rather wrestle with the tension and potential that work toward *coherence* brings. The self-examination is not meant to mold a justification for existing practices, but instead to look more intently at them with an "ethos of nonprescription, situatedness . . . and play" (Lenzo 1995, 19). This ethos encompasses elements of moral obligation and ethical responsibility integral to classroom choice making but not always evident or accessible when single practices are the focus of reflection.

Suggestions for Exploration: Question Set B

"When such patterns are not seen, alternatives are not envisioned" (Buchmann and Floden 1993, 36). Looking at the responses for each of the four questions in Set A, there are many different lenses which can be used to explore patterns within the choice making. A review of those responses can be used to initiate thinking about the following questions:

1. When you look at the authors or books identified as significant enough to merit a serious recommendation to colleagues, what perspectives do they have in common? What view of education do they put forth or represent? What characterizations are made of students? Of teachers?

2. When you look at the elements identified as significant school stories in your life as a student, what roles are played by the student? What roles are played by the teacher?
3. When you look at the elements identified as successful instructional strategies, what roles are played by the students? What roles are played by you as teacher? What constitutes success?
4. In looking at the students whose stories are memorable enough for you to identify as part of your own story, can you see coherent elements in the situations? In attitudes? In personality? In actions? In outcomes?

Questions like these invite me inside my own teaching to learn things that student course evaluations and supervisory reviews cannot offer. The inextricable threads of the art and science in teaching, of action and intent, of intended and unintended consequences, combine to make me nervous about taking the popular advertising slogan "Just Do It!" as a mantra for education. I don't want to be lost in some labyrinthian analysis, but I also don't want to presume that my well-intentioned choices automatically bring only the consequences I envision.

Suggestions for Elaboration: Question Set C

The tangle of intentions, consequences, motives, and assumptions is threaded—even knotted—through methodological choices. Even as I became more aware of my teaching as purposeful action, I looked for ways to understand the origin of its textures: "[the teacher's] intentions will be inevitably affected by the assumptions he [sic] makes regarding human nature and human possibility. Many of these assumptions are hidden; most have never been articulated . . . to achieve clarity and full consciousness, the teacher must attempt to make such assumptions explicit; for only then can they be examined, analyzed, and understood" (Greene 1973, 69–70). Varying the first four questions (from Set A) can provide another way to look for the texture in the patterns that might be emerging. The responses can then be explored with the other sets of questions as well as with any number of observations for comparison.

1. What are the names of three books or authors you would be reluctant to recommend to educational colleagues?
2. In your own history as a student, what are three events that you might have *expected* to be significant but which, in reality for you, were not?
3. In your life as a teacher, what are three instructional practices that you have tried but discarded over the years as being less than successful?

4. In your life as an educator, who are three students who are on the edge of your memory, students whose stories have not been or are not likely to be a part of the storehouse of images that constitute your own story making about teaching?

While such explorations can provide opportunities to illuminate some of the patterns formed by the accumulation of choices, the impetus underlying the choices is less easily accessible, but no less important. In "Prospective Immigrants Please Note," poet Adrienne Rich writes about the consequences presented by the decision to open actual and metaphorical doors, and she warns, "If you go through / there is always the risk / of remembering your name." Then, after acknowledging that it "is possible / to live worthily" without going through the door, she writes that such a choice means "much will blind you, / much will evade you, / at what cost who knows?" (59). What values underlie the choices I make in the classroom related to content, students, practices, achievement, sanctions? Because I am a teacher, observation is an integral and undeniable part of everything I do, but what if I observe the very nature of my observations?

Looking more closely at even the term "observation" makes the sham of its neutrality visible. One philosopher says we all have a "moral squint" that characterizes how we observe:

> We focus. We scan. We search. We scrutinize. We stare. We give dirty looks. When we look into things, we may take close looks, quick looks, hard looks, long looks, or honest looks. We look with favor and disfavor. We can look around; we look askance; and we overlook things. We look down on people, up to people, and out for people (McGrath 1994, x).

Coupling the how-to's of my work with a deliberate how-too asks me to be more conscious of the "moral squint" I bring into the classroom practices I use, to find the ground and the horizon upon and within which my professional practices are set.

Professional Growth and the *How-Two*

During one summer's leisure reading I wrote down a line paraphrased from one of Douglas Adams's books (I think it was *Hitchhiker's Guide to the Galaxy* [1991]): "I only know as much about myself as my current state permits." It seems the foreground and background of my work as an educator are in continual motion in relationship to the multiple contexts of the day, the circumstance, and the students, as well as to my own willingness to go through the door alluded to in Rich's lines. This incrementally self-reflexive process has many names in the professional literature: e.g., Maxine Greene (1973) talks about bringing a "wakefulness" to teaching, William Hare (1985) defends "open-mindness," Max Van Manen (1991) calls it "pedagogic thoughtfulness," and Dewey (1910) explicates "reflection." Each explanatory version, however, points to the importance of doing "more than making an individual aware of his or her life situation . . . it requires using narratives to invite *critical engagement*" (McLaughlin and Tierney 1993, 239).

Given that I had found help in my search for how-to's in the work of other teachers, it is not surprising to me that the teaching stories of other educators helped my initial understanding of the critical engagement characterizing the how-too. Kindergarten teacher Vivian Gussin Paley provides skillful insight into her own process in many books. The ongoing dialogue she engages in with her students and herself is dramatically illustrated in the recent book, *Kwanzaa and Me* (1995), which is itself prompted by the remarks of a returning student about whom she had written nearly two decades earlier in *White Teacher* (1979). Paley is tenacious in her exploration and examination of the impetus for and consequences of her teaching, and she eloquently presents the stories of the students and parents who are her partners in this examination. In doing so, she illustrates *engagement with* rather than *isolation from* as a significant characteristic of *how-too* in the school context.

Suggestions for Examination: Question Set D

"My discovering my identity doesn't mean that I work it out in isolation but that I negotiate it through dialogue, partly overt, partly internalized, with others" (Taylor 1991, 47). These *others* can, in fact, be colleagues met in print and not just those in the immediate school community. Here are a few reflection prompts along with examples of varied passages from the professional literature that illustrate the potential for dialogue that the results of the how-too can provoke.

1. Read each of the following passages with this question in mind: Do the patterns of my practices resonate with, contradict, or exclude the perspectives of what I read in professional literature?

> There is a pedagogical optimism that expects too much of parents and teachers, and too little of the child in how and what the child contributes to his or her own growth and development (Van Manen 1991, 221).

> Contemporary school practices of all kinds seem to encourage the more passive kind of cognition. One set of school practices

favors passivity by continually telling students what to do. The opposing set of practices favors passivity by encouraging students to follow their spontaneous interests and impulses. Largely absent, scarcely even contemplated, are school practices that encourage students to assume responsibility for what becomes of their minds (Bereiter and Scardamalia 1987, 361).

We want to define teachers as an active community of participants whose function is to establish public spaces where students can debate, appropriate, and learn the knowledge necessary to live in a critical democracy. By public space we mean, as Hannah Arendt did, a concrete set of learning conditions where people come together to speak, to engage in dialogue, to share their stories, and to struggle within social relations that strengthen rather than weaken possibilities for active citizenship (Giroux and McLaren 1986, 237).

2. What does each finding about my teaching enable and constrain in student learning?

3. From what ground do my actions arise? From what understandings do my explanations emerge?

Receding and Expanding Horizons

In the play *Peer Gynt* (1867), Ibsen gives us a story of the consequences of unreflective habit. When Aasse Gynt tells her young son fanciful stories to entertain him during difficult times, she assumes he doesn't need to understand their origin or her intent. Then when, as a consequence, he grows into a woefully unreflective adolescent relying on increasingly fantastic fabrications as evidence of his own biography, she laments: "Who would have thought the stories would cling to him so?" As an educator, what stories, in their tellings and retellings, in their construction and their reconstruction, cling to me so? What is the impact of this on the students with whom I work? By understanding my own horizons, what can I contribute to an environment that invites others to do the same?

And when I wonder if there is enough time in my teaching schedule for the how-too, I am reminded of Israel Scheffler's words. While philosopher Charles Taylor links knowledge of the horizons which influence our daily actions with the ethics of authenticity, Scheffler (1991, ix) points specifically to our classroom contexts: "Education is at once the most intimate and the most far-reaching of human endeavors.... It challenges us to be clearer in our thinking, more responsible in our beliefs, and more alive to the aims and consequences of our actions."

References

Adams, Douglas. 1979. *Hitchhiker's Guide to the Galaxy.* New York: Pocket.

Bartolome, Lilia I. 1994. "Beyond the Methods Fetish: Toward a Humanizing Pedagogy." *Harvard Educational Review* 64 (2): 173–193.

Bereiter, Carl, and Marlene Scardamalia. 1987. *The Psychology of Written Composition.* Hillsdale, NJ: Erlbaum.

Buchmann, Margaret, and Robert Floden. 1993. *Detachment and Concern: Conversations in the Philosophy of Teaching and Teacher Education.* New York: Teachers College.

Dewey, John. 1916. *Democracy and Education.* New York: Macmillan.

Dewey, John. 1910. *How We Think.* Boston: Heath.

Giroux, Henry, and Peter McLaren. 1986. "Teacher Education and the Politics of Engagement: The Case for Democratic Schooling." *Harvard Educational Review* 56 (3): 213–38.

Greene, Maxine. 1973. *Teacher as Stranger.* Belmont, CA: Wadsworth.

Hare, William. 1985. *In Defense of Open-Mindedness.* Montreal: McGill-Queen's University Press.

Ibsen, Henrik. [1867] 1989. *Peer Gynt.* Translated by Johan Fillinger. World's Classics edition. Oxford, England: Oxford University Press.

Lenzo, Kate. 1995. "Validity and Self-Reflectivity Meet Poststructuralism: Scientific Ethos and the Transgressive Self." *Educational Researcher* 24(4): 17–23.

Macedo, Donaldo. 1994. "Foreword." Pages xiii–xviii in *Politics of Liberation: Paths from Freire,* edited by Peter McLaren and Colin Lankshear. New York: Routledge.

McGrath, Elizabeth Z. 1994. *Art of Ethics: A Psychology of Ethical Beliefs.* Chicago: Loyola University Press.

McLaughlin, Daniel, and William Tierney. 1993. *Naming Silenced Lives: Personal Narratives and the Process of Educational Change.* New York: Routledge.

Neruda, Pablo. [1958] 1993. *Extravagaria.* Translated by Alastair Reid. Austin: University of Texas Press.

Paley, Vivian. 1995. *Kwanzaa and Me: A Teacher's Story.* Cambridge, MA: Harvard University Press.

Paley, Vivian. 1979. *White Teacher.* Cambridge, MA: Harvard University Press.

Perrone, Vito. 1991. *A Letter to Teachers: Reflections in Schooling and the Art of Teaching.* San Francisco: Jossey-Bass.

Rich, Adrienne. 1963. *Snapshots of a Daughter-in-Law: Poems 1954–1962.* New York: Harper.

Ricoeur, Paul. 1978. "Unity of the Voluntary and Involuntary as a Limiting Idea." In *The Philosophy of Paul Ricoeur: An Anthology of His Work*, edited by Charles Reagan and David Stewart. Boston: Beacon.

Scheffler, Israel. 1991. *In Praise of Cognitive Emotions.* New York: Routledge.

Taylor, Charles. 1991. *Ethics of Authenticity.* Cambridge, MA: Harvard University Press.

Van Manen, Max. 1991. *The Tact of Teaching: The Meaning of Pedagogical Thoughtfulness*. Albany: SUNY Press.

Editors

Louann Reid taught junior and senior high school English, speech, and drama for nineteen years. She is associate professor of English and director of English education at Colorado State University. She teaches undergraduate and graduate courses including adolescents' literature; methods of teaching language arts; teaching composition; theories of teaching literature; and theories of language, literacy, and learning. She works with secondary school teachers in Colorado on standards and assessment, literature instruction, censorship issues, and teacher research. A frequent presenter at state and national conferences, she is author and co-author of several articles in state and national English and speech journals. With Fran Claggett and Ruth Vinz, she has written six supplemental textbooks for high school students, emphasizing processes and projects that help students reflect and connect. She has served as a member of the NCTE Committee on Classroom Practices and the Information Literacy Committee and is chair of the Conference on English Leadership.

Jeffrey N. Golub is associate professor of English education at the University of South Florida in Tampa. For the previous twenty years, he taught English, speech communication, and writing classes at both the junior and senior high school levels in Seattle, Washington. In addition to his teaching, Golub works extensively with NCTE. He has served on the Council's Executive Committee, the Secondary Section Committee, and the Commission on the English Curriculum. He has written one book, *Activities for an Interactive Classroom*, and has edited two Classroom Practices volumes, *Activities to Promote Critical Thinking* and *Focus on Collaborative Learning*. Currently he chairs the Information Literacy Committee for NCTE and is a past member-at-large for the Conference on English Leadership. Golub has given several presentations and workshops at NCTE conferences and for teachers in school districts around the country. His topics include the interactive classroom, computers and writing instruction, and responding to poetry and other literature.

Golub and Reid emphasize constructive, reflective approaches in their methods classes. They collaborate frequently, presenting workshops and writing articles for publication. One of their articles won the *English Journal* writing award in 1989.

Contributors

Brandi J. Abbott was a student at Westmoreland Community College when she co-wrote her chapter in this volume. Presently she is a psychology major also earning teaching certification in elementary education at Seton Hall College in Greensburg, Pennsylvania. She anticipates pursuing an M. A. in elementary education.

Stephen Adkison is a teaching fellow in the Composition and Rhetoric program at the University of Nevada, Reno. He is especially interested in interdisciplinary modes of learning and teaching and has presented papers on this topic at both regional and national conferences. He has taught "reading and writing the culture" approaches in the Huron Shores Writing Institute and Mühlhausen Initiative International Writing Workshop in Mühlhausen, Germany, and in the Truckee River Project (Reading and Writing the West Institute) closer to home.

Jacob Blumner directs the writing center and teaches at Kent State University–Stark Campus in Canton, Ohio. His research interests include writing centers, writing across the curriculum, and comparisons of cultures through writing. He has participated in the Huron Shores Writing Institute and Mühlhausen Initiative International Writing Workshop in Michigan and in Mühlhausen, Germany, and he has published articles on writing across the curriculum and assessment.

Kelly A. Carameli is a single mother enrolled in the nursing program at Westmoreland County Community College, Youngwood, Pennsylvania. She enjoys reading, writing, and gardening. Another current project is raising quail to be used in training bird dogs.

Meta G. Carstarphen, assistant professor of journalism at the University of North Texas in Denton, was selected as a 1993 CCCC Scholar for the Dream for her research on race, rhetoric, and the media. Carstarphen teaches courses in mass media theory, public relations, and contemporary issues in journalism.

Dan Chabas has been teaching English for more than eleven years and is currently at Douglas County High School in Castle Rock, Colorado. He's *this* close to finishing his master's degree in English and the teaching of writing, with a focus on the ways in which students make connections with the curriculum. He's part of a unique teacher-researcher program, the Douglas County Higher Literacy Project, that is sponsored by the district's staff development office. He writes approximately one poem every three years and could be convinced to call himself "a peripheral visionary" (Stephen Wright).

Richard H. Fehlman is associate professor in the English department at the University of Northern Iowa where he teaches courses in general education as well as English methods. A high school English teacher for over twenty years, Fehlman has taught film and mass media courses as well as written a number of articles and made numerous conference presentations about the importance of developing students' media literacy skills. A former member of NCTE's National Media Commission and past chair of NCTE's Assembly on Media Arts, he is currently working on methods for integrating the development of critical viewing skills into English language arts curricula, K–12.

Francis Fritz is a graduate fellow in the Composition and Rhetoric program at the University of Nevada, Reno. His interest in the social interactions that inform writing has led to his participation in the Mühlhausen writing workshops. Fritz is also a poet who has been published most recently in *California English*. He is in his sixth year of teaching composition.

Bruce Goebel taught middle school language arts and science for several years, and he now teaches English education and American literature for the Department of English at Western Washington University. His articles have appeared in *English Journal, Philological Quarterly,* and *Journal of American Culture*, and he edited, along with James Hall, a collection of pedagogical essays titled *Teaching A "New Canon"? Students, Teachers, and Texts in the College Literature Classroom* (1995).

Claudia Greenwood has taught literature and composition at the Ashtabula campus of Kent State for nearly thirty years. With the teaching of children's and adolescent literature classes, she supports the associate-degree education curriculum. She accomplishes additional articulation with the secondary schools through a grant for teacher retraining in writing instruction.

Carol Jago teaches English at Santa Monica High School in Santa Monica, California. She also directs the California Reading and Literature Project at UCLA and has served as director for the NCTE Commission on Literature. Writing a weekly education column for a local newspaper and regular op-ed pieces for the *Los Angeles Times* has given her a unique perspective on teaching the reflective essay.

Larry R. Johannessen is associate professor of education and serves as secondary education coordinator at Benedictine University in Lisle, Illinois. He taught high school English and history for twelve years and has directed workshops and inservice programs for teachers in writing, thinking, and literature instruction. In addition to his journal articles, book chapters, and textbooks, he is the author of *Illumination Rounds: Teaching the Literature of the Vietnam War* (1992) and co-author of two popular NCTE publications: *Writing about Literature* (1984) and *Designing and Sequencing Prewriting Activities* (1982). He is a frequent speaker at NCTE conventions and affiliate conferences.

Daniel L. Kain is assistant professor of secondary education at Northern Arizona University in Flagstaff. He currently teaches methods of secondary teaching and evaluation of learning. Prior to teaching at the university, he taught English, speech, and history at the junior high and high school levels in Bozeman, Montana. His article in this volume reflects his interest in cooperative learning and student-centered projects, as well as teaching speakers and writers to attend to their audiences.

Barbara King-Shaver received her doctorate in education from Rutgers University, where she worked with Janet Emig on the original New Jersey Writing Project. King-Shaver has been a classroom teacher for more than twenty-five years, teaching students from fifth grade through graduate school. She currently is supervisor of English and social studies in South Brunswick, New Jersey, where she also teaches Advanced Placement English. In addition, King-Shaver has taught courses in reading, and in reading and writing across the curriculum, at Rutgers Graduate School of Education in New Brunswick, New Jersey. She has published articles on English and assessment in *English Leadership Quarterly* and *Focus on Education*.

Cynthia G. Kuhn is a doctoral student at the University of Denver. She received a B.A. in English from the University of Kansas and an M.A. in rhetoric and the teaching of writing from the University of Colorado at Denver, where she taught composition and held the position of assistant director of the writing program.

Sheryl Lain, director of the Wyoming Writing Project, has taught secondary English since 1968. She teaches part-time and coordinates K–12 language arts curriculum for Laramie County School District #1. Lain also serves as WyATE's NCTE liaison officer and as the editor of the WyATE newsletter *Sage*. She is a poet and creative nonfiction writer, and her work appears in national, regional, and state magazines, including *Christian Century, Inland Journal, Crone Chronicles,* and Delta Kappa Gamma's *Bulletin*. She co-authored an illustrated history of Wyoming, *Wyoming the Proud Land*, and she edited *Let Your Light Shine*, a collection of biographies of Wyoming pioneer educators.

Maria Madruga is a graduate student at the University of Nevada, Reno, where she teaches composition and a youth Native American writing workshop. She is interested in cross-cultural education as her thesis focuses on bridging Native American values with mainstream education. In addition, she teaches for the Huron Shores Writing Institute international writing program in Mühlhausen, Germany.

Kathryn Megyeri has been an English teacher in Maryland for more than thirty-three years. She has combined the study of writing and gerontology to publish intergenerational writings by her students and elderly persons. Her freelance work has appeared in journals such as the *Maryland English Journal, English Journal, Delaware Magazine, The Journal* *of Nursing Care, Journal of Reading, Perspectives on Aging,* and *Das Altenheim.* She has received two National Endowment for the Humanities grants and is a Maryland Student Service Alliance fellow on a grant from the Commission on National and Community Service. She has received the Outstanding Alumna Award from her college and the Dworkin Award for Outstanding Service to Youth. She writes a monthly column on education issues for *Women Today* magazine.

David S. Miall was educated in England, where he taught for ten years. Since 1990 he has worked at the University of Alberta, where he is associate professor of English. He has written a number of papers about student learning and teaching methods in the literature classroom and is currently completing a book on the topic. Other interests include empirical study of readers' responses to literary texts, and the literature of the romantic period, including Coleridge, Wordsworth, and Gothic fiction. He is also author of *Romanticism: The CD-ROM* (1997), which contains a hypertext anthology of texts, art, and photographs relating to the romantic period.

JoAnne P. Miller, a public school teacher for more than twenty-one years, currently offers Reading Workshop, Writing Workshop, and math to sixth graders at Davis Middle School in Hillsdale, Michigan. Miller has been involved in the Future Problem Solving Program, publishing articles on the program in *For Coaches by Coaches, Creating More Creative Students,* and *The Brainstormer.* She has also published "Going Through the Change" in *Literacy Consortium Magazine,* focusing on how she has moved from "teacher of the text" to "teacher of students" in a writing workshop.

Patrick Monahan is a teacher of English and is department head at Downers Grove South, a large suburban high school in Illinois. About his interest in assessment, Monahan explains, "I have the opportunity to observe good teachers and good students at work almost every day and through them I have really come to appreciate and respect classroom learning." He presents regularly at state and national conferences on topics ranging from large-scale literature assessment to performance-based learning in the writing workshop. Most recently he published an article on portfolios in *Assessment and the Learning Organization* (1995). He has served as a member-at-large of the Conference on English Leadership.

Dana Nevil holds B.A. and M.A. degrees in English from the University of Georgia and is a doctoral student at Georgia State University, where she is working on a degree in language and literacy. Dana has been teaching high school English for more than ten years in Atlanta, Georgia, at Lithonia High School. She has presented her experiences with multicultural poetry in the classroom at NCTE and GCTE conferences and is currently writing her dissertation on this topic.

Thomas Philion is assistant professor of English and the assistant director of the secondary English teacher education program at the University of Illinois at Chicago. A former middle school teacher, he has participated in a variety of collaborative research projects with urban educators. His current interests lie in portfolios, methods of teacher research, and adolescent literacy.

Leslie Richardson received her M.A. from The Johns Hopkins University and completed a Ph.D. in literature and creative writing at the University of Houston. She developed the project described in her article when she taught writing in the Houston public schools through the Writers in the Schools Program. For four years, she created weekly writing projects for students, modeling the teaching of creative writing for their teachers. She teaches a creative writing workshop in poetry as well as courses in composition and rhetoric at Southern Methodist University.

Erika Scheurer is assistant professor of English at the University of St. Thomas in St. Paul, Minnesota. She teaches writing, writing theory, and literature at all levels and is interested in the areas where composition and literary studies intersect. In her current book-length project, she is exploring the letters and poems of Emily Dickinson in light of contemporary voice theory.

Darrell g.h. Schramm is a poet and writer as well as a composition and poetry instructor who has taught for more than twenty-six years in the U.S. and abroad. Currently he teaches part-time at the University of San Francisco. A consultant for the Bay Area Writing Project, he has given workshops on college and high school composition, on portfolios and writing assessment, and on reader response. In addition to poems, stories, book reviews and nonacademic articles, he has published work in *California English, English Journal* and *Kansas English*.

Renate Schulz is assistant professor at the University of Manitoba, Canada, where she teaches language arts in the Teacher Education Program of the Winnipeg Education Centre. She has been involved in the professional development of language arts teachers in Zimbabwe and is currently working with teachers in a school-university partnership. She has presented and published in the areas of language arts, teacher education, and teacher development, and is the author of *Interpreting Teacher Practice: Two Continuing Stories* (1996).

Jeff Schwartz is the co-editor of *Students Teaching, Teachers Learning* (1992) and co-author of *Word Processing in a Community of Writers* (1989). His articles on teaching and his poems have appeared in a variety of journals and edited collections. Since 1988 he has been teaching at Greenwich Academy in Connecticut.

Linda Shadiow is professor of English and educational foundations at Northern Arizona University. She has taught junior and senior high school English in Minnesota and Montana. She has worked on a number of NCTE committees and been a presenter at numerous state affiliate and national conferences. Her articles have been published in national and affiliate journals and she has published book chapters on the history of young adult literature and the history of teaching English in the United States. Her current work is on ethics and cultural pluralism; she chairs the NCTE Code of Professional Ethics Committee.

Helen Collins Sitler holds a Ph.D. in rhetoric and linguistics and teaches in the English department at Indiana University of Pennsylvania. "Letters from Emily," published in *Language Arts* in 1995, and her dissertation, completed in 1997, also consider the use of dialogue journals in the classroom. She taught ENG 255, the literature class described in her chapter, for Westmoreland County Community College in Youngwood, Pennsylvania.

Kathleen Strickland, associate professor of Education at Slippery Rock University of Pennsylvania, teaches undergraduate and graduate courses in reading, language arts, and teacher research. She has published *Literacy, Not Labels: Celebrating Students' Strengths through Whole Language* (1995). Her husband, **James Strickland**, a professor of English at Slippery Rock University, teaches undergraduate and graduate courses in composition and rhetoric. From 1988 to 1994, he was the editor of *English Leadership Quarterly*, a publication of the NCTE Conference on English Leadership. He has published *From Disk to Hard Copy: Teaching Writing with Computers* (1997). Together, the Stricklands are co-authors of *UN-Covering the Curriculum: Whole Language in the Secondary and Post-Secondary Classroom* (1993) and *Reflections on Learning: The Role of Assessment and Evaluation in Secondary Classrooms* (1998). They have also written several chapters for edited collections and for *English Journal*.

Susan Tchudi is professor of English and director of the Core Writing Program at the University of Nevada, Reno. She has taught three workshops for the Huron Shores Writing Institute—two in Mühlhausen, Germany, and one in Rogers City, Michigan. Her books include *Integrated Language Arts in the Elementary School* (1994) and (co-authored with Stephen Tchudi) *The English/Language Arts Handbook* (1991) and *The Young Writer's Handbook* (1984). Although she has conducted workshops and presented papers at both state and national conferences, her favorite activity is working with young people in writing and drama workshops.

Cynthia Walters, a twenty-four year veteran, teaches English at Ashtabula High School in Ohio. She received her M.Ed. in curriculum and instruction from Kent State and has presented at workshops locally, nationally, and internationally, focusing on the use of prereading strategies and on responding to literature. Walters is a member of the Ohio Council of Teachers of English and Language Arts, NCTE, IRA, and the Ashtabula County Language Arts Leadership Team (a committee that examines and discusses current trends in the teaching of English and language arts, shares classroom strategies, plans staff development projects, and develops ideas for implementation in curriculums around Ashtabula County).

Ann Wheeler has taught secondary English in small, rural high schools for more than twenty years. Arthur High School, her "home-away-from-home" for the past eighteen years, has 135 students in the entire school, with 90 of those passing through her classroom daily. Though some would find teaching in a "country" school too confining, she appreciates the academic freedom allowed her and the chance to watch students grow and develop from their sophomore year until graduation.

*This book was typeset in Palatino and Helvetica by
Electronic Imaging.
The typefaces used on the cover were Trajan and Cloister.
The book was printed on 50 lb. offset by Edwards Brothers.*